Foreign Investment In China

Understanding the Corporate Legal Landscape

ROBERTO GILARDINO

The Choir Press

First published in the United Kingdom in 2025 by
The Choir Press

ISBN Paperback 978-1-78963-428-0
ISBN Hardback 978-1-78963-429-7

Contents

1. Introduction

In 1978 China opened the door to foreign investment through the reform and opening-up policy initiated by Deng Xiaoping. Since then, China has transformed from a third-world country to a global economic superpower and shifted its economic model from centrally planned to market orientated. Simultaneously, the regulatory landscape has rapidly matured in line with international practice and improved the business environment.

In the first foreign-investment era, policies focused on economic growth and spurred foreign investors to leverage low labour costs and export incentives. As a result, foreign companies benefitted from operating in a growth market and developing regulatory frameworks. Today China's economy has slowed down from double-digit gross domestic product (GDP) growth. Both domestic and foreign companies face an immensely different business environment and regulatory landscape; namely, the adopted digital ecosystem for corporate and tax procedures enables greater access to company records between national and local bureaus. Enforcing bodies can easily identify and investigate alleged violators. Equally, global political tensions between China and the West are rising. With both sides asserting direct criticisms and adopting national security laws to regulate cross-border investment and exports, companies must navigate an increasingly complex transnational legal environment. For companies in China, it is crucial to understand that the current corporate legal landscape is primarily shaped by the three aspects outlined below.

1. Compliance

   Since 2016, rapidly adopted regulations have simultaneously strengthened protection for companies and elevated regulators to enforce the rule of law. Particularly in areas such as cyber and data security and intellectual property infringement and competition, enforcement is active and violators face stricter penalties. Moreover, big data is increasingly leveraged to investigate company conduct. With the introduction of the Dishonest Entities List and the Enterprises with Abnormal Operations List to regulate company disclosure, violators are permanently held on record and publicly disclosed until they make all corrections, pay all outstanding debts, fulfil all necessary legal obligations and apply for removal from such list. Therefore, the changing legislation significantly paves a sophisticated legal framework in which compliance is prevalent.

2. Socialism with Chinese characteristics

   In the 19th National Congress of the Communist Party of China (CPC) President Xi Jinping initiated the concept of 'socialism with Chinese characteristics' in the new era (New Era), noting that as China advances in the economic landscape, both in China and abroad, it faces a new situation and outlook, and new challenges. Equally, the policy objective of 'common prosperity' was introduced at the meeting and focuses on reducing the gap between the wealthy and poor regions in China. In practice, sustained economic growth that develops the whole society is the emphasis and is implemented into the national and local legal framework; for example, the revised Anti-monopoly Law in August 2022 imposes stricter civil penalties and introduces criminal liabilities for the parties involved to further regulate larger companies from dominating the market and eliminating smaller competitors.

3. Geopolitics

   With escalating tensions between China and some Western countries, especially the U.S., many headquarters in Europe and America are facing greater scrutiny and difficulty in multi-national business management due to the judicial and administrative obstacles as a result of such tensions. Specifically, the US's ban on Xinjiang cotton, enacted in June 2022, resulted in many US companies, even without political stance, having to diversify supply chains and suppliers out of China; while in China, multinationals supporting the ban on Xinjiang cotton will face reputational damages locally and penalties under the Anti-foreign Sanctions Law (AFSL). Geopolitics is increasingly shaping regulations in export controls, data transfer, import tariffs, and merger and acquisition controls. These days it is not with whom you are doing business but in which country your business is established.

Today China bolsters a progressively sophisticated legal framework that leverages big data to regulate and investigate companies. Since Deng Xiaoping opened the doors to foreign investment, China's economy and international presence have risen extraordinarily. With the accession of China to multiple world organisations – including the United Nations, the World Trade Organization, the World Intellectual Property Organization, and so forth – legislation has been adopted and revised in line with international practice, and more currently with Chinese characteristics in the New Era under the leadership of President Xi Jinping. Therefore, companies doing business in or with China shall understand that the corporate legal landscape has significantly evolved and continues to evolve. China still offers ample opportunities for foreign investors, with the rising middle class and growing economy, though companies must align business models and practices with current and forthcoming legislation or face legal liabilities.

2 Past: Types of Foreign Direct Investment Entities 1979–2019

2.1 Introduction

In past years, laws and regulations concerning foreign investments in China have rapidly changed. Increased open market and regulation changes have led to a stable and optimised business environment for foreign direct investments. In the current economic climate, the direction is steered towards a more sustainable economic growth and innovation specifically focused on environmental, infrastructure, health and services industries, as well as new sectors related to elderly care and green technology. Foreign investment in China is generally determined by industry, and there are two essential lists – the Negative List and the Encouraged Catalogue – that establish the sectors encouraged, prohibited and restricted for foreign investment in China.

2.1.1 Negative List

The Special Administrative Measures on Access to Foreign Investment (Negative List) outlines sectors that are either prohibited or restricted for foreign investment. 'Restricted', in essence, means that foreign investors **must meet specific conditions** – such as shareholding limits – stipulated by the Negative List.

2.1.1.1 Negative List 2021

The National Development and Reform Commission (NDRC) and the Ministry of Commerce (MOFCOM) have jointly issued two updated Negative Lists on 27 December 2001, effective from 1 January 2022. They are the General Negative List and the Special Administrative Measures for Foreign Investment Access in Pilot Free Trade Zones (FTZ Negative List). The updated versions of the Negative Lists **reduce the numbers of restricted sectors** from 33 to 31 and 30 to 27 respectively. The main sectors with relaxed restrictions include:

Industries	Relaxed Restrictions
Manufacturing	The restrictions on the share ratio of foreign investment in commercial vehicle manufacturing have been reduced.
	Lifted restrictions on foreign investment in satellite television broadcasting ground receiving facilities and the production of key components.

2.1.2 Encouraged Catalogue

The Catalogue of Industries for Encouraged Foreign Investment (Encouraged Catalogue) establishes a list of encouraged sectors for foreign investment. Encouraged industries come with preferential incentives established by both national and local governments. They include tax incentives, streamlined approval procedures and discounted land prices.

2.1.2.1 Draft of the 2022 Encouraged Catalogue

On 10 May 2022 the NDRC and the MOFCOM issued the draft of the 2022 Encouraged Catalogue, which **has been expanded** by 200 industries. Primarily, there are three main areas emphasised in the catalogue.

Industries	Encouraged Areas
High-end manufacturing	This includes manufacturing of certain raw materials, certain components and parts, and end products, with a focus on the automobile, computer, communications and electronics industries.
Production-oriented service industries	This includes research and development, commercial services, modern logistics services and information services.
Investment in China's central, western and north-eastern provinces	The Catalogue for these regions has expanded relevant items according to each province's local conditions.

Foreign investment within the encouraged sectors shall benefit from preferential treatment, including **tariff exemptions** on imported equipment, access to **preferential land prices** and **looser regulations of land use**, and **lower corporate income tax**, among other advantages.

2.2 Types of Foreign-invested Enterprises in China

Prior to 1 January 2020, foreign investment was divided into 'foreign direct investment' and 'other foreign investment'. Generally, 'foreign direct investment' refers to investment activities establishing new entities or purchasing existing entities, while 'other foreign investment' refers to foreign investment activities that fall outside the scope of foreign direct investment. There were five main primary forms of foreign direct investment in China, which were subject to separate governing laws and related rules and regulations. Foreign-investment laws, rules and regulations are equally applicable to investors from Hong Kong, Macau Special Administrative Region and Taiwan district.

1979

Equity Joint Venture 中外合资企业 (zhōng wài hé zī qī yè)
From 1979, equity joint ventures were permitted to be established and were often selected for Sino-foreign joint ventures. The shareholders of such a company hold a respective percentage of the share in the company according to their respective capital contribution; for example, in Company X, Shareholder A contributes 49% of the registered capital and holds 49% of the share in the company, while Shareholder B contributes 51% of the registered capital and holds 51% of the share in the company.

1980

Representative Office 常驻代表机构 (cháng zhù dài biǎo jī gòu)
A representative office (RO) was the first form of 100% foreign-investment entity in China. On 30 October 1980 the Interim Regulations by the State Council of the People's Republic of China Concerning the Control of Resident Representative Offices of Foreign Enterprises was promulgated. An RO is not viewed as an independent legal person; rather, the foreign company overseas establishing the RO in China bears the legal liabilities of the RO. The scope of activity for ROs is limited to liaison and marketing activities in China, while profit-making business operations are prohibited.

1986

Wholly Foreign-owned Enterprise 外资企业 (wài zī qǐ yè)
From 1986, a wholly foreign-owned enterprise (WFOE), in which the capital of the company is 100% foreign generated, was permitted to be established. When the WFOE Law was first adopted, WFOEs were restricted to manufacturing only and the sale of goods manufactured. From 3 November 2016, the WFOE Law was revised to permit distribution and import and export within the WFOE business scope. A WFOE may establish a 100% Chinese enterprise with its profits, as the capital of the new Chinese enterprise is generated in China, not abroad. The new Chinese enterprise is governed by Chinese Company Law, not the WFOE Law. However, any injection of foreign capital into a Chinese company shall change the company into a foreign company.

1995

Contractual Joint Venture 中外合作企业 (zhōng wài hé zuò qǐ yè)
From 1995, foreign capital was allowed to be invested with Sino capital in a contractual joint venture. A contractual joint venture is a venture defined and established by a contract between the parties of the venture. A contractual joint venture could face difficulties, as the Sino-foreign contractual joint venture law provisions stipulate that the governance and regulation of the venture be governed by the contract. Therefore, where one party was not fully represented by its lawyer, the contract could be unbalanced and not in favour of all parties. Compared with equity joint venture, contractual joint venture is more flexible. It does not have to be a legal person, and its management can be determined by the contract between the parties.

Foreign-investment Commercial Enterprise 外商投资商业领域 (wài shāng tóu zī shāng yè lǐng yù)

2004

Prior to 11 December 2004, foreign investors were permitted to establish wholly foreign-owned enterprises or joint ventures, and both enterprise structures were restricted to certain business activities, such as importing and exporting products. The foreign-investment commercial enterprise (FICE) was introduced to allow foreign investors to establish a foreign entity for the commission agency, wholesale and retail (import and export), and franchising, subject to approval by the authority. FICEs were permitted to obtain import and export licences without utilising an import and export agent. As a result, many foreign investors subsequently established a WFOE for manufacturing purposes and a FICE for distribution. From 3 November 2016, FICEs were abolished and the business activities of foreign-invested enterprises (FIEs) (trading, buying and selling of goods in China) were permitted within a WFOE. Therefore, the revision enabled a large business scope within one enterprise structure.

From 1 January 2020, the Foreign Investment Law of the People's Republic of China (FIL) became effective. The FIL, adopted at the Second Session of the Thirteenth National People's Congress, marks a significant era for foreign investment in China. Primarily, the three main bodies of laws that regulate the four forms of foreign direct investment shall be simultaneously repealed.

1. The Law of the People's Republic of China on Sino-foreign Equity Joint Venture (EJV Law) governs equity joint ventures established between a foreign party and a Chinese legal entity
2. The Law of the People's Republic of China on Wholly Foreign-funded Enterprise (WFOE Law) governs wholly foreign enterprises that are wholly established by one, or with other, foreign investors
3. The Law of the People's Republic of China on Sino-foreign Cooperative Joint Venture (CJV Law) governs contractual joint ventures established between a foreign party and a Chinese enterprise or other economic organisation

The FIL unites both foreign direct investment and other foreign investment into one unified law governing foreign investment, as well as paving more consistency between domestic and foreign entities by regulating the most common aspects of both foreign-invested and domestic-invested companies under the Company Law.

3 Past: Wholly Foreign-owned Enterprises

3.1 Introduction

A wholly foreign-owned enterprise (WFOE) is a solely foreign-invested entity incorporated and registered in China. The Law of the People's Republic of China on Wholly Foreign-owned Enterprise (WFOE Law), adopted in 1986 and last revised in 2016 by the Standing Committee of the National People's Congress, governs and regulates WFOEs. Under the WFOE Law, WFOEs are structured to expand foreign economic cooperation and technological exchange, as well as promote the development of the Chinese economy. Foreign enterprises and other economic organisations or individuals (hereinafter referred to as 'foreign investors') are permitted to establish WFOEs within China. When the WFOE Law was first adopted, WFOEs were restricted to manufacturing and the sale of goods manufactured. From 3 November 2016, the WFOE Law was revised to permit distribution and import and export within the WFOE business scope. Today foreign companies investing in China without a Chinese partner or sole shareholder usually establish a WFOE, which is 100% foreign owned, and such a WFOE is subject to provisions of the Foreign Investment Law and is regulated in a similar manner to domestic companies.

3.1.1 Definition

WFOEs are referred to in the WFOE Law as enterprises established within the territory of the People's Republic of China in accordance with applicable Chinese laws, solely using capital input from one or more foreign investors. Branches established in China by foreign investors do not fall under the scope of a WFOE.

The WFOE Law encourages wholly foreign-owned enterprises in the following fields:

- Utilisation of advanced technology and equipment
- Engagement in the development of new products
- Achievement of product upgrades and replacement
- Economising on the use of energy and raw materials
- Exportation

All foreign-investment entities are subject to the Special Administrative Measures on Access to Foreign Investment (Negative List). For investment in industries outside of the Negative List, online record-filing management for incorporation and alteration administration can proceed, while restricted or prohibited foreign-investment sectors within the Negative List are subject to approval formalities.

3.1.2 Legal Form

A wholly foreign-owned enterprise is normally organised as a limited liability company (LLC) and stated in the articles of association (AoA). The legal form is effective upon approval by the examination and approval authority. 'Limited liability' refers to the liability of the foreign investor, with respect to the enterprise, as being limited to the amount of capital contributed.

3.1.3 Independence

The WFOE Law permits a WFOE to operate and manage without government interference and according to the approved scope of the business. The investments, profits and other interests of foreign investors in China **are protected by Chinese law**, although foreign investors shall adhere to Chinese laws and regulations and not harm the public interest of China. Equally, the assets of a WFOE may, in accordance with legal procedures and appropriate compensation, be expropriated by the State in special circumstances for public interest.

3.2 Establishment

The establishment procedure of a WFOE is as follows:

STEP 1	**Pre-registration of Company Name** As the first legal step, it is necessary to pre-register the company name with the competent company registration authority. Pre-registration is valid for three months and may be extended for another three months, during which it shall have exclusive rights to the name.
STEP 2	**Filing** Effective as of 1 October 2016, the Provisional Measures on Administration of Filing for Establishment and Change of Foreign-invested Enterprises (repealed) altered the previous establishment administrative formalities by implementing a filing system for all types of foreign-invested enterprises (FIEs) that are not subject to the Special Administrative Measures stipulated by the State (industries that do not fall into the Negative List of prohibited and restricted categories). A WFOE is subject to the Special Administrative Measures for the Examination and Approval of Foreign Trade and Economic Relations or an agency authorised by the State Council. Within 90 days upon receipt of the application, the designated agency shall decide whether or not to approve the WFOE.
STEP 3	**Registration** Upon approval and receipt of the approval certificate, the foreign investor shall apply for registration with the State Administration for Market Regulation within 30 days. Once the WFOE is registered, the business licence shall be issued, and the date of the business licence shall be the enterprise's date of establishment.

3.2.1 Registered Capital

The definition of 'registered capital of a wholly foreign-owned enterprise' is the total amount of capital contributed by the foreign investor as registered with the authority. Registered capital may not be reduced but may, however, be increased upon approval by the examination and approval authority. Any such change shall be registered with the local office of the State Administration for Marketing Regulation (SAMR).

The proportion of registered capital in the total amount of investment of a WFOE shall adhere to relevant provisions. Mortgages or assignments of property by a WFOE shall also be approved by the examination and approval authority and reported to the local office of the SAMR.

3.2.2 Forms of Capital Contribution

Capital may be contributed in the form of foreign currency, machinery, equipment, industrial property, proprietary technology and, on approval, yuan renminbi (CNY). Capital contribution shall be made pursuant to the articles of association of the WFOE.

When the capital is not contributed in local or foreign currency, it shall satisfy all of the following requirements:

Industries	Conditions
Machinery and equipment	• Shall be necessary for production in the enterprise • Shall not be capable of being manufactured in China within delivery time requirements of the enterprise
Industrial property and proprietary technology	• Shall be owned by the foreign investor • Shall be used to produce new products urgently required by China or used to produce products that have a ready export market

Machinery and equipment for capital contribution shall be inspected by a Chinese commodity inspection organisation upon arrival at a port in China. If a discrepancy is found upon inspection, the examination and approval authority has the power to 'demand rectification' of such discrepancies within a specified period of time. Valuation shall be consistent with the international market value of similar equipment. Machinery and equipment for contribution shall be described in detail and submitted along with the application for establishment of the enterprise.

Industrial property and proprietary technology shall be accompanied by certificates of ownership and validity, together with information on technical performance and practical value. The basis and standard used for valuation shall be specified, along with any other information requested by the examination and approval authority. This information shall be included with the application for establishment of the enterprise. The examination and approval authority also has the power to conduct further inspections after industrial property and proprietary technology have been put into operation, and to demand rectification if any discrepancies from its claimed usefulness are discovered during such an inspection.

3.3 Corporate Governance

The shareholders of a WFOE are the highest authority of the entity. The shareholders shall establish the articles of association (AoA). In the articles of association, items such as the governing rules of the company, management of its internal affairs, conduct of its business, and relationship between its members and the company are established. The provisions of the articles of association legally bind the company and its shareholders, directors, supervisors and senior officers. The articles of association is formulated by the shareholders of the company, and upon agreement of it, the shareholders shall affix their signatures or seals on it.

The methods of deliberation and voting procedures at shareholders' meetings are also governed by the company's articles of association. Any revision to the company's articles of association in the shareholders' meeting is adopted when there is a vote of two-thirds or more. Shareholder voting rights are based on each shareholder's respective capital contribution unless the articles of association specifies otherwise.

In a WFOE, there is a two-tiered daily governance system:

- The board of directors is the highest governing body, determining and controlling all major issues concerning the venture
- The managerial staff manages the daily operations of the venture according to the resolutions of the board of directors

In addition, there is a board of supervisors – or one supervisor in a relatively small company – appointed by negotiation between the parties. The role of the supervisor is not only important in supervising the company operation for the interest of the shareholders (as noted in the Company Law chapter), but also in mediating the cultural difficulties between foreign and Chinese parties.

3.3.1 Board of Directors

Under the Company Law, **the minimum number of members on the board of directors is three** (the number of directors shall be odd numbers, with a maximum of 33 members), and members of the board shall be appointed and replaced by the board of directors. The number of board members determined by each shareholder does not represent the share of the shareholder; for example, the majority shareholder may waive the right to appoint board members, while the minority shareholder may appoint three board members.

The board of directors is provisioned to **perform duties based on the principles of equality and mutual benefit**. Its powers and functions are governed by the provisions of the articles of association of the joint venture and include the following:

- Development plans
- Production and business plans
- Budget
- Distribution of profits
- Labour and remuneration plans
- The cessation of business activities
- The appointment or recruitment of the general manager, the deputy general manager, the chief engineer, the chief accountant and the auditors

3.4 Labour

Employment matters are governed by the relevant labour laws and regulations. Matters concerning the employment, dismissal, remuneration, welfare benefits, labour protections, labour insurance, and so forth, of the employees of a joint venture shall be stipulated in a contract in accordance with the relevant law. WFOEs may also employ Chinese staff and are required to sign employment contracts. Employment contracts shall clearly stipulate the terms of employment, dismissal, remuneration, welfare, labour protections and labour insurance.

Employees of a WFOE are provisioned with the right to establish a trade union organisation in accordance with the law and conduct trade union activities and safeguard the lawful rights and interests of employees. WFOEs are required to provide their trade unions with the necessary conditions for union activities. In practice, WFOEs shall 'actively support' the labour union, such as providing office premises for the union and facilitating cultural, educational and athletic activities.

3.5 Operations

3.5.1 Bank Accounts

After having obtained a business licence, WFOEs are required to open renminbi deposit accounts with the Bank of China or other designated banks. Any foreign exchange shall be kept in an account with a bank or other financial institution authorised by the State Administration of Foreign Exchange to engage in foreign-exchange business. Any insurance policy taken out by a joint venture shall be taken out with an insurance company within Chinese territory.

3.5.2 Accounting

An accounting system shall be established in China in accordance with Chinese laws and regulations and in accordance with the procedures of Chinese financial authorities. The system shall be reported for approval to the financial and taxation authorities in the place where the WFOE is located. The fiscal year begins on 1 January and ends on 31 December.

Accounting documents shall be written in Chinese, and in the case of accounting vouchers, books or statements written in a foreign language, a Chinese translation shall be provided. Annual accounting statements shall be prepared in accordance with Chinese financial and taxation regulations and procedures. Although the currency of denomination is renminbi, foreign-currency-denominated accounts may be prepared simultaneously. A Chinese registered accountant shall be engaged to prepare an audit report on the annual accounting statements. The regulations prescribe the time limits for presentation of accounting statements to the examination and approval authority and to the local office of the SAMR. When accounting records are not made available for supervision and inspection by the financial and taxation authorities at the location of a WFOE, the financial and taxation authorities can impose fines and the local office of the SAMR has the power to order suspension of business activities or revocation of the business licence.

Allocations to a reserve fund shall be at least 10% of after-tax profits, and no more allocation is mandatory if the accumulative reserved amount reaches 50% of the registered capital. Allocations to a bonus and welfare fund for employees may be determined by the enterprise itself in coordination with its union.

3.5.3 Purchasing

Within their approved scope of operations, and on the principles of fairness and reasonableness, WFOEs may have the choice to purchase raw materials, fuel and other requirements from both domestic and international markets. WFOEs are to be treated in a manner equal to other domestic enterprises with regard to prices for purchasing materials in China and the price and fees charged for services such as water, electricity, gas, heat, goods transportation, labour, engineering, consultation, advertising, and so forth.

3.5.4 Taxation

Enterprise Income Tax (EIT) rate = 25%

WFOEs are subject to a fixed enterprise income tax rate of 25% by virtue of the national Enterprise Income Tax Law. However, they may be entitled to a tax reduction if they engage in industries favoured by the State, such as agriculture, utilities, environmental protection, energy conservation and water conservation, among others. Wholly foreign-owned enterprises are also subject to value-added tax, customs duties, stamp tax, consumption tax and other taxes, such as urban real estate tax, vehicle and vessel licence tax, and so forth, where relevant.

All employees of a WFOE (including management personnel) are required to pay individual income tax in accordance with the Chinese laws and regulations.

3.5.5 Distribution of Profits

Distribution of profits is based on calculation of the after-tax net profit of the WFOE and deduction of allocations to the statutory collective reserve fund, welfare fund, reserve fund and employee incentive and enterprise development funds (if any). The balance remaining after such deductions may be distributed to the foreign investor(s) in proportion to their capital contributions.

3.5.6 Foreign Exchange

A WFOE may remit abroad its net share of profits and any other funds distributed to it. Foreign-exchange remittance formalities are governed by the Administrative Regulations of the People's Republic of China on Foreign Exchange.

Wages and other lawful income earned by expatriate employees of WFOEs may, after the payment of individual income tax in accordance with the tax laws of the People's Republic of China, be remitted abroad in accordance with the Administrative Regulations of the People's Republic of China on Foreign Exchange.

3.5.7 Mergers and Division

Division, mergers and other major changes in a WFOE are subject to approval by the authority that approved the enterprise's establishment. The management structure of a WFOE is as set forth in its articles of association.

3.6 Term and Termination

3.6.1 Term

A WFOE shall have a specific term, approved by the examination and approval authority. There is no limitation in the WFOE Law specifying the compulsory duration of a term. WFOEs typically have a term of 15 to 25 years.

For a WFOE that is subject to the Special Administrative Measures stipulated by the State, the term is extendable upon written application submitted to the approval authorities 180 days prior to the expiry of the term. The approval authorities shall make their decision on whether or not to approve the application for extension within 30 days of the date of receipt of the application. If an extension is approved, the extension shall be registered with the local office of the SAMR within 30 days of the date of receipt of the approval.

Effective as of 1 October 2016, for an extension of the term of operation, a WFOE that is not subject to the Special Administrative Measures stipulated by the State only needs to complete the filing formality with the approval authorities and does not need to seek approval.

The term of a WFOE shall expire upon the occurrence of the following circumstances:

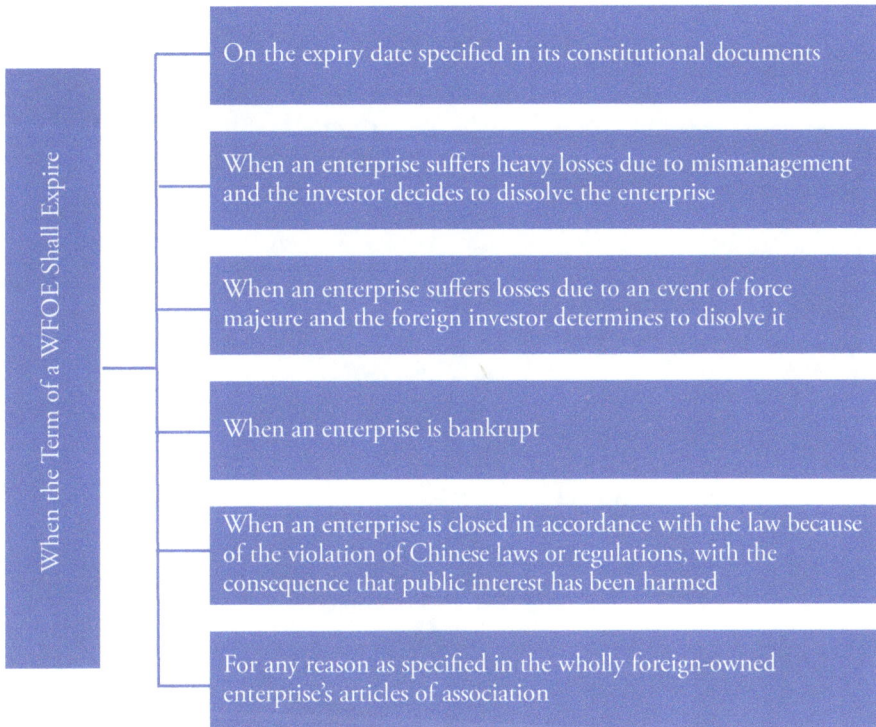

When the Term of a WFOE Shall Expire

On the expiry date specified in its constitutional documents

When an enterprise suffers heavy losses due to mismanagement and the investor decides to dissolve the enterprise

When an enterprise suffers losses due to an event of force majeure and the foreign investor determines to dissolve it

When an enterprise is bankrupt

When an enterprise is closed in accordance with the law because of the violation of Chinese laws or regulations, with the consequence that public interest has been harmed

For any reason as specified in the wholly foreign-owned enterprise's articles of association

3.6.2 Termination

In cases of termination due to mismanagement, *force majeure* or bankruptcy, the WFOE shall submit a written application for termination to the examination and approval authority. The approval date is the official date of termination.

In cases of termination on expiration of term, or termination due to a reason specified in the articles of association, in addition to notification of creditors, a public announcement shall be made within 15 days of the date of the termination. A liquidation proposal shall be submitted to the examination and approval authority within 15 days of issuance of the public announcement of the termination, together with a statement of the procedure and principles for liquidation. The candidates for the liquidation committee and other details, and all relevant documents, shall be approved by the examination and approval authority prior to commencement of the said liquidation.

4 Past: Foreign Investment Commercial Enterprises

4.1 Introduction

Prior to 11 December 2004, foreign investors were restricted from importing and exporting products with their wholly foreign-owned enterprises (WFOEs) or joint ventures established in China. In 2004 the Measures for the Administration of Foreign-invested Commercial Enterprise (FICE), effective from 1 June 2004, was promulgated by the Minister of Commerce. The FICE structure enables foreign investors to establish a foreign entity, namely a foreign-funded commercial enterprise, for the trading, buying and selling of goods in China. FICEs are permitted to obtain import and export licences without utilising an import and export agent. As a result, many foreign investors subsequently established a WFOE for manufacturing purposes and a FICE for distribution.

Effective from 3 November 2016, the Measures for the Administration of Foreign-invested Commercial Enterprise was abolished by the Minister of Commerce. The WFOE Law, which previously prohibited both production and service activities, was revised to permit distribution and import and export within the WFOE business scope. This revision enables foreign investors to gain access to combine service and manufacturing within one enterprise structure.

4.1.1 Definition

Foreign-funded commercial enterprises shall refer to enterprises with foreign investment that undertake the following commercial activities:

Commission agency	Agents, brokers, auctioneers or other wholesalers for sale of goods who sell goods to someone else and provide relevant attached services through collecting fees on the basis of contract
Wholesale	Selling goods to retailers, customers of industry, commerce and organisations or to other wholesalers, or providing relevant attached services
Retail	Selling goods for consumption and use of individuals or groups or providing relevant attached services in fixed places or through television, telephone, mail order, internet and automats
Franchising	Vesting other people with using its trademark, trade firm or mode of management by signing contracts for the purpose of gaining remunerations or franchising fees

A foreign investor is required to establish a FICE if it wishes to engage in these distribution activities. Investors in FICEs can be foreign companies, enterprises or other economic organisations, as well as foreign individuals. Foreign investors may establish a FICE with a Chinese party as a joint venture or on their own as a wholly foreign-owned enterprise. However, not all FICEs may be wholly owned by a foreign investor. A FICE with more than 30 outlets dealing in certain specified products of different brands that are sourced from different suppliers shall generally take the form of a joint venture, in which the maximum share of the foreign investor is limited to 49%. 'Specified products' includes books, newspapers, periodicals, pharmaceutical products, pesticides, mulching films, chemical fertilisers, processed oil, staple foods, vegetable oil, edible sugar, cotton, and so forth. Also, FICEs are prohibited from engaging in the wholesale of salt and tobacco and in the retail of tobacco.

4.1.2 Conditions

Foreign investors should credit and comply with the People's Republic of China's law. Foreign investors with substantial financial strength, advanced experiences, marketing techniques in business management, and broad international networks are encouraged. Under the Measures for FICE, FICEs are required to meet the following conditions:

- The minimum registered capital shall accord with the relevant provisions of the Company Law
- They are required to conform to the relevant provisions on the registered capital and total investment of enterprises with foreign investment
- The term of operation of a foreign-funded commercial enterprise shall not exceed 30 years in general, and the term of operation of a foreign-funded commercial enterprise established in the middle and western regions shall not exceed 40 years in general

Although there is no statutory requirement of minimum registered capital, the authority in charge of approving the establishment of a FICE may require a certain amount of registered capital to match the proposed scale of business of the FICE. The investment must comply with the minimum debt to equity (registered capital) ratios imposed under the law of the PRC. The term of operation should not normally be longer than 30 years but may be extended to 40 years if the FICE is established in the central and western regions of China.

4.1.3 Permitted Business Activities

Foreign-funded enterprises may deal with the following business upon approval:

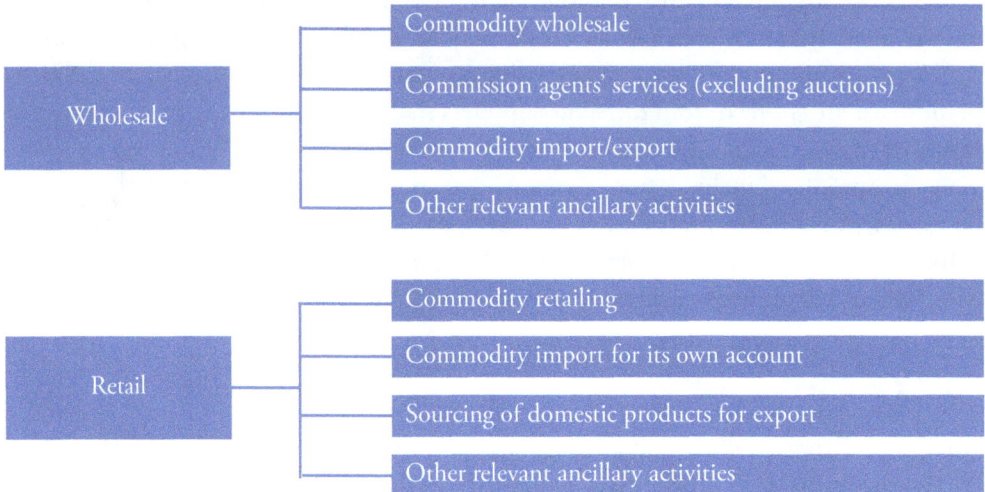

Wholesale	Commodity wholesale
	Commission agents' services (excluding auctions)
	Commodity import/export
	Other relevant ancillary activities

Retail	Commodity retailing
	Commodity import for its own account
	Sourcing of domestic products for export
	Other relevant ancillary activities

A FICE may engage in one or more of the business activities set forth above and may authorise third parties to open franchise shops.

4.1.4 Range of Products

A FICE must specify the range of products it distributes in the business scope of its corporate establishment documents. A FICE is only permitted to deal in those types of products listed in its business scope.

The import and distribution of certain categories of products in China is subject to various forms of state control. If the products that the FICE produces are subject to special state regulations or are import/export products that are subject to quota or licensing controls, the FICE must comply with the relevant licensing requirements.

4.2 Establishment

While the MOFCOM is the principal approval authority for FICEs, it has delegated its approval powers with respect to most types of FICE to the provincial-level departments in charge of commerce (provincial commerce authorities). Within the scope of these delegated powers, the provincial commerce authorities can autonomously approve the establishment of FICEs, and they are only required to report the matter to the MOFCOM for record. A FICE is still subject to the MOFCOM's approval if:

- its mode of operations involves sales without setting up shops (outlets), such as through television, telephone, mail order, etc.
- it wholesales audiovisual products or distributes books

In such instances where approval by the MOFCOM is required, an application for the establishment of a FICE must first be submitted to the provincial commerce authority in the proposed investment location. After preliminary examination, the provincial commerce authority shall forward the application to the MOFCOM within one month. The MOFCOM shall then have three further months to decide whether or not to approve the application.

4.2.1 Procedures

FICEs are required to adhere to the following provisions in order to be established:

- A one-off application and approval of the start-up, feasibility study report and establishment of foreign-funded commercial enterprises
- Submission of the following documents (see Table 1 on the next page) to the competent commerce department at the provincial level where the foreign-funded commercial enterprise is to be established[1]

Where documents are signed by a person who is not the legal representative, the power of attorney of the legal representative shall be shown.

4.2.2 Establishment of Outlets

FICEs may set up shops (outlets) on the following conditions:

- Land rights are obtained for commercial use by way of public invitation of bidding, auction or listing in accordance with the provisions of the relevant laws and administrative regulations of the State on land management
- Establishment complies with the regulations regarding urban development and urban commercial development

---

[1] Except in the circumstances listed above where it is still subject to the MOFCOM's approval, in which case the establishment shall report and recorded to the MOFCOM.

The MOFCOM is the approval authority for the opening of new outlets by a FICE. Provincial commerce authorities are, however, authorised to approve new outlets under the following two situations:

1. The area of a single outlet does not exceed 3,000 m2 and there are not more than three outlets in total, and the foreign investor has not opened more than 30 outlets in the same class in China through a FICE.
2. The area of a single outlet does not exceed 300 m2 and there are not more than 30 outlets in total, and the foreign investor has not opened more than 300 outlets in the same class in China through a FICE.

Under the above circumstances, the provincial commerce authorities are only required to report the approval for the establishment of outlets to the MOFCOM.

Where a FICE is already established and plans to open an outlet, it is required to submit the documents in Table 1 below to the competent commerce department at the provincial level where the foreign-funded commercial enterprise is established:

TABLE 1

	FICE Establishment	Outlet Establishment
a)	Application letter	Application letter
b)	Feasibility study report signed by all the investors together	Feasibility study report on opening the store
c)	Contract, articles of association (for a foreign-funded commercial enterprise, only the articles of association should be submitted) and the attachment. Any licence contract for use of a trademark or a business name, technology transfer contract, management contract and service contract signed, and other legal documents, shall be submitted as the attachment of the contract and are to be deemed as the attachment of the articles of association.	The revised contract or articles of association shall be submitted in case the amendments to the contract or articles of association are involved

FICE Establishment	Outlet Establishment
d) Bank credit certificates of all investors, registration certificate (photocopy), certificate of the legal representative (photocopy). If the foreign investor is an individual, his identity certificate shall be provided.	Resolutions of the board of directors on opening the store
e) The audit report of all investors in the recent year, which is audited by accountancy firms	The audit report of the enterprise in the most recent one-year period
f) The evaluation report on state-owned assets invested into the Sino-foreign equity joint venture or contractual joint venture commercial enterprises by Chinese investors	Registration certificate (photocopy) of all the investors, and the certificate of the legal representative (photocopy)
g) Catalogues of import and export goods of the planned foreign-funded commercial enterprise	Certificate documents of the usufruct of the land that is used for the store to be opened and/or the house lease agreement (photocopy), except when the business area of the store opened is less than 3,000 m²
i) Name list of the members of the board of directors of the planned foreign-funded commercial enterprise and the power of attorney for directors of each investor	
j) Notice of pre-approval of the enterprise name as issued by the State Administration for Market Regulation	
k) The certificate documents (photocopy) of the usufruct of the land used for the planned store and/or the house lease agreement (photocopy), except when the business area of the store to be opened is less than 3,000 m²	

	FICE Establishment	**Outlet Establishment**
l)	The documents of statement of conformity with the requirements for city development and urban commercial development as issued by the competent commerce department of the government at the locality of the store	The documents of statement of conformity with the requirements for city development and the commercial development of the city as issued by the government where the planned store is located
Note	Within one month after receiving the Certificate of Approval, the investor shall go through the registration formalities at the State Administration for Market Regulation together with the Certificate of Approval for Foreign-funded Enterprises.	

Where the document is signed by someone who is not the legal person, the power of attorney of the legal representative shall be issued.

4.3 Special Provisions

Where FICEs manage certain specified goods, the following prescriptions shall be confirmed in addition to the provisions of the Measures for FICE:

- Where a foreign-funded commercial enterprise manages books, newspapers or periodicals, it shall accord with the Measures for the Administration of Foreign-funded Distribution Enterprises of Books, Newspapers or Periodicals
- Where a foreign-funded commercial enterprise manages gas stations and undertakes the retail of refined oil, it shall have a stable channel of supply of refined oil, conform to the construction plan of the local oil station – with the business establishments thereof corresponding with the state standards and the provisions on computation and checking procedures – and meet the requirements for fire control and environmental protection, and so forth. The specific implementation measures shall be formulated by the Ministry of Commerce separately
- Where a foreign-funded commercial enterprise manages drugs, it shall conform to the relevant standards for the administration of drug sale. The specific implementation measures shall be formulated by the Ministry of Commerce separately

- Where a foreign-funded commercial enterprise manages automobiles, it shall manage within the approved business scope. The specific implementation measures shall be formulated by the Ministry of Commerce separately
- With the exception of the specific provisions in Article 18 of the present Measures and the present Article, if foreign investors establish commercial enterprises of farm products and by-products and agricultural production materials, they shall not be restricted in region, proportion of share or the amount of investment
- No wholesaling foreign-funded commercial enterprises may manage drugs, pesticides or agricultural films before 11 December 2004, nor shall they manage fertilisers, refined oil and crude oil before 11 February 2006
- No retailing foreign-funded enterprises may manage drugs, pesticides, agricultural films or refined oil before 11 December 2004, nor shall they manage fertilisers before 11 December 2006
- No wholesaling foreign-funded commercial enterprises may manage salt or tobacco, and no retailing foreign-funded commercial enterprises shall manage tobacco

4.3.1 Special Provisions Regarding Hong Kong and Macau Service Suppliers

Under the provisions of the Closer Economic Partnership Arrangements that Mainland China have concluded with Hong Kong and Macau, qualified Hong Kong and Macau service suppliers (collectively referred to as 'SAR suppliers') are granted greater access to the distribution sector than other service suppliers.

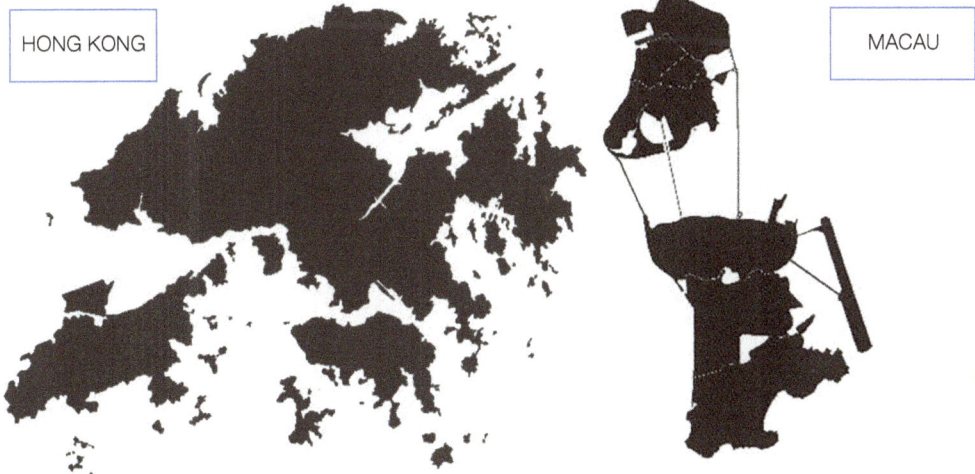

- Commercial service providers of Hong Kong and Macau may establish foreign-funded commercial enterprises in the Mainland after 1 January 2004
- The regional scope of retail enterprises established in the Mainland by Hong Kong and Macau commercial service providers shall be extended to cities at the prefecture level, and the cities at the county level in Guangdong Province
- Commercial service providers of Hong Kong and Macau may, according to the relevant articles of the Measures for FICE, apply after 1 January 2004 to establish commercial enterprises that undertake automobile retail business. However, the average sales volume per annum in the past three years before application shall be no less than USD 100 million, and the amount of capital in the previous year before application shall be no less than USD 10 million. The minimum registered capital of an automobile retailing enterprise established in the Mainland shall be CNY 10 million, and the minimum registered capital of an automobile retailing enterprise established in the middle and western districts shall be CNY 6 million
- Chinese citizens among the Hong Kong and Macau permanent residents are allowed to establish individual business, according to relevant laws, regulations and rules, to undertake commercial retail activities (excluding franchising). The business areas thereof shall not exceed 300 m²
- The Hong Kong/Macau commercial service providers shall correspond with the definitions of and the relevant requirements for 'service providers' as prescribed in the Mainland and Hong Kong Closer Economic Partnership Arrangements and the Mainland and Macau Closer Economic Partnership Arrangements

5 Past: Sino-foreign Equity Joint Ventures

5.1 Introduction

A Sino-foreign equity joint venture (EJV) is a limited liability company incorporated and registered in China by one or more foreigners with one or more Chinese investors. The Law of the People's Republic of China on Sino-foreign Equity Joint Ventures (Equity Joint Venture Law or EJV Law), adopted in 1979 and last revised in 2016 by the Standing Committee of the National People's Congress, governs equity joint ventures in China. The Equity Joint Venture Law provides the basic outline of applicable corporate law, with provisions relating to capital contribution, registered capital, transfer of equity interests, management structure and dissolution of the equity joint venture company.

Under the EJV Law, EJVs established within the territory of China shall promote the economic development of China and the enhancement of science and technology, as well as facilitate socialist modernisation and construction. All foreign-investment entities, including equity joint ventures, are subject to the Special Administrative Measures on Access to Foreign Investment (Negative List). For investment in industries outside of the Negative List, online record-filing management for incorporation and alteration administration can proceed, while restricted or prohibited foreign-investment sectors within the Negative List are subject to approval formalities.

5.1.1 Legal Form

The Equity Joint Venture Law permits foreign companies, enterprises, other commercial organisations and individuals (hereinafter referred to as 'foreign parties') to form joint ventures with Chinese companies, enterprises and other commercial organisations (hereinafter referred to as 'Chinese investors'), although Chinese individuals are prohibited from forming a joint venture with a foreign party or parties. Each party to the joint venture is liable to the joint venture within the limits of the capital subscribed. Equally, profits, risks and losses of the joint venture shall be shared in proportion to each party's registered capital contribution.

An EJV is a foreign-invested enterprise and shall be granted a legal-person status upon registration of the enterprise with the State Administration for Market Regulation (SAMR) or a local delegate. A legal person has the right to own, use, reap benefit from and dispose of property; the right to carry on management and production independently; and the capacity to sue and be sued in a court of law. Equally, a joint venture is governed and protected by Chinese laws. An equity joint venture shall have the right to independently conduct business and management within the scope prescribed by Chinese laws and regulations and by the agreement, contract and articles of association of the joint venture.

5.2 Establishment

5.2.2 Preliminary Documents

Equity joint ventures should be considered by foreign companies wishing to accelerate the growth of their products or services in China with the assistance of a local partner; for example, a foreign company could offer the history and technology of the products, while the Chinese partner could offer the Chinese market expertise. In this way, there is an equilibrium and exchange between the two parties, which may lessen the cultural clashes between them.

Prior to establishing an EJV with a Chinese partner, the following preliminary documents should be completed to safeguard both parties and start the EJV on a legally sound basis.

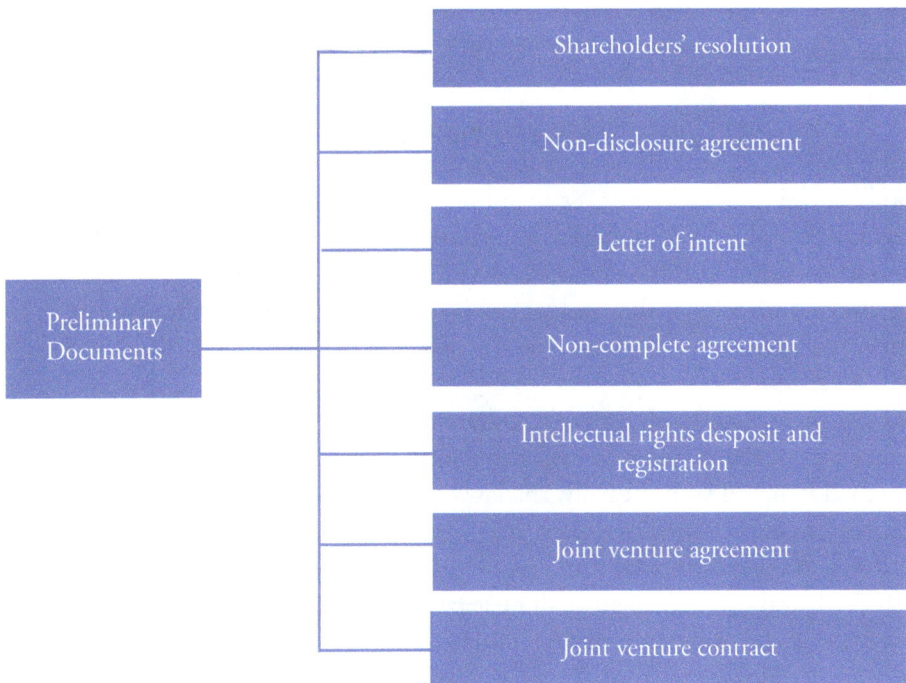

```
Preliminary          ┌──── Shareholders' resolution
Documents            │
                     ├──── Non-disclosure agreement
                     │
                     ├──── Letter of intent
                     │
                     ├──── Non-complete agreement
                     │
                     ├──── Intellectual rights desposit and
                     │     registration
                     │
                     ├──── Joint venture agreement
                     │
                     └──── Joint venture contract
```

5.2.2.1 Shareholders' Resolutions

Upon the identification of a joint venture partnership, or partnerships, the shareholder of each party should conclude a resolution to establish a joint venture. The shareholders' resolution should confirm the necessary or appropriate reason, with supporting evidence, in order to establish a joint venture.

Case study

Company A intends to form an EJV with Company B. The shareholders of Company A conclude a resolution that states that, based on the expertise of Scientist C, in order to expand research and development of Company A, it is deemed appropriate and in accordance with the internal compliance to form a joint venture with Company B.

Analysis

In this case, the foreign party under the governing foreign law has no provision for a shareholders' resolution; the highest and equivalent governing corporate body, such as resolutions of the board of directors, is suffice. The shareholders' resolution shall be affixed with the corporate seal, the legal representative seal, and seals of each shareholder. Such a shareholders' resolution shall be accepted by the full majority of shareholders, as it is deemed under the Chinese law as an important decision.

Where there is no resolution of the shareholders containing the seals and signatures of the decision to establish a joint venture, the joint venture can be deemed null and void. Equally, the lawyers of the parties cannot legally proceed with the establishment of the joint venture. If the shareholders' resolution is foreign and under foreign law, only the signature of the chairman is required, and the document shall be legalised and apostatised by the Chinese Embassy to be recognised under Chinese law.

5.2.2.2 Non-disclosure Agreement

The non-disclosure agreement should include the monetary penalties of a disclosure violation. Without such a clause, the value is open to negotiation. The defined amount of the liquidated damages shall be reasonable and appropriate to the company; otherwise, in court the judge may not accept a high amount from a relatively small company because it is not justifiable. Usually, the value of liquidated damages is a third of the company's turnover. Any amount higher or lower shall be clearly explained, with supporting evidence, and related to damages caused.

5.2.2.3 Letter of Intent

The letter of intent (LOI) should not be treated as a memorandum of understanding. The LOI should be a statement of the intent to pursue the establishment of the EJV. In practice, detailed contractual terms should be negotiated by the parties and not expressed in the LOI, as it may be difficult to define the details of the joint venture, since it could be difficult to renegotiate the terms later in the EJV contract. Rather, the LOI should be non-binding and determine the prerequisite and conditions on which the EJV will be based.

Case study

Party A intends to establish a joint venture with Party B based on the prerequisite and conditions in the following points . . .

Analysis

In this manner, if such prerequisites and conditions were false, Party A could claim liquidated damages from Party B on the basis of the letter of intent.

5.2.2.4 Non-compete Agreement

A non-compete agreement can prevent one party from competing with an existing company in the same market. Usually, such a party should liquidate the existing company so that the joint venture is the sole focus. If a non-compete agreement is not implemented, it could reflect that one party has agreed to allow the existing company of the other party to compete with the joint venture.

5.2.2.5 Intellectual Rights Deposit and Registration

The Trademark Law of the People's Republic of China utilises a first-come-first-served approach in filing an application at the Trademark Bureau, with approved applicants having priority over the subsequent application of trademark in similar classes of goods. Generally, companies seek to extend their trademark to China. However, it is often the case that the trademark is only extended to the boundary of China, and not within the territory of China, which results in potential risks to trademark rights due to the territorial limitation of trademark rights. In court proceedings, a trademark not registered in China may not be recognised or protected by the court.

It is advised that a further registration be made at the Customs Bureau. Once the registration is completed, the Customs shall prohibit any exportation and importation of goods of the registered trademark that are not sent from the registered address of the originator. The Customs shall also inform such companies of any trademark violations.

5.2.2.6 Joint Venture Agreement

'Joint venture agreement' refers to the document detailing the contractual principles for the establishment of the joint venture, although it is not required to be binding and is not required by law. Therefore, the joint venture contract could be concluded without the joint venture agreement.

5.2.2.7 Joint Venture Contract

'Joint venture contract' refers to the document in which a consensus is reached by the parties to the joint venture on their mutual rights and obligations. Usually, a joint venture agreement includes the following:

- Parties to the joint venture
- Purpose and scope of the joint venture
- Total investment capital and registered capital
- Change and transfer of registered capital
- Responsibilities and obligations of each party
- Ownership
- Board of directors
- Supervisors
- Business management office
- Labour management
- Tax, finance, accounting, auditing and profit distribution
- Duration of the joint venture

- Dissolution and liquidation
- Breach of contract
- Confidentiality
- Applicable law and dispute resolution
- Effectiveness of contract

5.2.3 Company Registration

As the first legal step, it is necessary to pre-register the company name with the competent company registration authority. The pre-registration is valid for three months and may be extended for another three months, during which it will have exclusive rights to the name.

Afterwards, for joint ventures that are not subject to Special Administrative Measures (industries that are not restricted or prohibited), joint venture agreements, contracts and articles of association concluded by the parties are required to be submitted to a record-filing management. For joint ventures within the Special Administrative Measures, joint venture agreements, contracts and articles of association concluded by the parties shall be submitted to the State Foreign Economic Relations and Trade Administrative Department (hereinafter referred to as the 'approval authority') for examination and approval. The approval authority shall decide whether to approve a joint venture within three months. Once the joint venture is filed or approved, it shall register with the State Administration for Market Regulation and obtain a business licence, and shall commence operations.

5.2.4 Registered Capital

'Registered capital' refers to the total amount of capital contributed by the parties and registered with the company registration authority. Registered capital is usually expressed in renminbi, although it may also be denominated in a foreign currency if the parties so agree.

The proportion of a joint venture's registered capital contributed by the foreign party shall generally be no lower than 25%. Foreign capital contributions of less than 25% may also be approved in some cases. In such cases, the enterprise's Foreign Investment Enterprise Approval Certificate will be marked 'foreign-investment ratio less than 25%'. These words will also be printed in the column of 'Type of Enterprise' of the foreign investment enterprise's business licence. The minimum registered capital threshold is not established, although companies in specific sectors may be subject to minimum registered capital in the relevant laws and regulations.

5.2.4.1 Forms of Capital Contribution

Capital contributions can be made in cash, machinery, equipment and intangible property, such as proprietary technology, trademarks and other industrial property rights, although technology or equipment contributed by a foreign party shall be advanced technology or equipment that is truly appropriate to China's needs. Capital contribution of imported patented or unpatented technology, materials and equipment is required to comply with the relevant laws and import laws and regulations. Any fraudulent acts through the international provision of outdated equipment or technology that causes losses shall be compensated. Additionally, the value of advanced technology or equipment as capital contribution is calculated in China by a valuation expert in China and is done so according to the Chinese market value.

The capital contributed by a Chinese investor may include the right to use a site provided for the joint venture during its operating term. Where the right to use a site does not constitute part of the investment made by the Chinese investor, the joint venture shall pay fees to the Chinese government for use of the site.

The various capital contributions shall be specified in the joint venture contract or the joint venture's articles of association, and the value of each contribution (excluding that of the site) shall be determined by the parties of the joint venture through consultation.

Practical Note: Business Plan

Prior to the establishment of the joint venture, it is important to evidence the will of the parties in the joint venture. In practice, a business plan or budget of the EJV can explain the appropriate reasons for the sum of capital contribution. This is particularly important in court, as the will of the parties could be used to demonstrate that the amount of the capital contribution was lawful and appropriate to the investment.

5.2.4.2 Capital Alterations

No joint venture may reduce its registered capital during the joint venture period. Where it is necessary to reduce the registered capital due to change in total investment sum or production and operational scales, approval shall be obtained from the approval authority. Any increase or reduction of registered capital shall be subject to resolution by the board of directors. Such an increase or reduction shall be reported to the competent authorities for approval and registration.

Any transfer of capital by one party of all or part of the registered capital requires the consent of the other party and the approval of the original approval-granting authority. In such cases, the other party has a pre-emptive right to purchase the share. If the other party declines to purchase the share, it can be offered to a third party, although the price may not be more favourable than that offered to the other party of the joint venture.

5.3 Corporate Governance

The parties to an EJV shall establish their articles of association, which is a tangible manifestation of the EJV contract. In the articles of association, items such as the governing rules of the company, management of its internal affairs, conduct of its business and the relationship between its members and the company are established. However, the parties are not regarded as the governing bodies after incorporation; for example, any revision to the company's articles of association is subject to the procedures for amendment of the articles of association, the unanimous agreement of the directors present at the board meeting and the approval of the supervising authority.

In an EJV, there is a two-tiered daily governance system:

- The board of directors is the highest governing body, determining and controlling all major issues concerning the venture
- The managerial staff manages the daily operations of the venture according to the resolutions of the board of directors

5.3.1 Board of Directors

Under the EJV Law, a board of directors shall be determined through negotiation between the parties of the joint venture and stipulated in the contract and the articles of association. The minimum number of board members is three (the number of directors shall be an odd number), and members of the board shall be appointed and replaced by the board of directors. Despite the fact that the number of directors to be appointed by each party shall be determined through consultation by the parties to the joint venture with reference to the proportion of their respective capital contribution, the number of board members determined by each party does not represent the share of the party; for example, the party holding the majority of shares may waive the right to appoint board members, while the party holding the minority of shares may appoint three board members.

The president of the board and vice-president of the board shall be determined through negotiation between the parties or shall be elected by the board of directors, although where the president of the board is assumed by one party of the joint venture, the other party of the joint venture shall assume the vice-president of the board. The president of the board of directors is, upon election, required to re-elect the board members. Therefore, even though the board of directors is nominated by the parties to the EJV, after the election of the president of directors, there is a possibility to amend the board of directors when the president re-elects the board members. There is no provision in the EJV Law or the laws and regulations concerning foreign investment in China that requires the president to re-elect the board members according to the election of the board.

The board of directors is provisioned to perform duties based on the principles of equality and mutual benefit. The powers and functions are governed by the provisions of the articles of association of the joint venture and include the following:

- Development plans
- Production and business plans
- Budget
- Distribution of profits
- Labour and remuneration plans
- Cessation of business activities
- Appointment or recruitment of the general manager, the deputy general manager, the chief engineer, the chief accountant and the auditors

5.3.2 Managerial Staff

The posts of the general manager and deputy general manager (or factory manager and deputy factory manager) are required to be split between the parties to the joint venture.

5.4 Labour

Employment matters are governed by the relevant labour laws and regulations. Matters concerning the employment, dismissal, remuneration, welfare benefits, labour protections, labour insurance, and so forth, of the employees of a joint venture shall be stipulated in a contract in accordance with the relevant law.

Employees of a joint venture are provisioned with the right to establish a trade union organisation in accordance with the law and conduct trade union activities and safeguard the lawful rights and interests of employees. Joint ventures are required to provide their trade unions with the necessary conditions for union activities. In practice, joint ventures are required to 'actively support' the labour union, such as providing office premises for the union and facilitating cultural, educational and athletic activities.

5.5 Operations

5.5.1 Bank Accounts

After obtaining a business licence, joint ventures are required to open renminbi deposit accounts with the Bank of China or other designated banks. On the strength of its business licence, the joint venture may open a foreign-exchange account with a bank or other financial institution authorised to engage in foreign-exchange business by the State Administration of Foreign Exchange. Any conduct of foreign-exchange business is required to be undertaken in accordance with the Administrative Regulations of the People's Republic of China on Foreign Exchange. Joint ventures may, in the course of their business activities, borrow funds directly from foreign banks. Any insurance policy taken out by a joint venture shall be taken out with an insurance company within Chinese territory.

5.5.2 Purchasing

Joint ventures, within their approved scope of operations and on the principles of fairness and reasonableness, may have the choice to purchase raw materials, fuel and other requirements from both domestic and international markets. Joint ventures are to be treated equally with other domestic enterprises with regard to prices for purchasing materials in China and the price and fees charged for services such as water, electricity, gas, heat, goods transportation, labour, engineering, consultation and advertising.

5.5.3 Selling

Joint ventures may sell their products inside or outside China. Distribution to foreign markets can be exported either directly or through appropriate agencies or Chinese foreign-trade organisations.

5.5.4 Taxation

Under the Enterprise Income Tax Law, equity joint ventures shall be subject to a uniform enterprise income tax rate of 25% on their worldwide net income. Equity joint ventures may still enjoy reduced income tax rates, but this shall not be based on their special 'joint venture' status but on their business engagement (i.e. the types of industries that are favoured by the State, such as agriculture, utilities, environmental protection, energy and water conservation and high technology). Any foreign party that reinvests its share of net profits within Chinese territory may apply for a refund of part of the income tax already paid.

5.5.5 Distribution of Profits

Distribution of profits is based on a calculation of the after-tax net profit of the joint venture and the deduction of allocations to the joint venture's statutory collective reserve fund, welfare funds, employee incentives and enterprise development funds. The balance remaining after such deductions may be distributed to the joint venture parties in proportion to their capital contributions.

5.5.6 Foreign Exchange

A foreign party to a joint venture may remit abroad its net share of profits and any other funds distributed to it under the following circumstances:

- On the expiry or suspension of a joint venture
- After performing its obligations as stipulated by the law
- In any agreement or contract

Foreign-exchange remittance formalities are governed by the Administrative Regulations of the People's Republic of China on Foreign Exchange.

Wages and other lawful income earned by expatriate employees of joint ventures may, after the payment of individual income tax in accordance with the tax laws of the People's Republic of China, be remitted abroad in accordance with the Administrative Regulations of the People's Republic of China on Foreign Exchange.

5.7 Term and Termination

The operating term of any joint venture is determined in accordance with its industry and individual circumstances. Dependent on the industry, the operating period may or may not be established. Generally, ventures engaging in investment projects that are encouraged and permitted by the State may choose to fix or not to fix an operational term in their joint venture contract. However, joint ventures falling within prescribed industries – such as service industries (including hotels, entertainment, catering, consultations, and so forth), land development, operation and management of real estate, exploration and exploitation of resources, and investment projects restricted by the State – are required to specify a fixed term in their contracts.

For a joint venture that is subject to the Special Administrative Measures stipulated by the State, if both parties have agreed to extend the term of operation, they shall submit an application to the approval authority at least six months prior to the expiry date of the operating period. The approval authority shall make a decision within one month of the date of receiving the application. For a joint venture that is not subject to the Special Administrative Measures stipulated by the State, both parties need only file the proofing material with the local agent of the Ministry of Commerce.

5.7.1 Early Termination

A joint venture may be terminated early under the following provisioned circumstances:

- The joint venture suffers heavy losses
- One party of the joint venture fails to perform its obligations under the contract or articles of association
- There is any occurrence of *force majeure*

The joint venture contract may be terminated by agreement of the parties and is subject to the approval of the approval authority and registration with the State Administration for Market Regulation. Where any economic loss is caused by a breach of contract, the party in breach shall be liable for the loss.

5.7.2 Disputes

Any dispute between the parties is required to be resolved by consultation with the board of directors. If the board of directors fails to resolve the dispute, the dispute can be resolved by conciliation or arbitration through an arbitral body in China or through arbitration by an arbitral body agreed upon by the parties. Where an arbitration clause in a cooperative contract has not subsequently reached an arbitration agreement in writing, legal proceedings can be instituted in a People's Court.

6 Current: Foreign-investment Law

6.1 Introduction

From 1 January 2020, the Foreign Investment Law of the People's Republic of China (FIL) became effective. The FIL, adopted at the Second Session of the Thirteenth National People's Congress, marks a significant era for foreign investment in China, and many foreign entities will be affected by the FIL. We will analyse the FIL to provide an in-depth understanding and main take-away points for foreign companies working in China.

6.2 Background

Foreign investment in China is governed by specific laws and regulations. Currently, foreign investment is divided into 'foreign direct investment' and 'other foreign investment'. Generally, 'foreign direct investment' refers to investment activities of establishing new entities or purchasing existing entities, while 'other foreign investment' refers to foreign investment activities that fall outside the scope of foreign direct investment.

In terms of foreign direct investment, there were three main bodies of laws that regulated the four primary forms of foreign direct investment:

1. The Sino-foreign Equity Joint Venture Law of the People's Republic of China (EJV Law) governs equity joint ventures established between a foreign party and a Chinese legal entity.
2. The Wholly Foreign-funded Enterprise of the People's Republic of China (WFOE Law) governs wholly foreign enterprises that are wholly established by one or with other foreign investors.
3. The Sino-foreign Cooperative Joint Ventures of the People's Republic of China (CJV Law) governs contractual joint ventures established between a foreign party and a Chinese enterprise or other economic organisations.

The adoption of the Foreign Investment Law (FIL) from 1 January 2020 simultaneously repeals the three laws above and unites both foreign direct investment and other foreign investment into one unified law governing foreign investment, as well as paving more consistency between domestic and foreign entities. It is important to note that the FIL shall also govern investments from Taiwan, Hong Kong Special Administrative Region and Macau Special Administrative Region.

Foreign-investment Governing Law Before 1 January 2020	Foreign-investment Governing Law After 1 January 2020
Sino-foreign Equity Joint Venture Law (EJV Law)	
Wholly Foreign-funded Enterprise Law (WFOE Law)	Foreign Investment Law (FIL)
Sino-foreign Cooperative Joint Venture Law (CJV Law)	

A unified foreign-investment law was first introduced in 2015 in the Consultation Draft of the Foreign Investment Law (Draft FIL), and on 26 December 2018, a new Draft FIL was deliberated at the Seventh Session of the Thirteenth NPC Standing Committee. A few months after the initial deliberation, the FIL was adopted at the National People's Congress.

6.3 Foreign Investment Law

Consisting of six chapters and 42 articles, the FIL regulates the new foreign-investment legal system and establishes fundamental provisions for investment form, promotion, protection, management and legal liability.

6.3.1 Forms of Foreign Investment

The FIL is applicable to both foreign direct and indirect investment in China. In Article 2 it states that foreign investment conducted by foreign investors may invest in China under the following circumstances:

1. A foreign investor establishes an enterprise within China (on its own or together with others)	2. A foreign investor acquires shares, or any other similar rights and interests of an enterprise within China
3. A foreign investor makes investment to initiate a new project within China (on its own or together with others)	4. Other forms stipulated under laws, administrative regulations and provisions of the State Council

6.3.1.2 Further Opening Up and Improved Mechanism for Foreign Investment

In the 2018 Forum, President Xi Jinping announced a new phase of opening up in China and outlined several key reforms to encourage foreign investment in China. For businesses, such reforms translate into reality and bring positive changes and opportunities in China. In Article 3, the Provisions reinstate the commitment to the opening-up policy through improving the business environment in the following areas:

- High-level investment liberalisation and convenience
- Investment promotion
- Level-play market environment

1. High-level Investment Liberalisation and Convenience

- **Special economic areas**
Currently, there are 12 pilot free-trade zones (FTZs) around China, including Shanghai, Tianjin, Guangdong, Fujian, Chongqing, Hubei, Henan, Liaoning, Sichuan, Shaanxi, Zhejiang and Hainan. These FTZs are special economy zones that act as experimental zones to test liberalisation reforms and enable foreign companies to operate in restricted and prohibited areas outside the FTZs. Article 13 demonstrates a commitment to establishing more special economic zones that support the opening-up policy and encourage further investment.

- **Preferential treatment**
While preferential treatment for foreign investment currently provides an incentive to invest in certain parts of China, some foreign investors have found that such preferential treatment may be beyond the actual authority of the local government. Under such circumstances, the preferential treatment could be removed or no preferential treatment shall actually be provided and the party may not have the legal rights to claim for respective performance or compensation. Articles 14 and 18 state that both national and local government are entrusted with the power to implement preferential policies to attract foreign investment according to the needs of the economic and social climate. In this manner, local government may legally implement respective promotional policies, and foreign investments may hold the corresponding legal rights.

2. Investment Promotion

- **Consistency between domestic and foreign investment**
The FIL provides greater consistency between domestic and foreign investment. From broadening market access to the operating stage of the investment, national treatment is applied to both domestic and foreign investment outside of the Negative List. Article 9 states that national policy supporting the development of enterprise shall equally apply to foreign investment, which in practice indicates that various investment activities of foreign investors should be eased, with less restrictions and greater enjoyment of the same rights as domestic investors.

- **Legislative consultation**
The FIL provides opportunities for foreign investors to consult with Chinese officials on new legislation, rules and regulations affecting foreign investment. In other words, foreign businesses may have more involvement in shaping and understanding new legislation that directly impacts their business in China.

3. Level-play Market Environment

- **Negative List**
  In 2016 the Negative List was first introduced as part of the reforms to limit case-by-case approvals for the establishment and change of foreign-investment administration systems. The Negative List establishes the industries in which foreign investments are prohibited or may only hold a limited share – usually 25% or 49%. Foreign investments that fall outside of the Negative List can incorporate companies through a record-filing system rather than the prior case-by-case approval system. In Article 4 the case-by-case approval system is officially abolished to create improved transparency and market access in an equal manner. With the exception of the prohibited and restricted industries outlined in the Negative List, national treatment shall be applied to all foreign investment.

  The Negative List is updated every year, and in the recent promulgation on 27 December 2021 the number of industries within the list was reduced to 31 items, with no new items added. Such reduction is a positive outlook for foreign companies looking to invest in areas once defined as prohibited or restricted.

  Equal treatment
  In terms of products and services produced in China by foreign investment, the government is required to treat such products and services as equal to domestic entities.

6.4 Investment Protection

6.4.1 Expropriation by the State

Investments made in China by foreign investors may be expropriated by the State as only for public use and only after fair compensation is made.

6.4.2 Free Repatriation

Free repatriation of the capital contributions, profits, capital gains, royalties and other compensation of foreign investors are allowed in renminbi or a foreign currency. The use of 'free' in Article 21 is the first time the word 'free' has been used in connection with the repatriation of gains derived from investments made by foreign investors in China. Under the existing laws, repatriation is:

- limited to legitimate profits, funds that remain after a dissolution, and other legitimate income
- allowed only after-tax clearance

6.4.3 Intellectual Property Protection

In response to foreign-investor concerns on intellectual property protection in China, Article 22 sets forth clear provisions on the protection of the legitimate rights and interests of holders of intellectual property. Any infringement is subject to legal liabilities, which in the recent reforms of the Trademark Law and Anti-unfair Competition Law of the PRC has raised the maximum penalty to CNY 5 million.

To address concerns that technology transfers are forced by Chinese policies requiring foreign investors to establish a joint venture with local partners, Article 22 explicitly states that no technology transfer shall be forced. Technology cooperation involving both a domestic and foreign party are required to work together with free will and business rules, and negotiation shall be performed with the principle of equality.

Furthermore, Article 23 requires Chinese officials who access trade secrets of foreign investment during the performance of their duties to maintain confidentiality. This is a positive step for commercial and trade secrets, with the revised Anti-unfair Competition Law – which specifically focuses on trade secrets – demonstrating China's commitment to protecting trade secrets and providing a stronger legal basis on which to hold infringers liable.

6.4.4 Complaint Mechanism

An official complaint mechanism shall be established so foreign-invested enterprises can file complaints against any government conduct that adversely affects their business. Foreign investment shall have the right to appeal to the appropriate authority across all phases of a foreign investment, from the establishment of a business entity to its dissolution.

The FIL aims to provide a stable, transparent, predictable and fair competitive market environment for foreign investors and foreign-invested enterprises, and it also includes provisions with clear policy directions to encourage and protect foreign investors. It also demonstrates that the Chinese government is addressing the concerns of foreign investors and paving the way to optimise the foreign-investment environment.

6.5 Investment Management

6.5.1 Corporate structure

In terms of wholly foreign-owned enterprises (WFOEs), there will be little impact, since the Implementation Opinion on Certain Issues Concerning the Application of Laws on the Approval and Registration Administration for Foreign-invested Companies requires WFOEs to adhere to the Company Law, while for equity joint ventures (EJVs) and cooperative joint ventures (CJVs) such revisions will have a major impact; namely, the corporate governance of both EJVs and CJVs considerably varies from the entities that adhere to the Company Law.

The table below summarises the corporate governance and structural differences between the laws.

Subjects	EJV Law	CJV Law	Company Law
Highest Authority	Board of directors	Board of directors or joint management committee	Shareholders
Powers and Duties of Highest Authority	All major issues, such as change to the articles of association, increase and decrease of registered capital, merger or spin-off, and dissolution	All major issues, such as change to the articles of association, increase and decrease of registered capital, merger or spin-off, and dissolution	Deliberating on and approving major matters, including the modification of the articles of association, the company's capital reduction, merger or division of the company, and dissolution and liquidation of the company
Voting Rules for Major Issues	Unanimous consent of all directors present at a board meeting	Unanimous consent of all directors or members of the joint management committee present at a meeting	Favourable votes of shareholders holding two-thirds or more of the voting rights
Number of Directors	No less than 3 directors	No less than 3 directors or members of the joint management committee	3 to 13 members of the board of directors or 1 executive director

Subjects	EJV Law	CJV Law	Company Law
Quorum	Two-thirds or more of all directors	Two-thirds or more of all directors or members of the joint management committee	As agreed by the shareholders (except voting for major issues where two-thirds is required, as mentioned above)
Term of Directors	4 years	No more than 3 years	No more than 3 years
Legal Representative	Chairman of the board	Chairman of the board or director of the joint management committee	Chairman of the board/executive director or general manager

6.5.2 Legal Person

Under the current CJV Law, CJVs are not required to be established as a legal person. Major elements of the partnership in a CJV are predominantly governed by the contractual joint venture contract, including investment or pre-requisite for cooperation, distribution of earnings or products, sharing of risk and loss, mode of operation and management, ownership of property upon termination of CJVs, and so forth. With the elimination of the CJV Law and the governance of the Company Law, CJVs without legal status should be established as a legal person and proceed in the required administrative formalities, such as articles of association, company incorporation, and so forth.

6.5.3 Corporate Governance

In both EJVs and CJVs, corporate governance is significantly impacted. Currently, the highest authority in EJVs is the board of directors, and in CJVs, the highest authority is either the board of directors or the joint management team. Now, under the Foreign Investment Law, such differences shall be unified to the provisions of the Company Law, that the corporate governance consists of the board of shareholders as the highest authority and the board of directors as the governance of the daily management and the board of supervisors. The board of shareholders convenes on the resolutions for the major issues of the company, and shareholder voting rights are based on each shareholder's respective capital contributions unless the articles of association specifies otherwise. The board of directors or one executive director is appointed by the board of shareholders to execute the resolutions of the board of shareholders and govern the daily management of the company.

With the highest authority of the company shifting from the board of directors or joint management team to the board of shareholders, the determination of the company shall rest on the board of shareholders. Any resolutions on major matters, including the appointment of the directors, supervisors and senior positions, are concluded with two-thirds of the majority voting rights. Therefore, such changes offer more flexibility in the decision-making mechanism and may decrease any deadlocks between shareholders, since a unanimous consent is no longer required. However, since the voting rights of shareholders is dependent on the respective capital contributions, minority shareholders may hold less influence than majority shareholders.

6.5.4 Share Transfer

Under the current EJV and CJV Laws, share transfers to a third party shall obtain the consent of all other shareholders, while under the Company Law, only the majority consent of shareholders is required. Again, the share transfer is much more flexible than before. However, any shareholders who disagree to the proposed transfer shall purchase the share to be transferred. Refusal to purchase the share shall be deemed as consent to transfer. Additionally, other shareholders shall have the right of first refusal on the purchase of the share.

6.5.5 Business Administration

From the effective date of the FIL, existing EJVs and CJVs are allocated a five-year transition period to implement such changes. Companies should complete any company alterations, such as articles of association, changes of directors and terms of directors according to record-filing procedures, as provisioned in the relevant laws, rules and regulations. Where joint ventures fail to complete such corporate changes, the competent department for commerce shall order such a company to make corrections within a prescribed time limit, and if such corrections are not made within the prescribed time, a penalty of no less than CNY 100,000 and not more than CNY 500,000 shall be imposed.

6.5.6 Collection of Information

Information of foreign investment submitted in the information-reporting system shall be both disclosed to the public and shared with various government authorities. In this manner, the foreign investors will no longer be required to prepare duplicate sets of the same application documents for different authorities, and efficiency of government review should increase, hence saving time and money for foreign investors. Government authorities are required to apply the same review standards with foreign investments as they do with domestic companies, except when otherwise required by law – which again demonstrates the Chinese government's commitment to equal treatment.

7 Current: Company Law

7.1 Introduction

The Company Law of the People's Republic of China (Company Law), adopted in 1993 and last revised in 2023 by the Standing Committee of the National People's Congress, and the five Provisions of the Supreme People's Court on Several Issues Concerning the Application of the Company Law of the People's Republic of China (Provisions) are the main legislations governing and applicable to corporate entities established in the People's Republic of China. The Company Law regulates the organisation and activities of companies, protecting the legitimate rights and interests of companies.

7.1.2 How 'Company' Is Defined Under the Company Law

The term 'company' in the Company Law refers to a limited liability company 有限责任公司 (Yǒuxiàn Zérèn Gōngsī) or a joint stock limited company 股份有限公司 (Gǔfèn Yǒuxiàn Gōngsī) established in the territory of the People's Republic of China. The Company Law is now applicable to both foreign- and Chinese-invested companies, though any specific law or regulation governing specific types of companies, such as state-owned companies, shall prevail over the Company Law.

7.1.3 Company Liabilities

Under the Company Law, a company is an enterprise legal person with independent legal-person property and property rights. A legal person, according to the Civil Code of the People's Republic of China, possesses 'civil legal capacity and capacity for civil acts and, according to the law, independently enjoys civil rights and assumes civil obligations'.

Where a company violates the law, the company can bear civil, administrative, and/or criminal liability according to the provisions of laws and regulations. If the liability is a civil one, the company shall pay compensation; if the liability is an administrative one, it shall pay corresponding fines and financial penalties imposed by the regulatory authority. Where the assets of a company are insufficient, the company shall firstly pay the compensation for such violation(s). Any crime in violation of the law shall be subject to criminal liability. Equally, if any person commits, in the name of a company, any serious violation of the law, threatening the security of the State, or injures the public interest or the interests of society, the business licence of the company shall be revoked.

> ### Practical Note: Investigating Companies in China
>
> Any company with a convicted penalty may be blacklisted. The companies in China can then be checked before a Sino-foreign joint venture or partnership is proceeded. To obtain the company documents, an investigation can be made through a Chinese lawyer filing a procedure at the State Administration for Market Regulation at the place where the inspected company is registered.

7.2 Limited Liability Company | 有限责任公司

Generally, 80% of companies in China are limited liability companies (LLCs). Limited liability companies may be comprised of either shareholders or one sole shareholder and may be private or wholly state-owned companies. A sole shareholder can be a natural or legal person. In the latest revision of Company Law (2023), the limitations in previous versions that a natural person may only establish one LLC, and no singular shareholder LLC shall establish another singular shareholder LLC have been removed.

Wholly state-owned companies are solely invested by the State, with capital contribution from the State-owned Assets Supervision and Administration Commission, as authorised by the State Council or the local People's Government of the same level.

Shareholders are capital contributors of the LLC and are entitled to a return on equity. Under an LLC, if there is no abuse of the independent legal status or similar violation of the law, the monetary liability of a shareholder is limited only to the amount of his capital contribution, while an LLC is liable for its debts to the extent of all its assets.

The number of shareholders is limited to 50.

Before establishment of a company, the following conditions shall be met:

- The number of shareholders shall constitute a quorum
- The articles of association shall be formulated collectively by shareholders
- The capital contributions of the company shall be compliant with the articles of association of the related company, which are subscribed to by all shareholders

- The company name and organisational structure shall be established under the requirements for limited liability companies
- The company domicile shall be established

7.2.1 Articles of Association

The articles of association of an LLC establishes the governing rules of the company, management of its internal affairs, conduct of its business and the relationship between its members and the company. The provisions of the articles of association legally bind the company and its shareholders, directors, supervisors and senior officers. The articles of association are formulated by the shareholders of the company, and upon agreement of the articles of association, the shareholders shall affix their signatures or seals on it. Mandatory items to be included in the articles of association include the following:

- Name and domicile of the company
- Business scope of the company
- Registered capital of the company
- Names of the shareholders
- Forms, amounts and dates of the capital contributions of each shareholder
- Institutions of the company and its establishment, functions and powers, and rules of procedure
- Legal representative of the company
- Any other matter deemed necessary by the shareholders of the company

In the case of wholly state-owned companies, the articles of association is required to be formulated by the State-owned Assets Supervision and Administration Commission or drafted by the board of directors and submitted to the State-owned Assets Supervision and Administration Commission for approval.

7.2.2 Name

An LLC established in accordance with the law shall include the words 'limited liability company' 有限责任公司 (Yōuxiàn Zérèn Gōngsī) or 'limited company' 有限公司 (Yōuxiàn Gōngsī) in its name.

7.2.3 Business Scope

The business scope describes each activity of the company. The title of each business activity is defined and approved by the State, and the shareholder or shareholders choose those that best conform to the business activities that are to be conducted by the company. Pursuant to the relevant laws or administrative regulations, certain business activities may be subject to approval by the authority. The business scope is defined in the articles of association and registered with the company administration authorities in accordance with the law. Any business activity outside of the registered business scope of a company is forbidden to be conducted unless the company changes the business scope by first amending its articles of association and then completing the formalities for the registration of changes.

> ### Practical Note: The Value of a Company in Relation to its Business Scope
>
> A company with a large scope of business activities could be appraised at a higher value, as it allows the company to operate in more streams of business, whereas a smaller scope of business activities may require more investment if acquired by another company in order to expand the business scope.

7.2.4 Capital Contribution

Prior to the establishment of a company, shareholders shall determine their respective capital contributions and subscribe their share subscription as determined by the articles of association.

Although under the Company Law there is no required minimum amount for registered capital of a limited liability company (including single-shareholder limited liability companies), special industries such as finance, securities and insurances may require a minimum amount of registered capital prescribed by relevant laws and regulations. Equally, any other relevant laws, regulations and decisions of the State Council in relation to minimum registered capital shall prevail over the provisions of the Company Law.

7.2.4.1 Form of Capital

A shareholder of a limited liability company may contribute capital in cash, in kind or using intellectual property rights, land use rights or other non-monetary assets. However, any assessment or ownership transfer of non-monetary asset value shall proceed in accordance with the law, except in instances where any other law or administrative regulation prohibits the use of the relevant assets to make capital contributions.

Prohibited forms of capital contribution include labour services, credit, the name of a natural person, credit standing or franchising rights, or property on which there is a guarantee, etc. on the basis of valuation.

7.2.4.2 Payment of Capital Contribution

Each shareholder in the prescribed time shall fully pay in the capital contribution amount as prescribed in the articles of association. The deadline for full contribution is within five years of the establishment of the company. Any shareholder's capital contribution made in cash shall be deposited in full into a temporary bank account opened in the name of the limited liability company. The appropriate transfer procedures for the property rights in any non-financial asset used to contribute capital shall be paid in accordance with the law.

A shareholder who fails to pay the capital contribution in full and on time shall pay the full amount to the company and be liable for compensation for any losses caused to the company. If a shareholder fails to make capital contributions in accordance with the provisions of the company's articles of association, or if the actual value of the non-monetary assets contributed is significantly lower than the subscribed capital, other shareholders at the time of company establishment shall bear joint and several liability within the scope of the insufficient contribution part.

7.2.4.3 Capital Verification and Issuance of Certification

All capital contributions surrendered by shareholders are subject to examination and verification conducted by the legally established capital verification institution. Generally, legally incorporated accounting firms, law firms and asset appraisal institutions, etc. are eligible capital verification institutions and are entitled to engage in capital verification. Once the verification is complete, a certification shall be produced stating the currency type and amount of monetary contribution or the certification of value equivalent to the prevailing market value for the non-monetary property. Regarding capital contribution made in instalments, the capital verification for each instalment shall be attached.

Any institutions of appraisal or verification of assets or a verification of certificates shall be legally liable under the following circumstances:

- Providing false materials
- Omitting any important matter from reports submitted

Any unlawfully gained profits from such violations shall be confiscated by the competent administrative department and fined between one and five times the value of any unlawfully gained profits. The competent administrative department may suspend business operations and cancel the qualification certificate(s) of the person(s) directly liable or revoke the business licence of the company.

Equally, in the instance that such institutions are proven to provide inaccurate appraisal results or proof-of-asset verifications or certificate verifications, and this subsequently causes loss to creditors of the company, such institutions shall be liable to compensate the creditors for the difference between the appraised or verified amount and the accurate value, unless they can prove that they are not at fault.

Practical Note: Selling of Shares

If a shareholder wants to sell his share in a company, before the sale of the share, the capital verification certificate is generally required as evidence for share value. Furthermore, if the shareholder is from overseas, the capital verification certificate shall identify the name of the overseas bank and account number. In this way, the capital of the share can be transferred back to the same bank account identified on the capital verification certificate. If the bank account is no longer open, the shareholder is required to conduct the formalities to change the bank account identified on the capital verification certificate, which may delay the return of the capital. Consequently, it is advisable to retain the original bank account.

7.2.4.4 Capital Registration

After the shareholders subscribe for the full amount of capital contributions according to the articles of association, the representative designated by the shareholders, or the agent appointed by the shareholders, shall submit such documents as a company registration application and articles of association to the company registration authority for registration of establishment. The company registration authority shall register the total capital contribution as the registered capital.

After the incorporation of a limited liability company, if the actual value of non-monetary assets submitted as capital contributions is found to be noticeably lower than the value specified in the articles of association, the shareholder or shareholders who contributed such capital are required to rectify the shortfall, and the other share-holders at the time of incorporation shall be jointly and severally liable. Where any fraudulent capital contribution is found, the company registration authority shall order the related shareholder to rectify the deficit and shall issue a fine of between 5% and 15% of the fraudulent capital contribution.

The board of directors shall verify the shareholder's capital contribution. If any shareholder is found to have not paid the capital contribution in full and on time according to the articles of association, the company shall issue a written call letter to such shareholder to call for the payment. The grace period for payment of the capital contribution may be specified in such call letter. If the shareholder still fails to fulfil its capital contribution obligations at the expiry of the grace period, the company may issue a written notice of deprivation of rights to the shareholder upon a resolution of the board of directors. From the date of the notice, the shareholder shall lose its share-holder's right over the unpaid part.

No shareholder shall withdraw their capital contribution following the incorpor-ation of the company and such violation shall be subject to the rectification from the company registration authority, and a fine of between 5% and 15% of the capital contribution that has been unlawfully withdrawn. Equally, the registered capital is required to be paid in before the company can be liquidated.

7.2.4.5 Capital Contribution Certificate

Following the incorporation of a limited liability company, each shareholder shall be issued with a capital contribution certificate, which shall specify the following items:

- Name of the company
- Date of incorporation of the company
- Registered capital of the company
- Name of the shareholder, the amount of subscribed and paid-in capital, the way of contribution, and the date of contribution
- Serial number and date of issue of the capital contribution certificate

The Capital Contribution Certificate shall bear the signature of the legal representative and the seal of the company.

7.2.4.6 Increased or Reduced Capital Contribution

Reducing the Registered Capital	• A balance sheet and schedule of assets are required to be prepared. • The company shall notify creditors within 10 days from the date of the decision and issue a public announcement through a newspaper or the National Enterprise Credit Information Publicity System within 30 days from the date of the decision. • Upon the notification of such reduction, a creditor may require the company to repay its debt in full or provide a corresponding guarantee within 30 days upon receipt of the notice or 45 days upon the date of the public announcement if no notice was received.
Increasing the Registered Capital	• The subscription of the shareholders for the increased amount shall be governed by the relevant provisions of the law.

Where a company increases or reduces its registered capital, the company shall handle relevant procedures for change with the company's registration authority in accordance with the law.

7.2.5 Shareholder Registration

A limited liability company shall prepare a register of members, which shall record the following items:

- The name and domicile of each shareholder
- The subscribed and paid-in capital amounts, the form of contribution, and the date of contribution of each shareholder
- The serial number of each capital contribution certificate
- The date of entitlement or loss of shareholder status for each shareholder

The shareholders recorded in the register of members may, pursuant to the register of members, claim and exercise shareholders' rights.

A company shall register the name of each shareholder with the company registration authority. In the event of any change in the registered details, the company shall handle the registration of the change. Any registration detail that fails to be registered or amended shall not be valid against any third party.

7.2.6 Company Registration

Registration of the establishment of a company is a legal act reflecting the effectiveness of the company establishment and emergence of the legal person. If the company is subject to approval under any provisions of the law or administrative regulations, the approval shall be obtained prior to the company registration. An application for the company registration is filed with the company registration authority in accordance with the law. If the application meets the requirements of the law, the company registration authority shall approve the registration of the company. Once the company is registered by the company registration authority, part of the registration details of the company can be inquired about by the public.

Any person who, in the course of registering a company, misstates its registered capital, submits false documentation or uses any other fraudulent means in order to conceal any important fact shall be ordered by the company registration authority to remedy the defect. Where the registered capital of a company is misstated, the company shall be fined between 5% and 15% of the amount by which the registered capital was misstated. Where false documentation is submitted or where any other fraudulent means are used in order to conceal any important fact, the company shall be fined between CNY 50,000 and CNY 2,000,000, and where the circumstances are serious, the company's business licence shall be revoked, and a fine between CNY30,000 and CNY 300,000 shall be imposed on any person directly in charge and other persons directly liable.

7.2.7 Business Licence

Once all establishment formalities are completed and approved, the company shall be issued with a business licence by the company registration authority. The business licence evidences establishment of the company, and the date of issuance is the date of the establishment of the company. The business licence shall include the following:

- Company name
- Company domicile
- Registered capital
- Business scope
- Name of the legal representative
- Other information

Any changes to the information recorded on the company business licence are subject to formalities for registration of changes. After the approval, the company registration authority shall reissue a new company business licence. Any company failing to handle the relevant procedures for registration of change in accordance with the law following any change in the company's registered details shall be ordered by the company registration authority to amend its registration within a specific period of time. If it still fails to make the required amendment, it shall be fined between CNY 10,000 and CNY 100,000.

Company registration is a legal requirement, and no business operations may be undertaken prior to the company registration and the issuance of the business licence. Any person conducting business in the name of an unregistered company or unregistered subsidiary shall be ordered by the company registration authority to rectify the violation or be subject to the company registration authority's enforcement procedures and may be fined up to CNY 100,000.

Equally, once the business licence is obtained as evidence of the company establishment, the company shall commence business operations within six months of incorporation. Failure to commence business operations without reasonable justification within six months of establishment, or suspension of business operation of its own volition for a period of six months or more, shall be liable to the revocation of its business licence, except where the company has fulfilled the procedure for closure of business in accordance with the law.

7.2.8 Shareholder Rights

Shareholders are capital contributors of the company and are entitled to return on equity and the following rights:

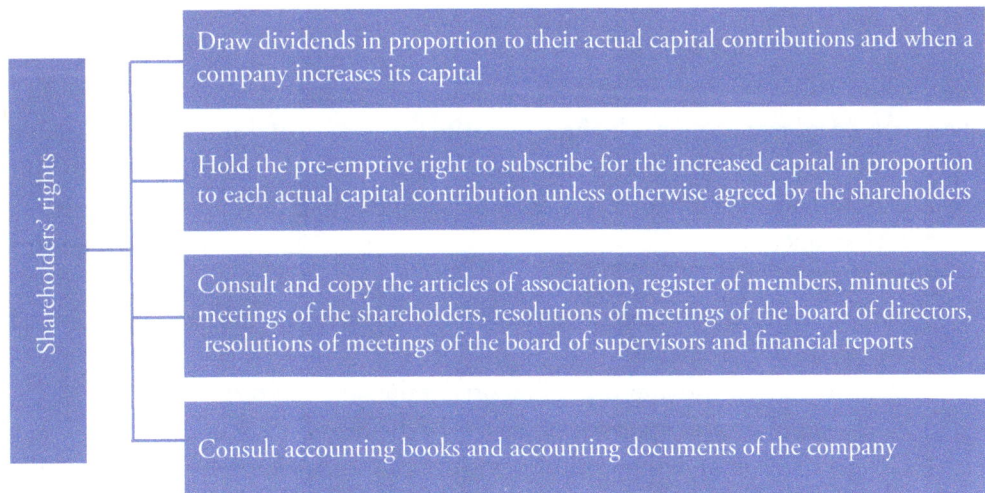

Shareholders' rights

Draw dividends in proportion to their actual capital contributions and when a company increases its capital

Hold the pre-emptive right to subscribe for the increased capital in proportion to each actual capital contribution unless otherwise agreed by the shareholders

Consult and copy the articles of association, register of members, minutes of meetings of the shareholders, resolutions of meetings of the board of directors, resolutions of meetings of the board of supervisors and financial reports

Consult accounting books and accounting documents of the company

Any requests to consult the accounting books of the company shall be submitted in writing to the company, clearly stating the purpose. If the company finds it reasonable to deem the request as improper, and that it may impair the legitimate interests of the company, the company may decline the shareholder's request and within 15 days upon the submission of the shareholder's written request issue the shareholder with a written reply stating the reasons thereof. If the company declines the request of any shareholder for consultation of the company's accounting books, the shareholder may initiate legal action at the People's Court.

7.2.9 Shareholder Liabilities

The Company Law stipulates that shareholders of a company shall abide by laws, administrative regulations and the articles of association and exercise shareholders' rights in accordance with the law. Shareholders are strictly prohibited from abusing shareholders' rights, the independent company's status as a legal person or the limited liability of shareholders. Any shareholder who causes loss to the company or to other shareholders by such abuse shall be liable for compensation. Equally, shareholders in evasion of debt payment by abusing the company's independent status as a legal person or the limited liability of shareholders, and such evasion results in serious damages to the interests of any creditor of the company, shall be jointly and severally liable for the debts of the company.

7.2.10 Limited Liability Company Corporate Governance

There are three main boards of corporate governance in an LLC: shareholders' meeting, board of directors and board of supervisors.

7.2.10.1 Shareholders' Meeting

The shareholders' meeting is the highest authority in the company and an indispensable organ in the corporate governance structure. The shareholders' meeting convenes on resolutions for major issues rather than the daily operations of the business and exercise the following functions:

- Election and replacement of directors and supervisors and determination of the remuneration thereof
- Deliberation on and approval of reports of the board of directors
- Deliberation on and approval of reports of the board of supervisors
- Deliberation on and approval of company profit-distribution plans and debt-recovery plans

- Making resolutions about any increase or reduction in the company's registered capital
- Making resolutions about the issuance of corporate bonds
- Making resolutions on any merger, demerger, dissolution, liquidation or change of company form of the company
- Revision of the articles of association of the company
- Any other functions or powers specified in the articles of association

The shareholders' meeting may authorize the board of directors to make resolutions regarding the issuance of corporate bonds.

In a wholly state-owned company, the State-owned Assets Supervision and Administration Commission shall exercise the functions and powers of the shareholders' meeting. The State-owned Assets Supervision and Administration Commission may authorise the company's board of directors to exercise some of the functions and powers of the shareholders' meeting and decide important matters of the company, although items relating to the combination, division or dissolution of the company, the increase or reduction of its registered capital or the issuance of corporate bonds must be decided by the State-owned Assets Supervision and Administration Commission.

7.2.10.1.1 Structure of the Shareholders' Meetings

The first shareholders' meeting is convened by the largest shareholder. This shareholder presides over the first meeting and exercises his powers in accordance with the Company Law. Shareholders' meetings thereby after the first assembly are convened by the established board of directors and are presided over by the chairman of the board of directors. Where a limited liability company has no board of directors, shareholders' meetings shall be convened and presided over by the acting director.

Shareholders are notified 15 days in advance of a meeting unless otherwise specified in the articles of association or agreed by all shareholders. Minutes shall be made of the decisions on matters discussed during the meetings, which shall be signed or sealed by the attending shareholders.

The methods of deliberation and voting procedures at shareholders' meetings are also governed by the company's articles of association.

A resolution of the shareholders' meeting shall be adopted by shareholders representing a majority of the voting rights. Any resolution to amend the articles of association, increase or decrease the registered capital, or regarding a merger, demerger, dissolution, or change of corporate form of the company shall be adopted by shareholders representing two-thirds or more of the voting rights.

The attendance of any director, supervisor or senior executive may be required for a meeting, but the member is a non-voting representative and answers the inquiries of the shareholders.

For any matters where the shareholders unanimously consent in writing to a resolution, the shareholders' meeting may not be required to convene, provided that the resolution document shall bear the signatures or seals of all the shareholders.

7.2.10.2 Board of Directors

The board of directors collectively handles corporate affairs. No director shall act individually; rather, the resolutions shall be the majority vote of the board. The board of directors is a permanent institution acting on behalf of the shareholders' meeting and may be subject to dismissal where it fails to work in a faithful and diligent manner. A relatively smaller limited liability company with fewer shareholders may establish a sole director with the same functions and powers as the board of directors. This director may serve concurrently as the manager.

7.2.10.2.1 Number of Directors and Length of Term

According to the latest stipulation of Company Law (2023), the board of directors of a limited liability company shall consist of three or more members, and may include any number of employees' representatives among them.

The articles of association specify the method for the appointment of a chairman and deputy chairman (if any) to preside over the board of directors. Furthermore, the articles of association shall stipulate the director's term of office, though it may not in any case exceed three years. Any director or supervisor may, after the expiry of his term of office, hold consecutive post on re-election.

7.2.10.2.2 The Functions and Powers of the Board of Directors

According to the Company Law of the People's Republic of China, the board of directors shall exercise the following functions:

- Convene shareholders' meetings and present reports thereto
- Execute resolutions made at shareholders' meetings
- Determine operational plans and investment plans
- Formulate the company's annual budgets and final account plans
- Formulate the company's profit-distribution plans and debt-recovery plans
- Formulate the company's plans for any proposed increase or decrease in its registered capital or on the issuance of corporate bonds
- Formulate the company's plans for any proposed merger, demerger, change in company form, dissolution, or similar
- Make decisions on the establishment of the company's internal management departments
- Make decisions on the appointment or dismissal of the company's manager and their remuneration and, according to the nomination of the manager, make decisions on the appointment or dismissal of the deputy manager(s) and the finance manager and their remuneration
- Establish the company's basic management system
- Any other function specified in the articles of association or granted by the shareholders' meeting

The board of directors mainly exercises its powers and functions through meetings convened and presided over by the chairman of the board of directors or the deputy chairman (if the chairman fails to perform his duties). In the meetings, directors shall make resolutions on issues submitted to be deliberated. Resolutions are made on the majority vote of the board of directors and are calculated on the system of 'one vote per director'. Thus, every director shall cast one vote on every issue submitted to the board of directors.

> ## Practical Note: Frequency of Board of Directors' Meetings
>
> Commonly, the board of directors should meet in the middle of the year to review the financial statement of the previous year and meet towards the end of the year to formulate next year's annual budget. However, this is not legally mandatory.

7.2.10.3 Board of Supervisors

The board of supervisors is an internal corporate supervision system set to protect the interest of the investors. It is a legally required standing agency to supervise and check the company's business activities. A limited liability company may establish a board of supervisors of no less than three members. The board of supervisors shall include shareholders' representatives and an appropriate proportion of employee representatives. Employee representatives shall account for at least one-third of the total members, and the specific proportion shall be stipulated by the articles of association. Employee representatives are elected by the employee assembly, or other forms of democratic elections.

The board of supervisors shall appoint one chairman, who shall be elected by the majority of all the supervisors. Meetings of the board of supervisors shall be convened and presided over by the chairman. If the chairman fails to perform the duties, the meeting shall be convened and presided over by a supervisor nominated by the majority of the supervisors.

No director or senior officer shall concurrently serve as a supervisor.

The term of office for a supervisor shall be three years and may be held as a consecutive post upon re-election.

For a relatively small limited liability company with fewer shareholders, it may appoint one supervisor without establishing a board of supervisors. Based on Company Law (2023), upon consensus of all the shareholders, such small company may also have no supervisor.

7.2.10.3.1 Authorities of the Board of Supervisors or the Supervisor

The company's directors, managers and other senior executives shall be regulated by the supervisory system. In such cases, directors and senior executives are required to faithfully provide relevant information and materials to the board of supervisors or to the supervisor. They may not obstruct the board of supervisors or any supervisor in the exercise of their powers

Supervisors of the board may exercise the following primary authorities:

- They may review the company's financial affairs by checking the company's account books and other accounting materials, financial reports, business reports, profit-distribution programmes and other accounting materials submitted by the board of directors to shareholders' meetings. Supervisors may perform a recheck in the event that questions pertaining to the company's financial affairs arise
- They may ensure that the company's operational and management activities are performed in line with the resolutions of the shareholders and supervise the performance of the directors and senior executives in their respective duties
- Where the director or senior executive violates the laws, administrative regulations, articles of association or resolutions of the shareholders' meeting, the board of supervisors may propose the removal of any director or senior executive who commits irregularities
- Where a director or senior executive damages the interests of the company, the board of supervisors may require them to stop and make correction
- They may propose certain topics and specific issues to shareholders' meetings for discussion and voting
- They may propose to convene over temporary shareholders' meetings, as well as convene and preside over shareholders' general meetings under special circumstances
- They may initiate litigation on behalf of the company where the board of directors or managers of the company neglect to protect the company interests
- Under the premise of not violating compulsory provisions of laws and administrative regulations, the company's shareholders' meetings may grant additional authorities to the board of supervisors through the articles of association based on the company's specific conditions

The board of supervisors may require directors and senior executives to submit reports about their performance of duties. Directors and senior executives shall provide relevant information to the board of supervisors truthfully and shall not obstruct supervisors from exercising their powers. All necessary expenses incurred by the board of supervisors in exercising its functions and powers shall be borne by the company.

7.2.10.3.2 Meeting of the Board of Supervisors

A board of supervisors shall hold regular meetings no less than once a year and may hold interim meetings. A resolution of the board of supervisors shall be **approved by 50% or more votes of the supervisors,** and the articles of association shall stipulate the methods of deliberation as well as the voting procedures.

7.2.10.3.3 Utilising the Role of the Board of Supervisors

The board of supervisors or sole supervisor is an internal corporate supervision system established to protect the interest of a company and its shareholders. It is a legally required standing agency, and its purpose is to safeguard and supervise the company's business activities according to the interests of the company and the shareholders. Supervisors are obligated to carry out responsibilities with a duty of loyalty and diligence. Where any director, supervisor or senior officer violates any law, administrative regulation or the articles of association in the course of performing his duties, they shall be liable to compensate the company for any loss thereby caused to the company.

Normally, the shareholder appoints a person of high trust for the role of supervisor, one who holds an understanding of the company so that they can effectively regulate its activities. Such appointment is required by law to be registered with the government. An additional best practice is signing a contract between the shareholders and the supervisor. In this manner, a replacement clause stipulating an agreed-upon timeline for replacing the supervisor upon his resignation can be included in the contract in order to limit risks.

Consequently, the role of the supervisor holds extreme importance and influence in a company. Where the supervisor is utilised in the correct and lawful manner, even a minority shareholder may hold great influence within the company management, operations and structure. However, if the majority shareholder does not fully utilise the supervisor correctly and lawfully, the control of the company may sway unfavourably to the majority shareholder.

7.2.11 Legal Representative (法定代表人)

The importance of the legal representative of a China-based company is too often overlooked. Often the role and responsibilities of the legal representative is underestimated, which may raise the risk potential for both the individual and the company.

The Civil Code of the People's Republic of China, effective from 1 January 2021, stipulates that the person with the responsibility of representing a "legal person" (i.e., an entity with independent legal status) in conducting civil activities in accordance with the law or the legal person's articles of association is the legal representative of the legal person. In other words, the legal representative is responsible for representing the company in exercising its functions and powers, as well as its daily management. The legal consequences of the civil activities conducted by the legal representative in the legal person's name shall be assumed by the legal person. Similar expression can also be found in the Company Law, that, the legal consequences of civil activities conducted by a company's legal representative in the name of the company shall be borne by the company.

The responsibilities of the legal representative include but are not limited to legally conserving the company's assets, executing powers of attorney on the company's behalf, authorising legal representation of and litigation by the company, and entering into contracts and taking responsibility for legal obligations in the company's name. Therefore, choosing a suitable, qualified legal representative to possess such broad powers and potentially be exposed to unlimited liability is extremely important in reducing potential risk.

The Company Law (2023) expands the scope of personnel that can be established as the legal representative – previously, only the chairman of the board of directors, the executive director or the general manager can serve as the legal representative; now, the restriction is relaxed – the legal representative can be a director or manager representing the company for the execution of company affairs .

The established legal representative is required to be registered in accordance with the law, and in the event of a change of the legal representative, the company shall register the change.

An option for foreign companies to consider is the utilisation of a professional, such as a lawyer. Although a lawyer may lack the corporate knowledge of the company as the legal representative, they may be highly effective in utilising the powers of the legal representative to govern the company; for example, the lawyer could ensure that contracts entered into correspond with the resolutions of the board of directors. The lawyer, as the legal representative, may also request that the senior officer report to the shareholders should any contract fail to correspond with the resolutions of the board of directors.

However, we note that the lawyer as legal representative should only govern the actions of the senior officer, and not manage the senior officers; for example, a lawyer as legal representative auditing contracts before their signing is governance, while a lawyer as legal representative requesting senior officers to audit contracts is management.

Since the legal responsibility calls for acting on behalf of the company, the law holds the legal representative to a higher standard of due diligence and care. A legal representative may face civil, administrative and criminal liabilities accrued by the company.

The definitions of liability assigned to the legal representative is as follows:

Liability	Details
Civil Liability	The civil activities of the legal representative in the name of the company are deemed as civil activities conducted by the company, with any consequences arising therefrom being borne by the company. Any restrictions stipulated in the articles of association or imposed by the governing body of the company affecting the legal representative's power to represent the company shall not be asserted against a bona fide third party. Where a legal representative of a company causes damage to others while performing responsibilities, the civil liability thus incurred shall be assumed by the company. After assuming the aforementioned civil liability, the company has the right to indemnification, in accordance with the law or its articles of association, against its legal representative who is at fault.
Administrative Liability	If a company violates any of the laws of the PRC, the legal representative of such a company may be subject to fines and punishment, in addition to any punishment passed to the company. Such punishment may also manifest as restriction in future career; for example, any former legal representative of a company or enterprise that has had its business licence revoked and has been ordered to close its business operations due to any violation of the law in circumstances where the former legal representative was personally liable for the revocation of the business licence shall not be eligible for appointment as a director, supervisor or senior officer of a company within three years. Where the violation is deemed serious, the legal representative may be subject to criminal liability.
Criminal Liability	The PRC Criminal Law imposes criminal liability on both the individual and the company the individual oversees, or is responsible for, that commits a crime. As the main principal of the company, the legal representative shall not be pursued with any criminal liability unless he has participated in the crime and is directly in charge of or is responsible for the crime committed by the company.

Overall, the legal representative is an essential role in the management of a company and should not be underestimated. Selecting an appropriate, trustworthy person as a legal representative is crucial to minimising risk. Selecting the wrong legal person may cause major damages to a company.

7.2.12 Senior Executives

The board of directors governs the senior executives to manage the company's day-to-day operations. Senior executives of a company include the general manager, deputy general manager, chief financial officer, and other persons designated by the company's articles of association. All senior executives are accountable to the board of directors and shall exercise responsibilities within the scope of the board of directors' authorisation.

Under the Company Law, the board of directors is responsible for appointing and dismissing the senior executives by an affirmative majority vote. It is advised that the selection of senior executives is crucially determined by individuals' qualification and competence. A limited liability company may have a manager, who shall be appointed or dismissed by its board of directors. If the board of directors deems a manager is no longer qualified for the position, in accordance with the law a meeting may be convened to decide on a manager's dismissal. Furthermore, if the board of supervisors of the company discovers that the conduct of any manager violates any applicable law, administrative regulation, the articles of association or any resolution of the shareholder's meeting, the board of supervisors can propose to dismiss such a manager.

7.2.12.1 Functions of Senior Executives

There are no mandatory items regarding the functions and powers for manager under the latest Company Law (2023). The manager shall exercise functions and powers as specified in the articles of association or as authorised by the board of directors, while the following powers are generally referred to in practice:

- Take charge of managing the production and business operations of the company and organise the implementation of resolutions made by the board of directors
- Organise execution of the company's annual operational plans and investment plans
- Draft plans on the establishment of the company's internal management departments
- Draft the company's basic management system
- Draft the company's specific policies
- Propose the appointment or dismissal of the company's deputy manager and chief financial officer
- Decide on the appointment or dismissal of executives for posts other than those decided by the board of directors
- Attend meetings of the board of directors as a non-voting representative
- Any other power conferred on the manager by the board of directors

7.2.12.2 Executive Meetings (not legally mandatory)

Many large companies, especially listed companies, have established executive meetings as a democratic and collective decision-making institution. During executive meetings, the senior executives of a company deliberate on day-to-day operational and management matters. Meetings are classified routinely on a weekly or monthly basis, or at special ad hoc meetings. Generally, the range of issues considered by an executive meeting includes strategic and policy issues concerning the overall operation and management of the company; issues concerning major by-laws of the company; personnel issues, and punishments and awards to employees; the establishment and adjustment of internal governance bodies of the company; issues concerning plans on major investments, major acquisition, restructuring and disposal of assets; and other issues for which the general manager deems necessary. Ad hoc meetings are convened where key issues regarding operation and management of the company are reviewed and decided.

As a rule, a managers' executive meeting is convened and presided over by the general manager. Any other senior executive of the company may convene and preside but is subject to approval or delegation of the general manager.

7.2.13 Capability of Directors, Supervisors and Senior Executives

A person shall not be appointed a director, supervisor or senior executive of a company under the following conditions:

- Any person without civil capacity or who has limited civil capacity[2]
- Any person convicted of a criminal offence in the nature of corruption, bribery, disseizing, misappropriation or disrupting the economic order of the socialist market and five years has not elapsed since any penalty imposed has been completed, or any person who has ever been deprived of his political rights due to any crime and five years has not elapsed since the penalty imposed was completed, or in the case he/she is sentenced to a period of probation, two years have not elapsed since the probation period was completed;
- Any former director, factory director or manager of a company or enterprise declared bankrupt and liquidated in circumstances where such a person was personally responsible and three years has not elapsed since the bankruptcy and liquidation of the company or enterprise was completed
- Any former legal representative of a company or enterprise that had its business licence revoked and was ordered to close business operations due to a

---

[2] Generally, in China a person will have full civil capacity when he is 18 years old.

violation of law in circumstances where the former legal representative was personally liable and three years has not elapsed since the date of revocation
- Any person who has significant unpaid due debts and identified as subject to enforcement for breach of credit by the people's court

Any election or appointment of any director, supervisor or senior executive made in violation of the provisions of the Company Law shall be invalid, and the said director, supervisor or senior executive shall be removed from his post.

7.2.14 Obligations of Directors, Supervisors and Seniors Executives

The Company Law stipulates obligations (also known as 'fiduciary duties') of senior executives, directors and supervisors to the company. Duties of a fiduciary are categorised under the duty of loyalty and the duty of diligence. The duties of loyalty are acts made according to shareholder, company and creditors' interests and are a conscience-based obligation characterised by moral consciousness. Directors, supervisors and senior executives shall avoid conflicts of interest between their own interests and the interests of the company, and shall not use their authority to seek improper benefits. The duty of diligence (also called the duty of care) is a requirement for the directors, supervisors and senior executives to act with goodwill, caution and reasonable care. Any director or senior executive in violation of any law, administrative regulation or the articles of association in the course of performing his duties shall bear the damages and compensation of such violations. Equally, acts of the director(s), supervisor(s) or senior executive(s) constituting a crime shall face criminal liabilities.

7.2.14.1 Negligence of Duties

The Company Law prohibits any director, supervisor or senior executive from taking any bribe or other illegal gains by taking advantage of his position or misappropriating company assets for personal use. Furthermore, the director or senior executive are prohibited from the following:

- Embezzling company property or misappropriating company funds
- Diverting company funds into an account held in his own name or in the name of any other individual
- Using authority to engage in bribery or accept other illegal income
- Personally accepting any commission on any transaction to which the company is a party
- Unlawfully disclosing confidential company information
- Acting in any way that is inconsistent with his duty of fidelity to the company.

Directors supervisors and senior executives directly or indirectly entering into a contract or engaging in a transaction with the company shall report to the board of directors or the shareholders' meeting, and obtain approval in advance according to the company's articles of association. The approval/disapproval shall be made by resolutions of the board of directors or the shareholders' meeting. This shall also apply to the close relatives of directors, supervisors, or senior executives, enterprises directly or indirectly controlled by directors, supervisors, or senior executives or their close relatives, and parties having other relationships as a related party with directors, supervisors, or senior executives.

Directors, supervisors, and senior executives shall not use their authority to seek any business opportunity that ought to belong to the company or operate businesses similar to those of the company, unless it has been reported to the board of directors or the shareholders' meeting and approved by the resolutions of the board of directors or the shareholders' meeting.

Any income received by any director or senior officer in violation of the above shall be treated as the property of the company.

Practical Note: Liability

Although the board of directors determines the company operations, financials and management, the mistakes of the daily management fall upon the senior executives. Therefore, it could be argued that the mistakes of the board of directors is traced back to the senior executives' mismanagement or failure to correctly implement the resolutions of the board of directors. The board of directors is still subject to liability, but the first degree of responsibility shall fall upon the senior executives and legal representative, as they are responsible for the daily management of the company.

7.2.14.2 Litigation

Director(s), supervisor(s) or senior officer(s) in negligence of the provisioned duties may face legal action initiated by the shareholders. The Company Law provisions shareholders of an LLC company to request in writing to the board of supervisors to initiate a legal action in the People's Court against the relevant director or senior executive; in cases where the supervisor is found to be negligent of its duties, the written request shall be made to the board of directors to initiate the legal action.

Shareholders may initiate action if the board of directors or board of supervisors refuses or fails to initiate legal action within 30 days of the request, or in an urgent situation in which failure to initiate a legal action forthwith will cause irreparable damage to the interests of the company. Equally, if any director or senior officer damages the shareholders' interests by violating any law, administrative regulation or the articles of association, the shareholders may initiate a legal action in the People's Court.

7.2.15 Corporate Governance in Practice

In practice, the corporate governance of a company in China is established in the utilisation of a company's corporate seals and corporate-seal policies.

The corporate seal (often called a 'chop') represents an unlimited power of attorney vested in the holder of the corporate seal(s). Once the seal is affixed to a document, the company is legally bound and effective, while signatures are not commonly used or recognised as a symbol of execution under Chinese legal practice. Therefore, as a matter of best practice, a corporate-seal policy should be formulated and implemented to instruct proper use and safeguarding of the company's corporate seals.

It can't be emphasised enough that a company without a proper seal policy and adherence to that policy can result in serious company mismanagement and failed governance.

Each company is required to hold a set of corporate seals, of which the specimens are registered and deposited at the public security bureau. If the company changes the seal, the company is required to once again perform the approval and registration procedures with the public security bureau.

Corporate seals may be produced cheaply by laser carving (Figure 1) or handcrafted (Figure 2). Handcrafted corporate seals are harder to replicate, since the depth of each cut differs. Through micro-fining, the depth of cut is easily exposed, and any copies can be recognised.

Figure 1

Figure 2

If the seal is damaged, it is required that the seal be destroyed. A new seal shall then be produced, and the registration procedures, similar to when the seal is changed, shall be carried out and followed accordingly.

7.2.15.1 Corporate Seal

The corporate seal is the representation of the company and is utilised to indicate that the company is willing to be bound by the document to which the corporate seal is affixed. Upon affixation of the corporate seal, the relevant document is concluded and effective. If the corporate seal by the power of attorney is entrusted to a person, and such an entrusted person concludes a document with the corporate seal, the responsibility and liabilities of such a document shall fall upon the company.

7.2.15.2 Legal Representative Seal

The legal-representative seal represents the will of the legal representative and is used for the performance of powers and duties of the legal representative. The legal-representative seal is commonly a part of the bank account signatures used for bank-related matters and required for payment transactions. In such cases, the bank shall not approve the payment without the legal-representative seal.

7.2.15.3 Invoice Seal

The invoice seal is utilised on debit notes and VAT invoices. The invoice seal verifies pro forma invoices as a debit note to the third party and the VAT invoice as evidence of the payment received by the company from the third party. Where the invoice seal is not affixed on the VAT invoice, there is no payment verification.

7.2.15.4 Department Seal

Department seals (the corporate seal with a department name and special use, such as 'quality department special use' written on the seal) and personal seals (the Chinese character name of the department manager or director) can be issued to each department director or manager as an additional safeguarding mechanism. In this manner, the risk of misuse of the seal is limited, as the use of the seal is restricted to each department; for example, the seal stating 'quality department special use' is restricted to quality-related documents. Any misuse of the seal is traced back to the department named on the seal.

If possible, a seal policy requiring the affixation of both the department seal and the personal seal of the department director or manager should be devised to safeguard the company. Equally, the seal policy may require the affixation of the legal-representative seal and corporate seal for major contracts.

Many foreign companies often lack firmly established seal policies or often misplace corporate seals, which leaves the company extremely vulnerable to mismanagement and risk. Therefore, proper corporate-seal management is a must in all companies.

Particularly for directors or senior officers or other decision-makers who do not partake in the day-to-day management of a company, a proper corporate-seal management policy will go a long way to ensuring the proper governance of the company.

7.2.16 Limited Liability Company Transfer of Stock Rights

Stock rights 股权 (Guquán) of shareholders may be transferred among shareholders in whole or in part. Under the latest Company Law (2023), if a shareholder is to transfer its stock rights to any person other than the existing shareholders, it shall provide written notice to other shareholders on details of transfer, including the quantity, price, payment method, and deadline for the transfer, and other shareholders shall have the right of first refusal to purchase on the same terms. If a shareholder does not respond within 30 days of receiving the written notice, it is considered a waiver of their right of first refusal. This latest revision no longer requires the consent of the majority of the other shareholders in advance to the transfer.

If two or more shareholders exercise the right of first refusal, they shall determine the respective purchase percentages by negotiation. In the event that negotiation is unsuccessful, the right of first refusal is exercised in proportion to their respective capital contributions at the time of transfer.

Apart from the above provisions, the Company Law also stipulates that the articles of association of a company may regulate the transfer of stock rights, prevailing over the above provisions. However, not all such provisions in the articles of association are recognised as effective in judicial practice, and there is no standard answer to this issue. Commonly, judicial practice renders that restrictions on equity transfer in the articles of association must be 'reasonable', and the provisions that excessively restrict or even prohibit the transfer of equity to external persons may be deemed invalid.

If the People's Court transfers the stock rights of a shareholder pursuant to a mandatory enforcement procedure provided by law, it shall notify the company, and the other shareholders may exercise the right of first refusal. If the shareholders do not exercise the right of first refusal within 20 days of receipt of a notice from the court, it is deemed as a waiver of the right of first refusal.

If a shareholder transfers their shares, they shall notify the company in writing and request a change in the register of members. If alteration registration is necessary, the shareholder shall request the company to apply for alteration registration with the company registration authority.

When the transfer of stock rights of the company proceeds as in the aforementioned paragraphs, the company is required to cancel the capital contribution certificate of the original shareholder and issue a capital contribution certificate to the new shareholder. The records of shareholders and their capital contributions in the articles of association and register of members shall be modified. No vote of the board of shareholders is required to modify the articles of association due to such a transfer of stock rights.

Under the following circumstances, any shareholder who votes against the relevant resolution of the shareholders' meeting may require the company to purchase his stock rights at a reasonable price:

- Where no profit is distributed to the shareholders for five consecutive years, but profits are made during such a period and conform to the profit-distribution requirements of the law
- In the event of any combination, division or transfer of the principal assets of the company
- Where the business term specified in the articles of association expires, or any of the other grounds for dissolution prescribed in the articles of association are satisfied, and the shareholders' meeting makes the company continue to exist by modifying the articles of association through adopting a resolution

Where the relevant shareholder and the company fail to reach an agreement on the purchase of stock rights within 60 days of the date on which the relevant resolution is adopted at the meeting of the board of shareholders, the shareholder may initiate a legal action in the People's Court within 90 days of the date on which the resolution is adopted at the meeting of the board of shareholders.

In the case of death, unless otherwise provided for in the articles of association, the lawful successor of a natural person may assume the qualifications of shareholders following that person's death.

7.2.17 Limited Liability Company Financial and Accounting policies

Financial and accounting policies are required to be established in an LLC in accordance with the laws, administrative regulations and the provisions of the finance department under the State Council. An accounting firm may be appointed as the company's auditor, and the company bears the responsibility to provide its appointed accounting firm accurate and complete accounting documents and books, financial reports, and other accounting information, accounting documents and books and financial reports. A financial report is to be submitted to each shareholder within the time limit prescribed in the articles of association.

Any sets of accounts separate from statutory accounting books or false records or concealment of important information in the accounting report will lead to the imposition of a penalty according to the Accounting Law of the People's Republic of China.

7.2.17.1 Distribution of Profits

The funds for distribution of shareholder dividends are forbidden to be withdrawn from company capital. Instead, a shareholder dividend is required to be drawn from the after-tax profits for the current financial year. The company is required to firstly offset any losses if the company's statutory reserve is insufficient to cover losses of the previous year. The company shall then withdraw 10% of company profits as the company's statutory common reserve, although a company with an aggregate common reserve of more than 50% of the company's registered capital may elect not to draw any statutory common reserve. The shareholders' meeting may also pass a resolution to withdraw funds for discretionary reserve. The remaining after-tax profits shall be distributed to shareholders according to their actual capital contribution, unless all shareholders agree otherwise. No profits may be distributed for shares held by the company itself.

If the company fails to comply with the rule of profit distribution, the profits distributed must be returned to the company. If losses are caused thereby to the company, the shareholders, as well as any directors, supervisors, and senior executives responsible for violation, shall be liable for compensation.

When the shareholders' meeting adopts a resolution on the distribution of profits, the board of directors shall distribute the profits within six months from the date of the resolution.

7.2.17.2 Capital Reserves

Any stock premium received by a company from the issuance of stock at a premium to par, and any other income to be included in the capital reserve account under any relevant provisions of the finance department under the State Council, shall be recorded as the company's capital reserve.

7.2.17.3 Use of Reserves

The company's reserves are mandated to cover losses made in past years, enhance the company's productivity and expand business, or to increase the registered capital.

When using a company's reserves to cover its losses, balances of discretionary reserve and statutory reserve shall first be used to cover such losses; if there is still a shortfall, the capital reserve may be used in accordance with regulations.

If the statutory common reserve is converted into capital, the value of the remaining common reserve shall be no less than 25% of the company's registered capital prior to the conversion.

7.2.18 Corporate Combination and Division

A corporate combination may be realised by merger or consolidation. The Company Law refers to a merger as the absorption of one company by another company, with the absorbed company being dissolved. Consolidation is referred to as the combination of two or more companies to establish a new company, with the existing companies being dissolved.

To carry out a corporate combination, an agreement between the parties to the combination shall be concluded and balance sheets and schedules of assets formulated. The parties to a combination are required to notify their respective creditors within ten days of passing the resolution on combination and make a public announcement in a newspaper or the National Enterprise Credit Information Publicity System within 30 days. Any creditor may, within 30 days of receiving such notice or within 45 days of the issuance of the public announcement if no notice is received, require the company to repay its debts in full or provide a corresponding guarantee. Failure to notify the creditors by notice or by public announcement of any combination, division, reduction of its registered capital or liquidation shall be ordered by the company registration authority to remedy the defect and may result in a fine of between CNY 10,000 and CNY 100,000.

In any corporate combination, the claims and debts of the parties to the combination shall be succeeded by the company that survives the combination or, in case of a consolidation, by the newly established company.

In a corporate division, the assets of the company shall be divided accordingly. To enable a division to proceed, balance sheets and schedules of assets are required to be formulated. The company shall inform its creditors within ten days of the date of the decision, and a public announcement in a newspaper or the National Enterprise Credit Information Publicity System is required within 30 days of the date of the decision. Unless otherwise agreed by the company and its creditors in any written agreement, the liability of company debts concluded prior to any division shall be jointly and severally borne by the companies resulting from the division.

7.2.19 Dissolutions and Liquidations

Enterprise dissolution refers to the legal act of any incorporated enterprise ceasing corporate operating activities due to the occurrence of any cause in the articles of association or legal cause and legally liquidating and settling creditors' rights and debts, distributing remaining properties to shareholders and handling formalities for corporate deregistration and business-licence revocation, finally eliminating the legal-person status of the company.

During the period, the status of a company as a legal person does not perish and the company is deemed as existing for the purpose of liquidation. Meanwhile, the company has restricted capacity and can only conduct activities relating to the liquidation. No other conduct, such as other operating activities irrelevant to the liquidation, shall be made. Any business activity unconnected with the liquidation shall be reprimanded by the company registration authority and any unlawful proceeds shall be confiscated.

Enterprise liquidation aims to protect the interests of shareholders and creditors. An enterprise dissolved shall be liquidated in accordance with the law unless the company is dissolved due to merger or division and the creditors' rights and debts are therefore inherited by the company subsisting or newly established after the merger or division; in which case, there is no need to conduct liquidation. Liquidation is a compulsory procedure for corporate termination, so enterprise dissolution and liquidation usually occur simultaneously.

A company may be dissolved under the following conditions:

- The term of business operation as prescribed in the articles of association expires or any dissolution event as prescribed in the articles of association of the company occurs[3]
- The shareholders' meeting resolves to dissolve the company
- Dissolution of the company is necessary due to any combination or division to which the company is a party
- The business licence is revoked or the company is ordered to close down or be dissolved in accordance with the law
- The company encounters serious difficulties in its operations or management, causing significant losses to the shareholders if the company persists, and the situation cannot be resolved by any other means. Shareholders representing 10% or more of the voting rights of the shareholders may petition the People's Court to dissolve the company

---

[3] Although the company may continue business operations by amending the articles of association, any amendment to the articles of association shall be subject to the consent of shareholders representing two-thirds or more of the voting rights.

If any of the causes for dissolution arises, the company shall disclose the cause for dissolution within ten days through the National Enterprise Credit Information Publicity System.

7.2.19.1 Liquidation Group

Except for corporate combination or division, a company shall be liquidated when dissolution happens. The directors are the liquidation obligors of the company and shall form a liquidation group within 15 days from the date that the cause of dissolution occurs. The liquidation group shall consist of directors, unless it is otherwise stipulated by the articles of association or resolved by the shareholders' meeting.

Where a liquidation group is not formed in time or fails to proceed with liquidation after formation, the company's creditors may petition the People's Court to appoint appropriate individuals to form a liquidation group. The People's Court shall accept such a petition and organise a liquidation group in order to liquidate the company in a timely manner.

The liquidation group is provisioned the following functions and powers for the liquidation period:

- Liquidate the company's assets and produce a balance sheet and schedule of assets
- Notify the company's creditors with a notice or public announcement
- Manage and clear the remaining business of the company
- Pay outstanding taxes and any tax liability incurred in the course of the liquidation
- Pay the company's accounts payable and recover its accounts receivable
- Dispose of the company's residual assets
- Represent the company in any civil litigation to which it is a party

Once the liquidation group is formed, the company's creditors are required to be notified within ten days and a public notification in a newspaper or the National Enterprise Credit Information Publicity System announcing the formed liquidation group shall be completed within 60 days. Any creditor, within 30 days of receipt of a notice or within 45 days of the public announcement in the event the creditor does not receive a notice, shall claim to the liquidation group on the debt owed to such a creditor. Claims of outstanding debts are required to describe the relevant details and provide supporting evidence. All debts claimed are recorded by the liquidation group. The liquidation group may not repay any creditor during the debt-claim period.

The liquidation group is required to firstly liquidate the assets of the company. Afterwards, a balance sheet and schedule of assets, as well as a draft liquidation plan shall be presented to the shareholders' meeting or the People's Court for confirmation.

Any remaining assets after payment of liquidation expenses, employee wages, social insurance premiums and statutory indemnity premiums, outstanding taxes and outstanding debts are distributed to shareholders on a pro rata basis in accordance with the respective proportion of capital contributed by each shareholder. No company assets may be distributed to any shareholder before the aforementioned items are concluded.

If the liquidation group finds that the company's assets are insufficient to cover its debts in full after liquidating the assets of a company and formulating a balance sheet and schedule of assets, it shall file a bankruptcy petition with the People's Court. In the instance that the People's Court accepts the bankruptcy application, the liquidation group shall hand over administration of the liquidation to the People's Court. Any company adjudicated bankrupt in accordance with the law shall be liquidated in bankruptcy in accordance with the relevant laws on bankruptcy.

On completion of any company liquidation, the liquidation group shall draft a liquidation report and submit it to the shareholders' meeting or to the People's Court for confirmation. The application for the cancellation of the registration of the company shall be submitted to the company registration authority, and a public announcement of the company's termination will be made. Failure to submit a liquidation report to the company registration authority in accordance with the provisions of the law, or concealment or emittance of any important fact in or from the liquidation report submitted, shall be ordered by the company registration authority to remedy the defect.

Members of a liquidation group owe an obligation to carry out duties in accordance with the law and shall fulfil liquidation responsibilities with a duty of loyalty and diligence. No member of a liquidation group may take advantage of his position, receive other unlawful payment nor misappropriate any company asset. Any member who causes any loss to the company or to any of its creditors, either intentionally or due to gross negligence, shall be liable to compensate the affected party.

7.3 Joint Stock Limited Company

A joint stock limited company is known as a company limited by the share of the company. Usually, joint stock limited companies are large companies. The original shareholders (referred to under the Company Law as 'promoters') of a joint stock limited company undertake to contribute money into the company at the time of establishment.

A limited liability company can be changed to a joint stock limited company if it satisfies the conditions for joint stock limited companies in the Company Law, with particular provision that the total amount of paid-in capital converted is not higher than its net assets. Any public offering of shares to increase the capital of the company shall be made in accordance with the law.

7.3.1 Establishment

A joint stock limited company may be established either by way of promotion or by way of stock flotation. Establishment of a company by way of promotion means that promoters of a company subscribe for all shares to be issued by the company to establish the company. Establishment of a company by way of stock flotation means that promoters subscribe for some of the shares to be issued by the company, with the remaining shares being offered to the general public or to particular classes of investors to establish the company.

The number of promoters is required to be ranged from one to 200, of whom a majority shall be domiciled within the territory of China.

The promoters are required to conclude a promoters' agreement clarifying their respective rights and obligations during the course of establishing the company and to carry out all necessary preliminary procedures relating to the establishment of the company. Under the Company Law, the joint stock limited company shall fulfil the conditions below:

- Meet the requirement on the number of promoters required by law
- The total share capital or total paid-in capital is subscribed for and raised by all promoters in compliance with the articles of association
- Issue shares and undertake preparations according to the law
- Promoters shall formulate the articles of association and, in the case of a joint stock limited company established by stock flotation, adopt the establishment meeting of the company
- Establish a name and organisational structure in compliance with the provisions for a joint stock limited company
- Establish a corporate domicile

7.3.2 Articles of Association (AoA)

The articles of association of a joint stock limited company shall specify the following matters:

- Name and domicile of the company
- Business scope of the company

- Form of company establishment
- Total number of shares issued, number of shares issued at the time of establishment, par value per share, and registered capital of the company
- For non-ordinary shares, the quantity of shares of each type and corresponding rights and obligations
- Name of each promoter, number of shares each promoter has subscribed for, and form and date of capital contributions made
- Rules relating to the composition, functions and powers, and rules of procedure of the board of directors
- Rules relating to determining and changing of the legal representative of the company
- Rules relating to the composition, functions and powers and rules of procedure of the board of supervisors
- Procedures for the distribution of company profits
- Causes for dissolution of the company and liquidation procedures
- Procedures of issuing company notices or public announcements
- Any other matter deemed necessary by the shareholders' meeting

7.3.3 Capital Contribution

Prior to the establishment of a joint stock limited company by promotion, the promoters shall subscribe for all shares to be issued at the time of the company's establishment according to the articles of association and shall pay full contribution for their subscribed shares before the establishment of the company. For a joint stock limited company by stock flotation, the promoters shall subscribe for no less than 35% of the total shares to be issued at the time of the company's establishment according to its articles of association, unless otherwise required in other specific laws or regulations.

If capital contributions are made with non-monetary assets, the promoters shall go through the relevant procedures for the transfer of property rights in accordance with the law. Any promoter who fails to make capital contributions on time and in full shall be liable for compensating the losses caused to the company.

The registered capital of a joint stock limited company shall be the total value of its issued shares as recorded by the company registration authority. No shares shall be offered to any other person before the shares subscribed for by the promoters are fully paid in.

7.3.4 Stock Flotation

The promoters in a public offering shall, together with the articles of association formulated by the promoters, publish a prospectus and prepare a share subscription form including the following details:

- Total number of shares to be issued
- Par value and issue price for par value shares, or issue price for non-par value shares
- Purposes of the raised capital
- Rights and obligations of subscribers
- Type of shares and their rights and obligations
- Offer period and a statement allowing subscribers to withdraw subscriptions in the event the offer is under-subscribed at the close of the offer period
- Number of shares subscribed for by the promoters

The public offering of the shares shall be underwritten by a lawfully established securities company with a concluded underwriting agreement.

Parties that purchase the offered shares are referred to as 'subscribers'. In order to purchase the shares of a public offering, subscribers shall fill in the number and price of shares to be subscribed and their domicile with the affixation of their seal, or signature on the subscription form. Subscribers shall contribute payment for their subscribed shares in full.

Payment of such shares is paid to an appointed bank for collection. An agreement on the collection of payments for shares on behalf of the company shall be signed with the appointed bank, which shall, according to such an agreement, receive and hold, as agent, payment for shares and issue receipts to the subscribers upon payment. Any appointed bank is obliged to produce evidence demonstrating the receipt of payments to the relevant authorities.

Where full payment is received for the public offering of shares, the subscriptions shall be verified and certified by a lawfully established capital verification institution. Within 30 days of receipt of all subscriptions, the promoters shall hold a company establishment meeting composed of the promoters and subscribers. In the event that shares offered to the public are not fully subscribed within the offer period disclosed in the prospectus, or the promoters fail to hold an establishment meeting within 30 days of receipt of all subscriptions, the subscribers may require the promoters to refund their subscriptions and pay interest calculated using the bank deposit interest rate for the relevant period.

The promoters shall notify each subscriber of, or publicly announce, the date of the establishment meeting no less than 15 days in advance of the meeting. The establishment meeting may not be held unless promoters and subscribers representing a majority of the total shares attend. The establishment meeting shall:

- deliberate the report on pre-establishment activities prepared by the promoters
- adopt the articles of association
- elect members of the board of directors
- elect members of the board of supervisors
- verify expenses incurred in establishing the company
- verify the value of any assets contributed by the promoters by way of capital contribution
- consider adopting a resolution of not establishing the company in the event of any *force majeure* or material change in operating conditions that may affect the establishment of the company

Any resolution made at the establishment meeting on any of the matters described above requires an affirmative vote passed by subscribers representing a majority of the votes of those attending the meeting.

Promoters and subscribers shall not withdraw any share capital after the payment for their subscribed shares or delivery of non-monetary assets as contributions, although share capital can be withdrawn under the circumstances that the issued shares are not fully subscribed for within the offering period, the promoters fail to convene the establishment meeting within the relevant time limit or the establishment meeting has resolved not to establish the company.

The board of directors shall, within 30 days of the conclusion of the establishment meeting, apply for registration to the company registration authority

7.3.5 Liabilities of Establishing a Joint Stock Limited Company

The liability of establishing a joint stock limited company in accordance with the Provisions is primarily borne by the promoter. Promoters are liable for two main aspects: the payment of the capital contribution and the establishment of the joint stock company.

7.3.5.1 Failure to Pay in Contributions

Promoters shall ensure the actual value of any non-monetary asset used as capital contribution is not significantly lower than the value of subscribed shares. If the actual value of non-monetary assets is found to be significantly lower than the stipulated value, the respective promoter is required to rectify the shortfall and other promoters shall be jointly and severally liable for the shortfall. Equally, in the instance of failure to pay in the capital contribution in full as stipulated in the articles of association, the respective promoter is required to pay the outstanding amount and other promoters shall be jointly and severally liable for the shortfall.

7.3.6 Joint Stock Limited Company Corporate Governance

Similar to an LLC, the corporate governance of a joint stock limited company comprises shareholders, directors, supervisors and senior executives. The highest authority of the company is the shareholders' meeting comprised of all shareholders who collectively exercise the rights of investors to define the decisions on major matters of the company in accordance with the Company Law.

7.3.6.1 Shareholders

A shareholder is a capital contributor or investor of a joint stock company. Shareholders have the right to attend the shareholders' meeting and the right to vote. Equally, shareholders are entitled to inspect the articles of association, the register of members, corporate-bond receipts, minutes of shareholders' meetings, minutes of meetings of the board of directors, minutes of meetings of the board of supervisors, and financial reports, and may put forward proposals and raise questions about the business operations of the company.

7.3.6.1.1 Controlling Shareholders

'Controlling shareholder' refers to any shareholder whose stock accounts for more than 50% of the total stock of a joint stock limited company, or a shareholder whose capital contribution or proportion of stock is less than 50% of the total capital or stock but holds sufficient voting rights to have significant influence on any resolution put to the shareholders' meeting.

7.3.6.1.2 Shareholders' Meeting

The shareholders' meeting is prescribed the same functions as the shareholders' meeting of a limited liability company and shall exercise the following functions:

- Election and replacement of directors and supervisors and determination of their remuneration
- Deliberation on and approval of reports of the board of directors
- Deliberation on and approval of reports of the board of supervisors
- Deliberation on and approval of company profit-distribution plans and debt-recovery plans

- Making resolutions about any increase or reduction in the company's registered capital
- Making resolutions about the issuance of corporate bonds
- Making resolutions on any merger, demerger, dissolution, liquidation, or change in company form of the company
- Revision of the articles of association of the company
- Any other functions or powers specified in the articles of association

7.3.6.1.3 Shareholders' Meeting

A shareholders' meeting is held annually, although under any of the following circumstances an interim general meeting is required to be held within two months:

- Where the number of directors falls below two-thirds of the minimum number of directors as required by the law or as specified in the articles of association
- Where the uncovered losses of the company reach one-third of its total share capital
- Where such a meeting is requested by a shareholder who holds, or by shareholders who collectively hold, 10% or more of the company's shares
- Where the board of directors deems such a meeting necessary
- Where the board of supervisors proposed such a meeting
- Any other circumstances specified in the articles of association

7.3.6.1.4 Notification of the Shareholders' Meeting

Shareholders are required to be notified **no less than 20 days** in advance of the shareholders' meeting. The notification shall include the time and place of the meeting and the matters to be deliberated at the meeting. Shareholders shall be notified no less than 15 days in advance of an interim meeting.

Any shareholder who holds, or shareholders who together hold, 1% or more of the shares of the company may put forward an interim proposal and submit to the board of directors in writing ten days in advance of a shareholders' meeting. Any interim proposal put forward shall include specific points for discussion and matters for resolution. The board of directors shall notify other shareholders of the interim proposal within two days as of the receipt thereof and submit the proposal to the general meeting for consideration, except for any proposals that are against the laws, administrative regulations, or the articles of association, or outside the purview of the shareholders' meeting. The statutory shareholding percentage required for proposing interim proposals is allowed to be increased at the company's discretion.

The shareholders' meeting shall not make any resolution on any matter not listed in the notice.

7.3.6.1.5 Convening and Chairing the Shareholders' Meeting

The shareholders' meeting is convened by the board of directors and is presided over by the chairman of the board of directors. Where the chairman is unable to or fails to perform his duties, the meeting shall be presided over by the deputy chairman of the board of directors. Where the deputy chairman of the board of directors is unable to or fails to perform his duties, the meeting shall be presided over by a director nominated by a majority of the directors. Where the board of directors is unable to or fails to fulfil its obligations to convene a shareholders' meeting, the board of supervisors shall convene and preside over the meeting. Where the board of supervisors does not convene or preside over the meeting, a shareholder who holds, or shareholders who together hold, 10% or more of the company's shares for 90 consecutive days or more may convene and preside over the meeting on their own initiative.

If a shareholder who holds, or shareholders who collectively hold, 10% or more of the company's shares, request the convening of an interim shareholders' meeting, the board of directors or the board of supervisors shall, within 10 days from the date of receiving such request, decide whether to convene the interim shareholders' meeting and provide a written response to the shareholder(s).

7.3.6.1.6 Attending the General Meeting

A shareholder may appoint an agent to attend a shareholders' assembly. The proxy shall specify the scope of authorization, power, and term of validity. The agent appointed shall present the proxy issued by the shareholder to the company and may exercise voting rights within the scope of his authorisation.

7.3.6.1.7 Voting Rights

Each share shall be entitled to one vote at a shareholders' meeting, except for non-ordinary shares. However, shares registered in the name of the company shall not carry voting rights. Any resolution proposed at a shareholders' meeting of shareholders shall be adopted by an affirmative vote of shareholders representing a majority of the voting rights of shareholders present, except resolutions proposing any modification to the articles of association or any increase or decrease in registered capital or any resolution about any proposed merger, demerger, dissolution or change in company form, which shall be adopted by shareholders representing two-thirds or more of the voting rights of shareholders present.

The shareholders' meeting may adopt a cumulative voting system for the election of directors and supervisors pursuant to the articles of association or by way of a resolution made at its meeting. The term 'cumulative voting system', as referred to in the Company Law, means a voting system whereby shareholders can multiply their voting rights by the number of candidates and cast their votes for one candidate for director or supervisor.

7.3.6.1.8 Minutes

The shareholders' meeting shall take minutes on decisions made and matters discussed at its meetings. The chair of the meeting and directors present shall sign the minutes, which shall be retained together with a list of signatures of shareholders present and any powers of attorney exercised.

7.3.6.1.9 Shareholders of a Listed Company

Where a listed company purchases or sells any major assets or provides any guarantee for any amount exceeding 30% of its total assets within one year, such a transaction shall be subject to a resolution of the shareholders' meeting passed by shareholders representing two-thirds of the voting rights of shareholders present.

7.3.6.2 Board of Directors

The board of directors is an institution comprising representatives elected by the shareholders' meeting for the interests of all shareholders over the management and guidance of company activities. The rules of composition of board of directors for a joint stock limited company are similar to that of a limited liability company. The board of directors may include employee representatives. Employee representatives who serve on the board of directors shall be democratically elected through the employee representatives' assembly, the employees' assembly, or otherwise. A listed company shall have independent directors, who shall be subject to any specific measures by the securities regulatory authority under the State Council.

The term of office and functions of the board of directors of a limited liability company shall apply to the board of directors of a joint stock limited company. Its functions include the following:

- Convene shareholders' meetings and present reports thereto
- Execute resolutions made at shareholders' meetings
- Determine operational plans and investment plans
- Formulate the company's annual budgets and final account plans
- Formulate the company's profit-distribution plans and debt-recovery plans
- Formulate the company's plans on any proposed increase or decrease in its registered capital or on the issuance of corporate bonds
- Formulate the company's plans on any proposed merger, demerger, change in company form, dissolution, or similar
- Make decisions on the establishment of the company's internal management departments
- Make decisions on the appointment or dismissal of the company's manager and their remuneration, and, according to the nomination of the manager, make decisions on the appointment or dismissal of the deputy manager(s) and the finance manager and their remuneration
- Establish the company's basic management system
- Any other function specified in the articles of association or granted by the shareholders' meeting

The board of directors shall appoint one chairman and may appoint deputy chairmen. The chairman and any deputy chairman (if any) shall be elected by a majority of all the directors.

A joint stock limited company with a small scale or few shareholders may appoint one director without establishing a board of directors to exercise the functions and powers prescribed for the board of directors.

7.3.6.2.1 Convening and Chairing the Board of Directors' Meeting

A meeting of the board of directors shall be convened and presided over by the chairman of the board of directors, who will also inspect the implementation of resolutions of the board of directors. Where the chairman of the board of directors is unable to or fails to perform his duties, the meeting may be convened and presided over by the deputy chairman of the board of directors. Where the deputy chairman of the board of directors is unable to or fails to perform his duties, the meeting shall be convened and presided over by a director nominated by 50% or more of the directors.

The board of directors shall convene no less than two meetings per year and shall notify all directors and supervisors no less than ten days in advance of the meeting. A proposal to hold an interim meeting of the board of directors may be put forward by shareholders representing 10% or more of the voting rights, or by one-third or more of the directors or the board of supervisors. The chairman of the board of directors shall, within ten days of receiving such a proposal, call and preside over a meeting of the board of directors. Where the board of directors holds an interim meeting, it may separately decide the method of and time limit applicable to notifications about meetings of the board of directors. No meeting of the board of directors may be held unless a majority of directors is present.

Directors shall attend meetings of the board of directors in person. If a director is unable to attend a meeting, the director may issue a written proxy appointing another director to attend the meeting on his behalf and stating the scope of his authorisation.

7.3.6.2.2 Resolutions of the Board of Directors

In board of directors' meetings, directors shall make resolutions on issues submitted to be deliberated. Resolutions are made on the majority vote of the board of directors and are calculated on the system of 'one vote per director'; thus, every director shall cast one vote on every issue submitted to the board of directors.

In listed companies, if any director has a relationship with any enterprise involved in a matter to be decided at a meeting of the board of directors, the respective director shall not vote on the relevant resolution either on his own behalf or on behalf of any other director. Any agenda item at a meeting of the board of directors shall not be discussed or voted on unless a majority of directors without any interest in the relevant matter is present at the meeting. Any resolution of the board of directors shall be adopted by the affirmative votes of a majority of directors without any interest in the relevant matter. Where less than three directors without any interest in the relevant matter are present, the matter shall be submitted to the listed company's shareholders' meeting for deliberation.

The board of directors shall take minutes on resolutions made and matters discussed at its meetings, which shall be signed by the directors present.

7.3.6.2.3 Duties and Responsibilities of Directors

Directors shall be responsible for resolutions of the board of directors. Where a resolution of the board of directors violates any law or administrative regulation, the articles of association, or any resolution of the shareholders' meeting and causes any serious loss to the company, the directors who participated in adopting the resolution shall compensate the company. Where a director is proven to have raised any objection to the relevant resolution and his objection is recorded in the minutes, the director may be exempted from liability.

Directors, supervisors and senior executives of a joint stock limited company are subject to similar liabilities as directors, supervisors and senior executives of an LLC. Directors, supervisors and senior executives shall comply with laws, administrative regulations and the articles of association and shall owe duties of fidelity and due diligence to the company.

No director, supervisor or senior executives shall take any bribe or other illegal gain by taking advantage of his position, nor may he misappropriate company assets for personal use.

As prescribed in the Company Law, no director or senior executive may:

- Embezzle company property or misappropriate company funds
- Divert company funds into an account held in his own name or in the name of any other individual
- Use authority to engage in bribery or accept other illegal income
- Personally accept any commission on any transaction to which the company is a party
- Unlawfully disclose confidential company information
- Act in any way that is inconsistent with his duty of fidelity to the company

Directors, supervisors, and senior executives directly or indirectly entering into a contract or engaging in a transaction with the company shall report to the board of directors or the shareholders' meeting and obtain approval in advance according to the company's articles of association. The approval/disapproval shall be made by resolutions of the board of directors or the shareholders' meeting. This shall also apply to the close relatives of directors, supervisors, or senior executives, enterprises directly or indirectly controlled by directors, supervisors, or senior executives or their close relatives, and parties having other relationships as a related party with directors, supervisors, or senior executives.

Directors, supervisors, and senior executives shall not use their authority to seek any business opportunity that ought to belong to the company or operate businesses similar to those of the company, unless it has been reported to the board of directors or the shareholders' meeting and approved by the resolutions of the board of directors or the shareholders' meeting.

Any income received by any director or senior executives in violation of the above shall be treated as the property of the company.

7.3.6.2.4 Secretary to the Board of Directors

The secretary to the board of directors in listed companies is responsible for preparation for the shareholders' meeting and the meeting of the board of directors, the document safekeeping and management of shareholders' materials internally, and the information disclosure issues of the company externally.

7.3.6.3 Board of Supervisors

A joint stock limited company shall establish a board of supervisors comprised of no less than three members. The term of office of the supervisors of a limited liability company shall apply to the supervisors of a joint stock limited company. The board of supervisors shall include shareholders' representatives and an appropriate proportion of employee representatives. The proportion of employee representatives shall be specified in the articles of association but in any event shall account for no less than one-third of the supervisors appointed. Employee representatives who serve as members of the board of supervisors shall be democratically elected through the employee representatives' assembly, the employees' assembly, or otherwise.

The board of supervisors shall have one chairman and may have a deputy chairman. The chairman and deputy chairman shall be elected by a majority of supervisors. The chairman of the board of supervisors shall call and preside over meetings of the board of supervisors. Where the chairman of the board of supervisors is unable to or fails to perform his duties, the deputy chairman of the board of supervisors shall call and preside over meetings of the board of supervisors. Where the deputy chairman of the board of supervisors is unable to or fails to perform his duties, a supervisor nominated by a majority of the supervisors shall call and preside over meetings of the board of supervisors.

No director or senior executive of a company may concurrently act as one of the company's supervisors.

7.3.6.3.1 Board of Supervisors' Meeting

The board of supervisors shall hold no less than one meeting every six months. The supervisors may call interim meetings of the board of supervisors. Unless otherwise specified in the law, the methods of deliberation and voting procedures of the board of supervisors shall be specified in the articles of association.

A resolution of the board of supervisors shall be passed by a majority of supervisors. The board of supervisors shall take minutes on resolutions made and matters discussed at its meetings, which shall be signed by all supervisors present.

7.3.6.3.2 Obligations and Responsibilities of Supervisors

The functions of a limited liability company shall apply to the board of supervisors of a joint stock limited company. The main functions of the board of supervisors include the following:

- Checking the financial affairs of the company
- Supervising compliance of the directors and senior executives with their respective duties and proposing the removal of any director or senior executive who violates any law, administrative regulation, the articles of association or any resolution of the shareholders' meeting
- Requiring any director or senior executive to take corrective action where they act in a way that damages the interests of the company
- Proposing the calling of interim shareholders' meetings and calling and presiding over shareholders' meetings where the board of directors does not exercise its functions in that regard as prescribed in the law
- Putting forward proposals at shareholders' meetings
- Initiating any action against a director or senior executive in accordance with the law
- Any other functions or powers specified in the articles of association

7.3.6.4 Senior Executives

'Senior executive' refers to managers, deputy managers, financial officers, secretaries to the board of directors of listed companies, or other personnel prescribed by the articles of association. A joint stock limited company shall have a manager, who shall be appointed or dismissed by the board of directors. The manager shall report to the board of directors and exercise functions and powers as specified in the articles of association or as authorised by the board of directors. The manager shall attend meetings of the board of directors but is not a non-voting attendee. The board of directors may appoint one of its members to serve concurrently as the manager.

7.3.6.5 Audit Committee

One major new update of Company Law (2023) is that it introduces the choice of having an audit committee in a joint stock limited company. A joint stock limited company may, instead of establishing a board of supervisors or supervisor, establish an audit committee within the board of directors composed of directors to exercise the functions and powers of the board of supervisors according to the law.

The audit committee shall consist of three or more members, and a majority of the members shall not hold any position in the company other than as a director and shall not be related with the company in a way that may affect their independent and objective judgment. The employee representative among the members of the board of directors may become a member of the audit committee.

The deliberation and voting procedures of the audit committee shall be governed by the company's articles of association. Any resolution of the audit committee shall be adopted by a majority vote of the committee members. Each member of the audit committee shall have one vote for any resolution of the committee.

7.3.7 Issuance and Transfer of Shares in a Joint Stock Limited Company

The capital of a joint stock limited company is divided into shares (股份), which may be either par value shares or non-par value shares, as stipulated by the company's articles of association. For par value shares, the value assigned to each share shall be equal. The company may convert all issued par value shares into non-par value shares or all non-par value shares into par value shares according to its articles of association.

Any issuance of shares is required to be conducted with fairness and impartiality, and shares of the same type shall be entitled to the same rights. In one issuance, shares of the same type shall be issued at the same price and with the same terms. The per-share price paid by subscribers for their subscribed shares shall be the same.

The company may issue the following classes of shares with different rights from ordinary shares in accordance with the provisions of the company's articles of association:

1) Shares with priority or inferior right to the distribution of profits or residual property.
2) Shares with more (or less) voting rights than ordinary shares.
3) Shares that are subject to transfer restrictions, such as the prior consent of the company.
4) Others specified by the State Council.

A company that publicly issues shares shall not issue the class 2) and 3) shares above, except those already issued before public offering. If a company issues the class 2) shares above, one exception is that, in terms of the election and removal of supervisors or audit committee members, the voting rights shall be the same for all shares as those of ordinary shares.

Companies issuing non-ordinary shares shall specify the following matters in the articles of association:

- The sequence of the distribution of profits or residual property for the non-ordinary shares
- The number of voting rights for the non-ordinary shares

- Transfer restrictions on the non-ordinary shares
- Measures to protect the rights and interests of minority shareholders
- Any other matters deemed necessary to specify by the shareholders' meeting.

The shares of a joint stock limited company may be listed and traded on the stock exchange and referred to as a 'listed company'. Listed companies are subject to publicly announcing matters relating to their financial status, business operations and any significant litigation to which they are a party, as well as to publishing their financial reports in a timely manner during each financial year, with the aforementioned obligation proceeding in accordance with the relevant laws and administrative regulations.

7.3.7.1 Share Certificates – Stocks

A company's shares shall be in the form of stocks. Stocks are certificates issued by a company to represent the ownership of shares held by shareholders. The stocks issued by a company shall be registered stocks and may be issued at a price equal to or at a premium to their par value, but shall not be issued at a price below par value.

Stocks shall be in paper form or other forms prescribed by the securities regulatory authority of the State Council. If the stock is in paper form, the following details should be specified:

- Company name
- Date of incorporation of the company or the time of stock issuance
- Class and par value of the stock, and the number of shares it represents; for non-par value stocks, the number of shares it represents

Stock in paper form shall also bear the serial number of the stock, the signature of the legal representative and the seal of the company, and share certificates held by promoters shall be inscribed with the words 'promoters' stock.

All share certificates are required to be delivered to the shareholders following the company's establishment, and no share certificate shall be delivered before such establishment.

7.3.7.2 New Share Offering

A proposal to issue new shares is subject to the resolution of the shareholders' meeting. The resolution is required to include the matters below:

- Class and number of new shares to be issued
- Issuance price of the new shares
- Offering period for the new shares

- Class and quantity of new shares to be issued to the existing shareholders
- In the case of issuing non-par value shares, the amount of capital from the new share offering to be included in the registered capital.

The offer price of new shares can be established according to the business operations and financial status of the company.

The articles of association or the shareholders' meeting may authorise the board of directors to decide the issuance of shares not exceeding 50% of those already issued within three years. But if non-monetary assets are used as capital contributions, they shall be resolved by the shareholders' meeting.

If the board of directors decides to issue shares in accordance with above, which leads to changes in the registered capital and the number of issued shares of the company, the modification of the items recorded in the company's articles of association does not need to be voted by the shareholders' meeting.

If the articles of association or the shareholders' meeting authorises the board of directors to decide the issuance of new shares, the relevant resolution of the board of directors shall be adopted by two-thirds or more of all the directors.

Any company offering new shares to the public shall register the offering with the securities regulatory authority under the State Council and publish a prospectus accompanied by the articles of association of the company, with the same details as those for stock flotation; thus, the public shares shall be underwritten by a lawfully established securities company with a concluded underwriting agreement, and payment of such shares shall be paid to an appointed bank acting on behalf of the company.

7.3.7.3 Share Transfer

Compared with a limited liability company, the transfer of shares in a joint stock company is more flexible. Any transfer of shares by a shareholder is required to be carried out by a lawfully established stock exchange or by other means prescribed by the State Council.

7.3.7.3.1 Transfer of Stock

A transfer of stock shall take effect by a shareholder's endorsement or by other means prescribed by the relevant laws or administrative regulations. Following any transfer, the company shall record the name and address of the transferee in the shareholders' register.

The shareholders' register may not be modified within 20 days preceding any shareholders' meeting or within five days preceding any ex-dividend benchmark date fixed by the company. Where any laws, administrative regulations, or the securities regulatory authority stipulate otherwise in relation to the changes to the shareholders' register of a listed company, those provisions shall prevail.

7.3.7.3.3 Restriction of Share Transfer

Where there are restrictions on share transfers in the company's articles of association, those restrictions shall apply.

Shares issued prior to any public offering of the shares shall not be transferred within one year of the date on which the shares of the company were first listed and traded on a stock exchange. Where any laws, administrative regulations, or the securities regulatory authority stipulate otherwise, those provisions shall prevail.

Directors, supervisors and senior executives of a company shall notify the company of the shares they hold and any changes therein. During their respective term of office, any shares transferred by any of the company's directors, supervisors and senior executives in any year shall not exceed 25% of the relevant individual's total stake in the company. Company shares held by any of the company's directors, supervisors and senior managers shall not be transferred within one year of the date on which the shares are first listed and traded on a stock exchange. Any of the aforesaid persons who cease to hold their post shall not transfer any shares within six months of the date on which they ceased to hold their post. Any other restrictions on transfers of shares held by directors, supervisors and senior executives may be specified in the articles of association.

If shares are pledged within the restricted transfer period, the pledgee shall not exercise the right during the restricted transfer period.

7.3.7.4 Share Repurchase

Under any of the following circumstances, shareholders who vote against the resolution of the shareholders' meeting may request the company to purchase their shares at a reasonable price, except for companies that publicly issue shares:

1. The company has not distributed profits to shareholders for five consecutive years, and the company has been continuously profitable for these five years and meets the legal conditions for profit distribution.
2. The company transfers its major assets.
3. When the business term specified in the articles of association expires or other reasons of dissolution in the articles of association occur, the shareholders' meeting adopts a resolution to amend the articles of association to keep the company exist.

If no agreement on the repurchase of shares is reached between the shareholder and the company within 60 days from the date of relevant resolution by the shareholders' meeting, the shareholder may initiate legal action within 90 days from the date of adopting the resolution.

A company is prohibited from purchasing its own shares unless it falls under any of the following circumstances:

1. The company reduces its registered capital.
2. The company plans to merge with a company that is one of its existing share-holders.
3. The purchase is pursuant to an employee share award incentive scheme or equity incentive plan.
4. The purchase is pursuant to a request from any shareholder to purchase his shares because of his objection to any company resolution concerning a merger or demerger made at any shareholders' general meeting.
5. The purchase is for the conversion of convertible corporate bonds issued by a listed company.
6. The purchase is necessary for a listed company to maintain its company value and protect its shareholders' equity.

Any company's purchase of its own shares for any reason specified in items 1 and 2 of the above list shall be subject to a resolution of the shareholders' meeting. Any company's purchase of its own shares for any reason specified in items 3, 5 and 6 of the above list may, according to the provisions of the articles of associations or upon authorisation by the shareholders' meeting, be subject to a resolution of the board meeting with more than two-thirds of directors present.

Shares repurchased for the reduction of registered capital are required to be cancelled within ten days of the purchase. Repurchases for mergers or by request of shareholders in the aforementioned circumstance shall be transferred or cancelled within six months of the purchase.

Shares purchased by the company for the purposes 3, 5 and 6 shall not exceed 10% of the total shares already issued by the company and shall be transferred or cancelled within three years of the purchase, and for listed companies, such repurchase shall only be made through the public centralised trading system; namely, no shares can be purchased privately by entering into an agreement with certain shareholders. In this way, manipulation from certain management personnel that might prejudice the interest of shareholders, especially minority shareholders, can be avoided.

Any repurchase of a company's own shares is subject to the information disclosures obligations, and no company may accept a pledge of its own shares.

7.3.8 Trading of Shares of Listed Companies

The shares of listed companies are required to be listed and traded in accordance with the relevant laws and administrative regulations and with the dealing rules of the stock exchange on which they are listed and traded.

7.3.9 Handling of Theft, Loss or Destruction of Registered Stocks

Where any registered stock is stolen, lost or destroyed, the relevant shareholder may request that the People's Court declare the stock invalid in accordance with the public notification procedure prescribed in the Civil Procedure Law of the People's Republic of China. Where the People's Court invalidates stock pursuant to this procedure, the relevant shareholder may issue an application with the company for the issuance of new stock.

7.3.10 Corporate Bonds of a Joint Stock Limited Company

'Corporate bonds' refers to negotiable securities issued by a company under the relevant statutory procedures, with guaranteed payment of principal and interest by a specified future date or dates. The issuance of corporate bonds may be public or private. No company may issue bonds without satisfying the issuance requirements specified in the Securities Law of the People's Republic of China.

A company conducting a public issuance of corporate bonds shall register the issuance with the securities regulatory authority and publish an offering circular including the following key information:

- Company name
- Purpose(s) for which the proceeds of the corporate bond shall be used
- Total amount of corporate bonds to be issued and the par value thereof
- Method for determining the coupon rate of the bonds
- Maturity date and method for principal and interest payments
- Any bond guarantee
- Issuance price of the bonds and the offer period
- Net assets of the company
- Total amount of the company's outstanding corporate bonds
- Underwriters of the corporate bonds

Any bond issued by a company in paper form shall state the company's name, the par value, the coupon rate, the maturity date, and other similar details. The certificate is required to bear the signature of the legal representative of the company and the company seal. Corporate bonds shall be issued in the form of registered corporate bonds.

7.3.10.1 Registered Corporate Bonds

'Registered corporate bonds' refers to corporate bonds on which the name of the bondholder is recorded. The company is required to maintain a register of bondholders with the following information:

- Name and address of the bondholder
- Date on which the bondholder acquired the bond and the serial number of the bond
- Total value, par value, coupon rate, maturity date and the method of payment of principal and interest
- Date on which the bond was issued

The registration and settlement institution for corporate bonds shall establish rules on registration, custody and acceptance of bonds, and on the payment of coupons.

Any transfer of a corporate bond shall be made by the bondholder's endorsement or by other methods prescribed in the relevant laws and administrative regulations, and after such transfer the company is obliged to record the transferee's name and address on the register of bondholders.

7.3.10.2 Convertible Corporate Bonds

A joint stock liability company may, pursuant to a resolution of a shareholders' meeting, (or a resolution of the board of directors if so authorised under the company's articles of association or by the shareholders' meeting) issue convertible corporate bonds with conversion method specified.

The template characters of convertible corporate bonds shall be indicated on the bonds when issuing such convertible corporate bonds, and the amount of convertible corporate bonds shall be recorded in the register of bondholders.

Any company that issues convertible bonds shall exchange its shares for convertible bonds held by bondholders in accordance with the conversion formula prescribed, provided that bondholders shall in any event retain an option to, or not to, convert their bonds.

7.3.11 Joint Stock Limited Company Financial and Accounting policies

Financial and accounting policies in a joint stock limited company follow similar provisions to those of an LLC.

Financial and accounting policies are required to be established in accordance with the laws, administrative regulations and provisions of the Ministry of Finance under the State Council. An accounting firm may be appointed as the company's auditor, and the company bears the responsibility to provide its appointed accounting firm with accurate and complete accounting documents and books, financial reports and other accounting information, accounting documents and books, as well as financial reports. A financial report is required to be prepared in the offices of the company 20 days in advance of the date of the shareholders' meeting. Any stock limited company with public shares shall publicise its financial report.

7.3.11.1 Distribution of Profits

Rules regarding distribution of profits for a joint stock limited company follows similar provisions to those of an LLC.

7.3.11.2 Capital Reserve

Rules regarding capital reserve for a joint stock limited company follow similar provisions to those of an LLC.

7.3.12 Corporate Combination and Division

Rules regarding corporate combinations and divisions follow similar provisions to those of an LLC.

7.3.13 Dissolutions and Liquidations

Rules regarding dissolutions and liquidations follow similar provisions to those of an LLC.

7.4 Subsidiaries and Branches

7.4.1 Subsidiaries

A subsidiary is an independent legal person with established assets and a separate company name, articles of association and authority. The subsidiary conducts business activities and engages in various civil activities autonomously, and independently bears civil liabilities in accordance with the law.

7.4.2 Branches

A company shall regard its main domicile as its registered address and may set up branches. A branch is an affiliated body of the company and does not possess a legal personality. The Company Law establishes the branch as an affiliated body dependent of the main company, and the legal liability is borne by the company (head office). Management of the branch is governed by the head office, although the branch is required to be registered with the company registration authority and to obtain a business licence with the name of the head office and the term 'branch office'.

7.4.2.1 Special – Branches of Foreign Companies

Branches of foreign companies are subject to specific regulations and upon approval of the Chinese government. It refers to the branches established within the territory of the People's Republic of China by foreign companies. The term 'foreign company' refers to a company established outside the territory of China under any foreign law. A foreign company is a foreign legal person, and its branch established within the territory of China shall not have the status of a Chinese legal person. All liabilities for the business activities conducted by the branches within the territory of the People's Republic of China shall be borne by the foreign companies.

7.4.2.1.1 Establishment

An application of establishment for a branch of a foreign company shall be submitted to the competent authority in China. The application is required to be supported by documents verifying the legal status of the foreign company. Such documents include the following:

- Articles of incorporation of the foreign company
- Certificate of incorporation as issued in its country of domicile
- Other documents of the foreign company as required by the authority

Examination and approval of branches of foreign companies are separately formulated by the State Council. Upon the approval of the establishment, the branch shall be registered with the registration authority in accordance with the law and obtain a business licence. The name of any branch of a foreign company shall indicate its country of domicile and its form of liability structure. Articles of incorporation shall be made available at the place of business of the branch.

Once the branch of the foreign company is established in the territory of China, a person must be designated as a representative or agent within the territory of China to manage the branch. Operating funds corresponding with the business activities or according to the minimum amount established by the State Council are required to be allocated from the foreign company to the branch.

7.4.2.1.2 Liquidation

Where closure of a branch of a foreign company occurs, the company is required to settle the debts of the branch in full in accordance with the law and shall liquidate the branch in accordance with the procedures for the liquidation of a company. No branch of a foreign company established in China may transfer any of its assets out of China before paying its outstanding debts in full.

7.5 External Investments and Compliance

7.5.1 External Investments

A company may invest in other enterprises. A company shall not become a capital contributor that shall bear joint and several liability for the debts of the invested enterprise if any specific regulation have such requirement.

If a company intends to invest in another enterprise or provide a guarantee for another person, a resolution is required to be passed – pursuant to the company's articles of association – by the company's board of directors or shareholders' meeting. The total amount of investments or guarantees, or the amount of a single investment or guarantee shall not exceed the limit established in the articles of association.

Where the company intends to provide a guarantee for any shareholder (or actual controller[4]) of the company, a resolution shall be passed by the shareholders' meeting. Such shareholder (or any shareholder under the control of such actual controller) shall not participate in voting on such investment, and resolution on such matter shall be adopted by a majority vote from the other shareholders attending the meeting.

7.5.2 Compliance with the Law

The shareholders of a company shall abide by laws, administrative regulations and the articles of association and exercise shareholders' rights in accordance with the law. They shall neither damage the interests of the company or other shareholders by abusing shareholders' rights nor damage the interests of any creditor of the company by abusing the company's independent status as a legal person or the limited liability of shareholders.

---

[4] A non-shareholder under an investment relation, agreement or other arrangement with the company may exercise control of the company.

Any shareholder of a company who causes any loss to the company or to other shareholders by abusing shareholders' rights shall be liable for compensation in accordance with the law.

Where any of the shareholders of a company evade the payment of debts by abusing the company's independent status as a legal person or the limited liability of shareholders, thereby seriously damaging the interests of any creditor of the company, they shall be jointly and severally liable for the debts of the company.

If a shareholder utilises two or more companies under their control to carry out activities specified above, each of these companies shall bear joint and several liability for the debts of any of the companies.

For a company with a sole shareholder, if the shareholder cannot testify the independence of the company's assets from its own, the shareholder shall bear joint and several liability for the company's debts.

No controlling shareholder, actual controller, director, supervisor or senior officer of a company may damage the interests of the company by taking advantage of his affiliated relationship.

Any person who causes any loss to the company by violating the above shall be liable for compensation.

Any resolution of the shareholders' meeting or board of directors of a company that violates any law or administrative regulation shall be null and void. Where the procedures for calling a shareholders' meeting or a meeting of the board of directors, or the voting method used therein, violates any law, administrative regulation or the company's articles of association, or where any resolution violates the company's articles of association, the shareholders may, within 60 days of the date on which the resolution is passed, petition a People's Court to nullify it, except where only minor defects occur in the procedure for convening the meeting or the voting method used in the meeting, with no material impact on the resolution.

8 Current: Contracts

8.1 Introduction

'Guanxi' (关系 *guānxì*) – pronounced *gwan-shee* – is one of the most potent forces in Chinese culture. Its direct translation is 'relationships'. However, the reality of *guānxì* is that it relates to 'connections' formed over time by the reciprocation of social exchanges and favours, the latter often related to business.

Foreigners doing business in China are often forced to wrestle with the concept of *guānxì* in their day-to-day activities and decision-making processes. One area where foreigners find themselves in trouble is when they mistake *guānxì* to suffice in business relationships and be more powerful than a written, legally binding contract in Chinese business; and while there maybe have been a time when this was the modus operandi for advancing business, it is no longer.

The current framework of contract legislation is built mainly on the Book III Contract of the Civil Code of the People's Republic of China, which came into effect on 1 January 2021, replacing the Contract Law, which was the governing law from 1999 to 2020, for over 20 years. The Civil Code mainly categorises contracts into the following types:

- Sales contract
- Utility supply contract
- Gift contract
- Loan contract
- Suretyship contract
- Lease contract
- Financial lease contract
- Factoring contract
- Work contract
- Construction project contract
- Transport contract
- Technology contract
- Custody contract
- Warehousing contract
- Entrustment contract
- Property management service contract
- Brokerage contract
- Intermediary contract
- Partnership contract

8.1.1 General Background

8.1.1.1 Basic Principle of a Contract

The word 'contract' in Chinese is written with the two characters 合同 (*Hétōng*): 合 (*hé*) means to join and 同 (*tōng*) means to be the same together. Therefore, the two characters combined signify parties in unification with the same purpose.

8.1.1.2 Counterparty Due Diligence

Before entering into contract negotiation, a company search of the Chinese party shall be performed. The company search should disclose corporate structure, business scope, internal corporate governance, registered capital, registered address, any company changes and any recorded offences. This procedure is employed to ensure that the Chinese party is a valid, registered business and that its registered business scope allows the company to perform the related business activities; for example, if a foreign party intends to conclude a contract with a Chinese party to export goods to Spain and no import or export activity is found under the business scope of the Chinese party, the Chinese party is prohibited from exporting goods but may utilise a third party with a proper import and export business activity and licence – which, naturally, may increase the price of goods.

8.1.1.3 Chinese Language

Although Chinese law permits the use of foreign languages in contracts, evidence submitted to court must be in Chinese. Therefore, it is encouraged to use bilingual contracts and establish Chinese as the prevailing language where the counterparty is a domestic company. If there is no governing language, a Chinese court or arbitration panel shall establish Chinese as the prevailing language. If there is no Chinese version of the contract, then the contract is required to be translated by an appointed translator of the State.

8.1.1.4 Corporate Seal

Relating to Chinese contracts, each page of the contract shall be affixed with a portion of the corporate seal. Corporate seals shall include the full Chinese registered name of the Chinese party. Signatures may accompany the seal on a contract, but the validity of contracts affixed with only signatures is controversial in legal practice, since a seal is the common proof of validity of a contract for Chinese companies. Besides, if a company has a contract seal engraved especially for affixing on contracts, the contract seal can be used instead of a corporate seal.

8.1.1.5 General Principles

Equality of Parties	Voluntariness	Public Interest
A contract is an agreement between equal parties, and parties to a contract are on the same footing in contractual relations. Neither party may impose its will on the other. In practice, should a party seek legal expertise to negotiate the contract while the counterparty does not, the counterparty could argue that the contract was not concluded with equal footing, since one party was advised by legal expertise and the other was not.	The parties to a contract enjoy the right to voluntarily conclude a contract according to the law, which should not be without illegal interference from any unit or individual, although if the State issues a mandatory assignment or a state procurement order, the relevant legal person(s) or other organisation shall conclude contracts based on the rights and obligations as provided for by the relevant laws and administrative regulations.	Parties shall abide by the laws and administrative regulations and respect public morals, as well as not disrupt the socio-economic order or act against public interests.
Fairness	**Good Faith**	**Full Performance of Contracts**
Rights and obligations of the contract parties stipulated in a contract must be fair.	The parties act honestly and in good faith when exercising rights and performing obligations under a contract.	The parties are required to perform their specific duties according to the contractual terms, and neither party may change or stop the performance of its duties unilaterally. Where a party cannot perform the contract according to the contractual terms, such a party is deemed in breach of the contract.

8.2 Formation of Contracts

A contract may be concluded in writing or in any form as agreed to by the two parties. A written contract may be in the form of contractual agreements, letters and electronic data contents, such as telegrams, telexes, faxes, electronic data exchanges and email.

However, a contract must be in writing where the contract parties or the laws or administrative regulations so require.

Practical Note: Electronic Data

Electronic data must be received by the receiver's server, and it must be clear that the sender has no access to such a server. Where electronic data is filed as evidence in court, prior to the filing, a public notary is required to notarise that the electronic data was received by the receiver on the receiver's server. Electronic data is required to be in Chinese, and other languages shall be translated by a government-designated translation company.

8.2.1 Basic Clauses of a Contract

The parties to a contract may decide the content of a contract themselves, but generally the following basic clauses should be included:

- Titles or names and domiciles of the contract parties
- Subject matter of the contract clearly defined
- Quantity requirements
- Quality requirements
- Price terms or payment
- Time limit, place and method of performance
- Liabilities for violation of the contact
- Methods of settlement of disputes

Various contract models may also be applied by contract parties.

8.2.2 Offer

An offer is defined as an expression of the desire to conclude a contract. To be a valid offer, the content of an offer has to be concrete and definite, and it should also indicate an intention of the offeror to be bound if the offer is accepted. Items such as price list, a public notice for auction or tender, and other commercial advertising are treated as an 'invitation to offer' rather than as an 'offer'. However, if the contents of a commercial advertisement meet the conditions of a valid offer, such a commercial advertisement shall be treated as an offer.

An offer takes legal effect upon the delivery to the offeree, and a contract is formed when an offer is effectively accepted. Where a contact is entered into electronically, the offer is delivered to the offeree when the relevant electronic data enters the receiver's designated computer; or, where no specific system is designated, the offer becomes effective when the data enters any system of the receiver.

8.2.2.1 Withdrawing and Revoking an Offer

An offer may be withdrawn provided that the offeror's notice of withdrawal reaches the offeree before or at the same time as the notice of offer.

An offer may be revoked except under any of the following circumstances:

- The offeror has explicitly indicated that the offer is irrevocable by specifying a time limit for acceptance or by any other manner
- The offeree reasonably believes that the offer is irrevocable and has prepared for the performance of the contract

Where an expression of intent to revoke an offer is made in a real-time communication, the content of such an expression of intent shall be known to the offeree before the offeree makes an acceptance. Where an expression of intent to revoke an offer is not made in a real-time communication, it shall reach the offeree before the offeree makes an acceptance.

An offer shall no longer be effective under the following circumstances:

- The offeree has rejected the offer
- The offeror has legally revoked the offer
- The offeree has not accepted the offer within the time limit for acceptance
- The offeree has materially changed the contents of the offer

8.2.3 Acceptance

The offeree's indication of agreement to the offeror's offer is acceptance. To accept an offer, the offeree must send a notice of acceptance. Silence does not constitute an acceptance. However, exceptions to this requirement of notice are allowed where trade practices have been established or where the offeror has indicated that an agreement may be expressed by performing an act without a notice to the offeror.

8.2.3.1 Time of Acceptance

An acceptance of an offer must reach the offeror within the time limit specified by the offer. Where there is no time limit, an acceptance to an oral offer made during conversation must be made immediately unless the parties have agreed otherwise. Acceptance to other offers must be made within a reasonable time, having regard to the circumstances.

The time limit for acceptance fixed by the offer in a telegram or a letter begins to run from the moment the telegram is handed in for dispatch or from the date shown on the letter, or from the mailing date shown on the envelope stamp if no such date is specified on the letter. If an offer is made by telephone, telex, or other means of rapid communication, the fixed time period for acceptance begins to run from the moment the offer reaches the offeree.

An acceptance is deemed to take legal effect when it reaches the offeror or, in accordance with trade practices of the requirements of the offer, the required performance of acceptance has been undertaken. A contract is concluded when an acceptance becomes effective. Acceptance by electronic means follows the same procedures as an offer made electronically.

8.2.3.2 Withdrawal of Acceptance and Late Acceptance

An acceptance may be withdrawn provided the notice of withdrawal reaches the offeror before or at the same time as the notice of acceptance. Generally, any acceptance beyond the established time limit is regarded as a new offer unless the original offeror notifies the offeree immediately that such an overdue acceptance is acceptable. However, an overdue acceptance is effective as an acceptance if the notice of acceptance has been sent within the fixed period of time and, under normal circumstances, such an acceptance would have reached the offeror in due time unless the offeror, without delay, has informed the offeree of his rejection of the late acceptance.

8.2.3.3 Modified Acceptance

An acceptance must be explicit and its contents must match those of the offer. Any material alteration to the terms of an offer – such as changes in subject matter, quantity and quality of the subject matter, price, payment, period of time for performance, place and method of performance, liability, and dispute settlement method – shall be regarded as a new offer. Nonetheless, a modified acceptance shall be effective if the alteration is non-substantial, and the contract shall be concluded on the basis of the modified acceptance unless the offeror objects to it in time or the offer clearly prohibits any alteration.

8.2.3.4 Conclusion of a Contract

1. Where the parties conclude a contract in the form of a written agreement, the contract is formed at the time the parties all sign, stamp or put their fingerprints on it. Prior to signing, stamping or putting their fingerprints thereon, where one of the parties has already performed the principal obligation and the other party has accepted the performance, the contract is formed at the time of such acceptance.
2. Where a contract is required to be concluded in writing in accordance with the laws or administrative regulations, or agreed by the parties and the parties fail to make the contract in writing, if one of the parties has already performed the principal obligation and the other party has accepted the performance, the contract is formed at the time of such acceptance.
3. Where the parties conclude a contract in the form of a letter, a data message, or the like, and a confirmation letter is required to be signed, the contract is formed when the confirmation letter is signed.

8.2.3.5 Place of Contract

In general, the place where the acceptance takes effect is the place where the contract is concluded. Such a place may be any of the following:

- The receiver's main business place, where the contract is made by way of electronic messages
- The receiver's domicile, where it has no main business place
- The place where the contracting parties sign or seal the contract, where a contract is made in a written form

127

If the place of conclusion shown in the contract is inconsistent with the place where the contract was actually signed or sealed, the place of conclusion as defined in the contract shall be deemed the place of conclusion. If no place of conclusion is specified in the contract and the relevant parties have signed or sealed the contract in a different place, the place where the contract was finally signed or sealed shall be deemed the place of conclusion.

8.2.4 Form

'Standard clauses' refers to the clauses that have been drawn up by one party in advance for the purposes of repeated use and that have been concluded without negotiating with the counterparty.

Where a contract is to be concluded with standard clauses, the party that provides such standard clauses shall determine the parties' rights and obligations in accordance with the principle of fairness and use reasonable means to draw the counterparty's attention to the clauses concerning the other party's major interests and concerns. Where the party providing the standard clauses fails to perform the aforementioned obligation of calling attention or giving explanations, thus resulting in the other party's failure to pay attention to or understand the clause concerning its major interests and concerns, the other party may claim that such a clause does not become part of the contract. Standard clauses are void if:

- there is any circumstance that constitutes voidness of a civil juristic act
- they cause physical injury to the other party or damage to the other party's property, intentionally or due to gross negligence
- the party providing the standard clauses unreasonably exempts or alleviates itself from liability, imposes heavier liability on the other party or restricts the main rights of the other party
- the party providing the standard clauses deprives the other party of its main rights

8.3 Validity of Contracts

8.3.1 Effectiveness of Contracts

In general, a contract comes into effect as soon as it is legally concluded unless otherwise provided by law or agreed by the parties. If laws or administrative regulations require that the effectiveness of a contract is subject to approval and registration procedures, such requirements shall be followed. Where the party obligated to complete application for approval or other procedures fails to do so, the other party may request that the former party bear the liability for breach of such obligation.

The contract parties may agree that a contract becomes effective or is terminated upon the occurrence of specified conditions stipulated in the concluded contract. However, if the conditions are unfairly prevented by a party for its own interests, such conditions shall be recognised as fulfilled. Equally, if a party unfairly facilitates the satisfaction of the conditions, such conditions shall be regarded as unfulfilled.

Contracts must be concluded by legal persons and natural persons with full civil capacity. A contract entered into by a person without civil capacity is void. A contract entered into by a person with limited civil capacity is valid only upon confirmation by that person's legal representative (i.e. such a person's legal custodian). Where a contract is entered into by a natural person with limited civil capacity, the other party to the contract may request such a person's legal representative to ratify the contract within 30 days. If the legal representative does not respond, he shall be deemed to have refused to ratify. Before the contract is subsequently ratified by a legal representative, the other bona fide party has the right to revoke the contract by giving notification. However, contracts that only grant benefits to the person with limited civil capacity or are appropriate to such a person's age, intellectual capacity or health status are deemed effective without the need for ratification by a legal representative.

A contract signed on behalf of a legal entity by a legal representative or by a person in charge of a legal entity exceeding the scope of their authority shall be valid unless the other party either knows or should have known that the person has so exceeded their authority. Similarly, where a contract is entered into by a person who has no agency authority, or by an agent who acts beyond the scope of their authority or whose authority has already been terminated, the contract shall only be valid if the other contract party reasonably believes that the person acting on behalf of the counterparty has the necessary authority of agency. In such cases, the principal is entitled to request that the agent who has no such authorisation compensate for all losses suffered as a result of the agent's unauthorised conduct.

Where a person disposes of another person's property without proper legal authority, the contract may still be valid if that person obtains such a right thereafter or the person with proper rights to the property ratifies the contract thereafter. Likewise, where an agent who has no power of agency enters into a contract in the name of the principal, the contract shall be deemed to have been ratified by the principal as long as the principal performs any of the obligations under the contract.

8.3.2 Void Contracts

The Book III Contract of the Civil Code sets forth circumstances under which a contract shall be deemed invalid, in part or entirely. Apart from the above specific stipulations in the Book III Contract, a contract is also invalid in any of the following circumstances where the civil juristic act shall be deemed invalid as per the Book I General in the Civil Code:

- It is performed by one person and another person based on a false expression of intent
- It is in violation of the mandatory provisions of laws or administrative regulations or offends the public order or good morals
- It is conducted through malicious collusion between a person who performs the act and a counterparty thereof and thus harms the lawful rights and interests of another person

8.3.4 Revokable Contracts

The party concerned may request that the court or an arbitration institution revoke the contract if it is:

- performed based on serious misunderstanding
- induced to be performed by fraudulent means against the party's true intention
- performed against the party's true intention owing to duress by the other party or a third person
- performed in situations where one party takes advantage of the other party in a desperate situation, or where the other party lacks the ability to make a judgment, which is obviously unfair

A party's right to revoke a contract is extinguished under any of the following circumstances:

- The party has failed to exercise the right to revocation within one year of the date when it knows or should have known of the cause for revocation, or within 90 days of the date when the party who has performed the act with serious misunderstanding knows or should have known of the cause for revocation
- The party acting under duress has failed to exercise the right to revocation within one year of the date when the duress ceases

- The party that becomes aware of the cause for revocation waives the right to revocation expressly or through its own conduct

The right to revocation is extinguished if the party fails to exercise it within five years of the date the contract has been performed.

A contract that is void or has been legally revoked has no effect from the very beginning. Where a contract does not take effect, or is void, revoked, or terminated, the validity of a clause concerning dispute resolution shall not be affected.

8.3.5 Effect of a Void or Revoked Contract

If a contract is void or is rescinded, property acquired by one party must be returned to the other party. If it cannot be returned or if it is not necessary for it to be returned, the property should be evaluated, and the evaluated amount must be paid to the other party as compensation. The party at fault must compensate the other party for the loss caused thereby. Where both parties are at fault, each must bear its appropriate liabilities.

In cases where a party intentionally conspires to harm the interests of the State, a collective entity or a third party, the property so acquired must be returned to the State, the collective entity or the third party.

8.3.6 Illegal Contracting Acts

Contracts shall be concluded for due purposes and shall not disturb socio-economic order or undermine national or public interests. Using contracts to seek unlawful gain in violation of the law is illegal, and contracts so concluded could be void *ab initio* or rescindable, depending on the seriousness of the circumstances, and the party that committed such acts shall be punished in accordance with administrative or criminal law.

8.4 Performance of Contracts

8.4.1 Basic Principle

Complete and full performance of a contract according to an agreed arrangement is a basic principle of the Contract Law. Both parties must fulfil their obligations in accordance with the nature and purpose of the contract, common commercial practices and the principle of good faith. In performing the contract, each party is obliged to cooperate with the other party, to inform the other party as required and to keep commercial secrets confidential.

8.4.2 Ambiguous Obligations

If the provisions in the contract relating to the quality, price, time of performance and place of performance are unclear, or if there are no such provisions in the contract, the contract parties may make supplementary agreements or determine the issues in accordance with relevant clauses or established commercial practice. If these methods fail, the ambiguity shall be solved in accordance with the following rules:

- Where provisions relating to quality are unclear, the contract shall be performed in accordance with a mandatory national standard, or a recommendatory national standard in the absence of a mandatory national standard, or the standard of the industry in the absence of a recommendatory national standard. In the absence of any national or industrial standards, the contract shall be performed in accordance with the general standard or a specific standard conforming to the purpose of the contract

- Where provisions relating to price are unclear, the contract shall be performed according to the market price at the place where the contract is performed, or, where it is so required, according to the government price or the price for which the government has issued guidance. If the government price is readjusted during the time limit of the delivery, the payment is calculated at the time of the delivery. If the delivery of the subject matter is delayed and the price is raised, the original price shall be adopted. In the same case and the price falls, the new price is adopted. If there is an overdue collection of the goods or there is an overdue payment and the price is raised, the new price shall be adopted. In the same case and the price is dropped, the original price shall be adopted
- Where provisions relating to place of performance are unclear and the payment is monetary, the place of performance is the place of the party receiving the monetary payment, transfer of real property is the place where the real property is located, and for other subject matters, the place of performance is the place where the party performing the obligation is located
- Where provisions relating to the period of performance are unclear, the obligor may perform his obligations at any time. The obligee may also at any time demand that the obligor perform his obligations within a reasonable period of time
- Where provisions relating to the method of performance are unclear, the performance shall be made according to the method that is beneficial to the realisation of the purpose of the contract
- Where provisions relating to the cost of performance are unclear, the obligor shall bear the cost. Where the expenses for performance are increased, and the increase is caused by the obligee, the obligee shall bear the increase

8.4.3 Performance Involving a Third Party

Where the parties agree that the obligor shall perform the obligation to a third person, if the obligor fails to perform the obligation to the third person or the performance does not conform to the agreement, the obligor shall bear default liability to the obligee.

Where it is provided by law or agreed by the parties that a third person may directly request that the obligor perform the obligation to him, and the third person does not explicitly reject it within a reasonable period of time, if the obligor fails to perform the obligation to the third person or the performance does not conform to the agreement, the third person may request that the obligor bear default liability. The defences the obligor has against the obligee may be asserted against the third person.

Where the parties agree that the obligation shall be performed to the obligee by a third person, if the third person fails to perform the obligation or the performance does not conform to the agreement, the obligor shall bear default liability to the obligee.

Where an obligor fails to perform an obligation, and a third person has a lawful interest in the performance of the obligation, the third person is entitled to perform it to the obligee on behalf of the obligor unless the obligation may only be performed by the obligor based on the nature of the obligation as agreed by the parties or as provided by law.

After the obligee accepts the performance of such an obligation by the third person, his claim against the obligor shall be assigned to the third person unless otherwise agreed by the obligor and the third person.

8.4.4 Order of Performance

Where the parties have mutual obligations to each other and there is an order of performance of the obligations, the parties shall perform the obligations at the same time. A party is entitled to refuse the demand of performance by the other party if the other party has not yet commenced to perform its contractual obligations or, if the party performs its obligations improperly, to refuse to perform the relevant obligations.

Where the parties have mutual obligations to each other and there is an order of performance of the obligations, and the party obliged to perform first fails in its performance, the other party is entitled to reject the demand of performance of that party or, if the former party performs its obligations improperly, to refuse to perform the relevant obligations.

8.4.5 Suspension of Performance

A party obliged to first perform the contract obligations may temporarily suspend performance of its obligations if there is solid evidence to show that the other party has:

- fallen into serious difficulty with its business operation
- transferred its assets or capital to evade repayment of debt
- lost commercial credibility
- lost or is likely to lose the ability to perform its obligations under the contract

The party that suspends performance should, however, immediately inform the other party and should resume its performance when the other party regains its ability to perform or offers an appropriate performance guarantee. If during the suspension of performance and within a reasonable time the other party fails to regain the ability to perform or to offer an appropriate performance guarantee, it shall be deemed to be an indication, through its act, that the party will not perform his principal obligation, and the party that suspends the performance may terminate the contract and may request that the other party bear default liability.

An obligor may also suspend his performance or place the subject matter in escrow where performance becomes difficult due to the obligee's failure to inform the obligor of the obligee's split, merger or change of address. However, neither party may refuse to perform contractual obligations on the grounds that either party's name or entity name, legal representative, responsible person, or person handling the contract has been changed.

8.4.6 Earlier or Partial Performance

Generally, performance shall be rendered in accordance with the terms of the contract. An obligee may reject an earlier performance or partial performance of the obligor unless such performance does no harm to the interests of the obligee. The obligor shall bear all the extra costs incurred from the earlier performance or partial performance.

8.4.7 Rights of Subrogation and Nullification

8.4.7.1 Right of Subrogation

Article 535 of the Civil Code allows the obligee to request that the People's Court allow him to exercise by subrogation the obligor's claim against the counterparty of the obligor in his own name where the obligor fails to diligently enforce its rights against the counterparty or an accessory right related thereto unless such a claim belongs exclusively to the obligor himself.

The scope of the right of subrogation is limited to the obligee's due claim. The necessary expenses for the obligee to exercise the right of subrogation shall be borne by the obligor.

Where the People's Court determines that the right of subrogation has been established, the counterparty of the obligor shall perform the obligation to the obligee. After the performance is accepted by the obligee, the corresponding rights and obligations between the obligee and the obligor, and those between the obligor and the counterparty, are terminated.

8.4.7.2 *Right of Nullification*

An obligee may apply to the court to nullify the following actions of an obligor if:

- the obligor gratuitously disposes of his proprietary rights and interests by waiving his claims, waiving the security for his claims or transferring his properties without consideration, and the like, or maliciously extends the period of performance of his due claim, and the enforcement of the obligee's claim is thus adversely affected
- the obligor transfers his property at an obviously unreasonably low price, takes another's property or provides security for another's obligation at an obviously unreasonably high price, and the enforcement of the obligee's claim is thus adversely affected

If an obligee petitions the People's Court to annul the obligor's action of abandoning due claims or transferring the property, and the People's Court finds that the obligor's action is improper and annuls it, the obligor's action shall be deemed invalid *ab initio* (from the beginning).

The necessary expenses incurred by the obligee in exercising the right of nullification, such as lawyers' fees and travel costs, shall be borne by the obligor.

8.8 Variation and Assignment

8.8.1 Variation

Contracts may be altered upon agreement by the parties, but if the contract is required to be approved by and registered with relevant authorities, variation to the contract must also be submitted to the original contract approval and registration authorities for approval and registration. To be effective, such variations must be clear.

8.8.2 Assignment

An obligee is permitted to assign all or part of his contractual rights to a third party, except where:

- the nature of the contractual rights prohibit assignment
- the contract parties have agreed to prohibit assignment
- the relevant applicable law prohibits assignment

Where the original contract is required to be approved and registered with certain authorities, the assignment, in addition to having the consent of the other party, must also be approved and registered with the original approval and registration authorities.

To ensure the validity of the assignment, the obligee must notify the obligor of such an assignment. Where an obligee assigns his claim but fails to notify the obligor thereof, the assignment is not effective against the obligor, and the notice of the assignment of a claim may not be revoked unless consented to by the assignee.

Where an obligee assigns his creditor's right, the assignee shall acquire the accessory right related thereto unless the accessory right belongs exclusively to the obligee. Failure to register the assignment of the accessory right, or failure to change the possession thereof, shall not affect the acquisition of the accessory right by the assignee.

The obligor may raise any defence against the assignee that he may have against the obligee/assignor after receiving the notice of assignment of a claim.

The obligor may also claim to offset his obligations to the assignee where (i) the obligor receives the notice of assignment and has a claim against the assignor that becomes due prior to or at the same time as the due date of the assigned claim, or (ii) the obligor's claim and the assigned claim are generated on the basis of the same contract.

Similarly, an obligor may also assign all or part of its obligations to a third party upon the consent of the obligee. The obligor or the third person may demand that the obligee gives his consent within a reasonable period of time. Where the obligee makes no indication, it shall be deemed as no consent given.

Where a third person agrees with the obligor to join in the obligation and notifies the obligee thereof, or a third person indicates to the obligee his willingness to join in the obligation, if the obligee fails to explicitly make a rejection within a reasonable period of time, the obligee may request that the third person assumes the joint and several obligations with the obligor to the extent of the obligation the third person is willing to assume.

The new obligor is entitled to raise any defence against the obligee that the original obligor would have. Where the original obligor has a claim against the obligee, the new obligor may not claim a set-off against the obligee.

8.9 Termination

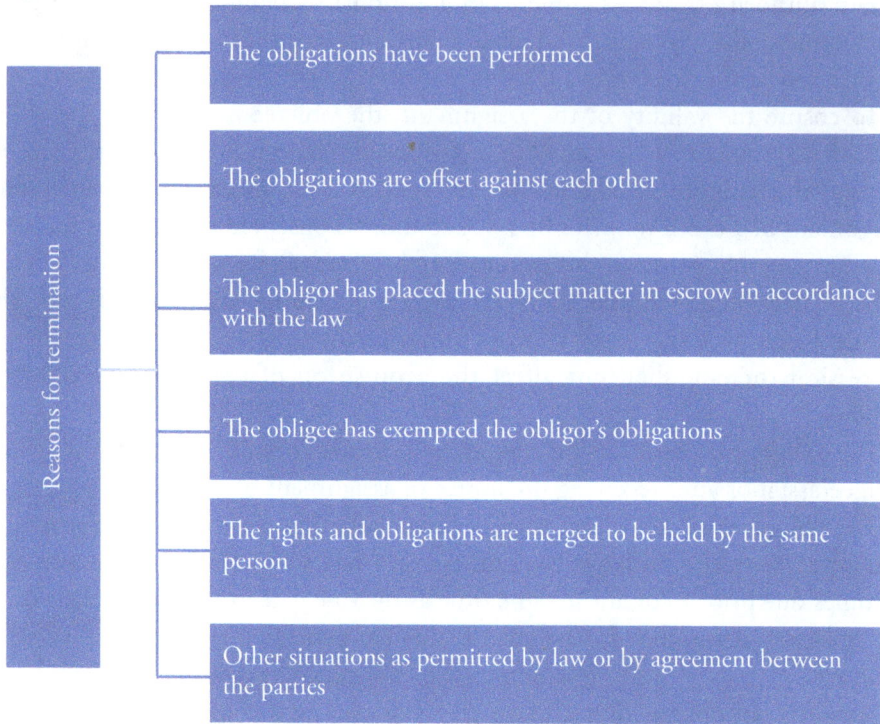

Reasons for termination

- The obligations have been performed
- The obligations are offset against each other
- The obligor has placed the subject matter in escrow in accordance with the law
- The obligee has exempted the obligor's obligations
- The rights and obligations are merged to be held by the same person
- Other situations as permitted by law or by agreement between the parties

The relationship of rights and obligations under a contract shall be terminated upon rescission of the contract. The parties may rescind the contract upon agreement through consultation. The parties may agree on the causes for rescission of the contract by a party. When a cause for rescission of contract arises, the party with the right to rescission may rescind the contract.

Article 563 of the Civil Code also sets out certain statutory conditions under which the parties may rescind the contract. These are as follows:

- The purpose of the contract cannot be realised due to a *force majeure* event.
- Prior to expiration of the period of performance, one of the parties explicitly expresses or indicates by his act that he will not perform the principal obligation
- One of the parties delays his performance of the principal obligation and still fails to perform it within a reasonable period of time after being demanded
- One of the parties delays his performance of the obligation or has otherwise acted in breach of the contract, thus making it impossible for the purpose of the contract to be achieved
- Other situations stipulated by the law

For a contract under which the obligor is required to continuously perform an obligation for an indefinite period of time, the parties thereto may rescind the contract at any time, provided that the other party shall be notified within a reasonable period of time.

The right to terminate a contract will elapse if the rights holder fails to exercise his termination right within a statutory or contractually agreed time limit. Where there is no such statutory or contractually agreed time limit, the termination right shall elapse if the party with the termination right does not exercise such a right within one year after it knew or should have known the causes for termination, or within a reasonable period of time after being demanded by the other party.

Where one of the parties requests to terminate the contract in accordance with the law, the other party shall be duly notified. The contract shall be terminated at the time the notice reaches the other party or, where the notice states that the contract shall be automatically terminated if the obligor fails to perform his obligation within a specified period of time, when the obligor fails to perform the obligation upon expiration of such a specified period of time. Where the other party has objections to the termination of the contract, either party may request that the People's Court or an arbitration institution determine the validity of the termination.

Once a contract is terminated, where the obligations have not yet been performed, the performance shall cease. Where the obligations have already been performed, the parties may, taking into account the performance status and the nature of the contract, request restoration to the original status or other remedial measures taken and have the right to request compensation for losses. Where a contract is terminated due to a default, the party with the right to terminate the contract may request that the breaching party bear default liability unless otherwise agreed by the parties.

After the principal contract is terminated, a security provider shall still be obligated to secure the obligee's liability unless otherwise agreed in the security contract.

Termination of the relationship of rights and obligations under a contract does not affect the validity of the contract clauses regarding settlement and liquidation.

A party may discharge its contractual obligations by offset where the parties have obligations to each other and the subject matter of the performance is of the same type and quality. A party wishing to carry out an offset must send a notice to the same effect to the other party. An offset must not contain conditions or time limits. If the parties to a contract have mutual obligations but the types and nature of the subject matters are different, both parties may also offset obligations through consensus consultation.

8.9.1 Placement of Subject Matters in Escrow

Where it is difficult to perform an obligation under any of the following circumstances, an obligor may place the subject matter in escrow if:

- the obligee refuses to accept the performance without justifiable reason
- the obligee's whereabouts cannot be determined
- the obligee dies, with his heirs or estate administrator not determined, or the obligee loses his capacity for performing civil juristic acts, with no guardian determined
- any other circumstances apply as provided by the law

Where the subject matter is not suitable for escrow or the expenses therefor are too high, the obligor may sell the subject matter through auction or sale and place the proceeds thus obtained in escrow in accordance with the law.

After a subject matter is placed in escrow, the obligor shall promptly notify the obligee, or the obligee's heir, estate administrator, guardian or custodian for his property.

After the subject matter is placed in escrow, the obligee bears all the risks arising and all costs incurred thereof. All proceeds derived from the subject matter during the escrow period shall belong to the obligee. The expenses thus incurred shall be borne by the obligee.

The obligee is entitled to collect the subject matter at any time. However, where the obligee owes due obligation to the obligor, the escrow agency shall reject the obligee's request for collecting it before the obligee performs such obligation or provides security therefor.

The obligee's right to collect the subject matter placed in escrow is extinguished if the said right is not exercised within five years of the date the subject matter is delivered to the escrow agency, and such subject matter shall be escheated to the State after the escrow agency's expenses are deducted. However, where an obligee fails to perform his due obligation to the obligor, or where the obligee waives their right to collect the subject matter placed in escrow in writing to the escrow agency, the obligor has the right to take back the subject matter after paying the escrow agency's expenses.

The right of the obligee to the subject matter lodged must be exercised within five years of the day of lodgement; otherwise, it will elapse. In such a case, the ownership of the lodged subject matter is passed to the State.

8.10 Liabilities for Breach of Contract

8.10.1 Breach of Contract

If a party does not perform its part of the obligations, or its performance does not comply with the agreed contractual terms and conditions, a breach of contract then arises. The breaching party shall bear default liability, such as continuing to perform its obligations, taking remedial measures or compensating for losses. Where a party explicitly expresses or indicates by its act that it will not perform its contractual obligation, the other party may request that the former party bear default liability before the expiration of the time period of performance.

Where a party fails to make payment in compliance with the terms of the contract, the other party may demand that the breaching party make the payment. Where a party fails to perform its non-monetary obligations or if the performance of a non-monetary obligation does not comply with the agreed terms, the other party is entitled to demand that the breaching party undertake specific performance or cure the breach unless:

- the obligation is, either in law or in fact, impossible to perform
- the subject matter of the obligation is not suitable for specific performance, or the cost for performance is too high
- the obligee fails to demand the performance within a reasonable period of time

In cases where the performance does not comply with the contract, the breaching party must bear liability for breach of contract in accordance with the agreed terms. Where there is no such term on default liability, or the terms are not clear, the aggrieved party may, according to the nature and amount of losses, request that the other party repair, exchange, reproduce, refund or reduce the price or payment.

Where a party fails to perform its contractual obligation, or its performance does not conform to the agreement, it shall pay compensation if after performing its obligation or taking remedial measures the other party still suffers loss.

Where a party fails to perform its contractual obligation, or its performance does not conform to the agreement, causing the other party to suffer loss, the amount of compensation shall be equivalent to the loss caused by the breach of contract, including the benefits expected to be obtained should the contract have been performed, except that it shall not exceed the loss that may be caused by the breach that the breaching party foresees or should have foreseen at the time of the conclusion of the contract.

8.10.2 Liquidated Damages

Parties to a contract may stipulate in the contract a set amount of money as liquidated damages. When there is a breach of contract, the breaching party shall be liable to pay the sum to the non-breaching party. The parties may also agree upon a method for calculating the damages in the contract. Where the agreed liquidated damages are lower than the loss caused, the People's Court or an arbitration institution may increase the amount upon the request of a party. Where the agreed liquidated damages are excessively higher than the loss caused, the People's Court or an arbitration institution may make an appropriate reduction upon the request of a party.

If the liquidated damages are made due to the delay of performance, the breaching party must continue the performance even after paying liquidated damages.

8.10.3 Deposit

The parties may agree that one party makes a deposit to the other party to secure its claim. A deposit contract becomes effective upon actual delivery of the deposit.

The amount of the deposit shall be agreed by the parties, except that it shall not exceed 20% of the value of the object of the principal contract, and any excessive part cannot be effected as a deposit. Where the amount of the deposit actually delivered is more or less than the agreed amount, the agreed amount of the deposit shall be deemed to have been changed.

After an obligor has performed his obligation, the deposit shall be calculated as part of the price or be refunded. Where a party paying the deposit fails to perform its obligation or fails to perform it in conformity with the agreement, so that the purpose of the contract cannot be achieved, it is not entitled to request a refund of the deposit. Where a party receiving the deposit fails to perform its obligation or fails to perform it in conformity with the agreement, so that the purpose of the contract cannot be achieved, it shall refund twice the amount of the deposit to the other party.

Where the parties agree on both liquidated damages and deposit when a party defaults, the other party may choose to apply either the clause on the liquidated damages or the clause on the deposit. Where the deposit is not sufficient to compensate the losses caused by one party's default, the other party may request compensation for the losses in excess of the amount of the deposit.

8.11 Dispute Settlement

8.11.1 General Principles

In general, and practically, when there are disputes arising from the contract, the parties are encouraged to resolve the disputes through negotiation for 30 days. If negotiation fails, mediation can be conducted for 10 to 15 days by a third party or the legal representative or the representative of the legal representatives. If the parties are unwilling to do so, or if such consultation or mediation fails, the parties may settle the case by bringing the case to the People's Court or an arbitration body in accordance with the arbitration agreement. If disputes arise from a contract with a foreign nexus, the parties may apply for arbitration to an arbitration body according to the arbitration agreement or clause. If there is no arbitration agreement or the arbitration agreement is invalid, the dispute can be brought to the People's Court. The court judgment, arbitration award or mediation agreement must be implemented by the parties. In cases of non-compliance by one party, the other party may petition the court for enforcement.

Practical Note: Dispute Resolution Best Practices

In the Chinese culture, negotiation or mediation is viewed as friendly dispute resolution in place of utilising the courts. Settling disputes in court is the last option, and evidence of an attempt to settle the dispute with negotiation or mediation beforehand is required. In terms of courts, Chinese parties often prefer the People's Tribunal, while foreign parties favour the Arbitration Court because they believe there are more advantages in the Arbitration Court. The more significant element in dispute resolution in court is the choice of lawyer. It is essential to choose a litigation lawyer with an international-law background and with previous cases involving a foreign element. Additionally, it is important to note that Chinese lawyers are strictly prohibited from receiving commission from litigation cases; such violations shall result in the loss of the certification to practise law.

When there is ambiguity in the words or expressions of a contract, the following rules are to be followed:

- The interpretation of any ambiguity in the standard form clause must be made against the person seeking to rely on the standard form clause, and any inconsistency between the standard form clause and non-standard form clause must be resolved by giving effect to the non-standard form clause
- Regarding disputes on the interpretation of terms of contract, the meaning of such terms must be determined in accordance with the actual words used in the contract, the relevant clauses, the purpose of the contract, commercial practices and customs, and the principle of good faith
- Regarding disputes on the interpretation of words or expressions in a contract that is written in two or more different languages and both are equally valid, the words or expressions shall be determined in accordance with the purpose of the contract
- If parties involving foreign interest have not agreed to a governing jurisdiction of the contract, the law of the country that the contract is most closely connected to shall apply. Any Sino-foreign equity joint ventures, Sino-foreign contractual joint ventures, Sino-foreign cooperative exploration and development of natural resources to be performed in China are subject to the laws of the PRC

8.11.2 Statute of Limitations

There is a special provision on the limitation of action for disputes arising from a contract for the international sale of goods and a contract for the import and export of technology, which is four years, while for other contracts the limitation of action is three years under most conditions.

Case Study: Governing Law and Dispute Resolution

One of the common mistakes is establishing the governing law and dispute resolution in Hong Kong or in a foreign party's jurisdiction. Often a foreign jurisdiction is chosen because the foreign party believes it is a safer option, since they are more familiar with the legal system. However, foreign parties may face difficulties in enforcing foreign awards in China, considering that the breaching party may claim objection, plus the court may have its own opinion. Equally, the procedure to enforce the foreign award based on multilateral and bilateral treaties similar to the Hague Convention on Foreign Judgement in Civil and Commercial Matters, entered between China and the jurisdiction of the government, could accumulate more expenses and prolong the time, which may allow the breaching party to dissipate assets before the award is enforced by a Chinese court.

9 Current: Labour

9.1 Introduction

Employing, managing and developing employees successfully is crucial to the long-term health and success of a company. The expeditious economic growth of China in past years has led to low unemployment rates and companies striving to retain good employees or struggling to terminate problematic employees.

Foreign companies should approach the employment of local labourers with cultural sensitivity rather than by applying Western methods. Primarily, the Chinese education system and parenting play a significant role in the behaviour of local employees and their career objectives. Due to the high population in China, the number of students in one class averages around 40 to 50 to one teacher and one assistant. This means that the individualised style of teaching in the West is not suitable for the mass number of students in one class. Rather, students of varying levels are taught with the same style and approach. Additionally, from the start of education, learning Chinese characters is an essential base on which to learn other subjects. With over 5,000 characters to master, and large class sizes, students are generally taught Chinese characters utilising repetency as the fastest method to learn. As a result, there is often no development of an individual's talents and skills, which leaves the labour force with little enjoyment in individual career development without monetary incentives.

Equally, staff turnover is extremely high in most companies. Many Chinese employees remain in one company for one or two years before moving to a higher-paid position. Therefore, companies may find nurturing and investing in employees challenging, and their investment may then move to a competitor.

Although companies face challenges in employment across the world, it is important to apply the laws, regulations and rules related to labour with a cultural understanding of China. Specifically, implementing strategies to retain and develop good employees and terminate difficult employees without a labour suit are essential to the corporate life cycle of a company.

9.2 Governing Laws

The Labour Law of the People's Republic of China, revised in 2018, and the Labour Contract Law of the People's Republic of China, revised in 2012, are the two primary laws governing employment in China. The two laws apply to enterprises, individual economic organisations (referred to as employers), employees within the territory of the People's Republic of China and the labour relationship between employers and employees.

The Labour Law of the People's Republic of China was first adopted in 1995, with the latest revision promulgated in 2018. The Labour Law regulates the labour system and protects the legitimate rights and interests of employees.

The Labour Contract Law of the People's Republic of China was first adopted in 2009, with the latest revision promulgated in 2012. This law establishes the contractual terms of labour contracts, defining each party's rights and obligations, conclusion, performance, amendment, cancellation or termination between the parties of a labour contract.

9.2.1 Labour Relationship

A labour relationship consists of the employee and the employer. The employee contributes to the production activities and complies with the internal labour rules of the employer, and the employer pays remuneration according to the quantity or quality of the employee's services and provides suitable working conditions.

'Employer' refers to a unit with the capacity and right to employ people. The employment of the employees shall be organised to conduct production and operation, and the employer provides remuneration and other benefits and treatments in return for labour. Employers include enterprises, privately owned economic organisations and private non-enterprise units within the territory of China, individual economic organisations that have employees, state organs, public institutions and social groups.

Employees are natural persons who are able to provide labour in line with the relevant rules and regulations.

9.3 Hiring

9.3.1 Fair Employment

Employees are prescribed with the equal right to employment and choice of occupation. Discrimination in employment is prohibited and equal conditions of employment shall be provided. Under the Labour Law, the following provisions are established for fair employment:

- There shall be no discrimination of ethnic groups, race, gender or religious belief in employment
- Women shall enjoy an equal right to employment, except in posts or types of work deemed by the State as unsuitable for women. On the basis of gender,

women cannot be refused employment or be subject to raised employment standards

- Special stipulations in laws, rules and regulations apply to the employment of disabled people, people of ethnic minority groups and demobilised army personnel

The minimum employment age is restricted to 16 years old. Employers – with the exception of institutions of literature and art, physical culture and special arts and crafts – are forbidden to recruit minors under 16 years old. Any units employing minors under 16 are required to be examined and approved in accordance with the relevant provisions of the State and to guarantee the minor's right to compulsory education.

9.3.2 Employment Applications

In the recruitment process, the employer is required to truthfully provide the scope of work, working conditions, place of work, occupational hazards, production-safety conditions, labour compensation, as well as other matters requested by the employee. Equally, the employer is entitled to request basic information about the employee in relation to the employment. However, the employer cannot retain the candidate employee's resident ID card or other documentation, nor demand that the employee provide security or collect property from him under the guise of another form.

Before confirming the appointment of employment, the employer shall check if the onboarding employee is still hired by the previous employer. The previous employer should issue a certificate of termination of labour relationship, which shall be submitted by the employee to the current employer as evidence.

9.4 Labour Contracts

9.4.1 Offer Letter

An offer letter shall be issued to the candidate employee as an interim measure before the labour contract is concluded. Usually, the offer letter outlines the nature of the position and the benefits, as well as the indication of employment. Although there is no statutory format or terms to be included in the offer letter, employers can legally bind the offer letter and explicitly stipulate major particulars similar to a labour contract, including the job (post), start date of employment, salary, contract duration (including the probation period) and relevant benefits and welfare of employees. Equally, the offer letter can provision the employment offer as conditional upon and subject to the fulfilment of certain criteria.

Once the offer letter is affixed with the company seal, the company cannot rescind the offer letter, although the candidate may choose not to accept the employment offer.

Offer letters may not replace labour contracts. If an offer letter is duly signed and no labour contract is concluded, the offer letter may not be recognised as the labour contract, even though the major terms are explicitly stipulated therein. Employers are encouraged to utilise a formal and written labour contract in order to avoid later disputes.

9.4.2 Contract

A labour contract is an agreement establishing the labour relationship between an employee and an employer. A labour contract defines the rights and obligations of the respective parties and is required to be concluded on or prior to the actual work commencement date, which is also normally the starting date of the validity term of the labour contract.

The formulation of the contract and any modifications after the contract conclusion shall follow the principles of equality, voluntariness and agreement through consultation. No contract can be concluded without the consent of both parties. Labour contracts shall be concluded with the affixation of each party's signature or seal. Once duly signed or sealed, the contract is legally binding and effective. Each respective party is required to fulfil its obligations as stipulated in the labour contract, and each party shall retain at least one original copy of the contract.

Written labour contracts are essential and shall be concluded at the latest within one month from the starting date. Failure to conclude such contracts shall result in unfavourable consequences to the employer. If an employer fails to conclude a written labour contract with an employee more than one month but less than one year after the work commencement date, the employer shall pay twice the salary to the employee each month. If an employer fails to conclude a written labour contract with an employee within one year of the work commencement date, he shall be deemed to have entered into an open-ended labour contract.

9.4.2.1 Collective Contracts

The employer and trade union, or the representatives nominated by the employees if there is no trade union, may conclude a collective contract. The collective contract primarily concerns matters of labour compensation, work hours, rest, leave, work safety and hygiene, insurance and benefits. The draft of the collective contract shall be presented to an all-employee representative congress or to all the employees for discussion and approval. The contract shall be concluded by the labour union representing the employees and employer or, if there is no labour union, the representatives nominated by the employees under the guidance of the labour union at the higher level. After conclusion, the contract is required to be submitted to the labour administration department. If there is no objection from the labour administration department, the contract shall become effective within 15 days of receipt.

The collective contract concluded in accordance with the law applies to all employees, as well as the employer. Additionally, where there is a collective contract, if the employer also enters particular labour contracts with certain employees and agrees upon different terms – such as labour compensation and standards for working conditions – such different standards shall not be lower than those stipulated in the collective contract.

If an employer breaches the collective contract and infringes upon the employees' labour rights and interests, the labour union may, in accordance with the law, demand that the employer assume liability. If a dispute arising from the performance of the collective contract is not resolved after friendly negotiations, the labour union may apply for arbitration and institute legal proceedings in accordance with the law.

9.4.2.2 Contractual Terms

A labour contract shall be concluded in written form and contain the following mandatory clauses.

Mandatory clauses

- Name, domicile and legal representative or main person in charge of the employer

- Name, residential address and number of the resident ID card, or other valid identity document number, of the employee

- Term of labour contract

- Scope of work and place of work

- Labour remuneration

- Social insurance

- Labour protection, working conditions and protection against occupational hazards

- Labour discipline

- Conditions for the termination of labour

- Liabilities for the violation of the labour contract

- Other issues required by laws and regulations to be included in the labour contract

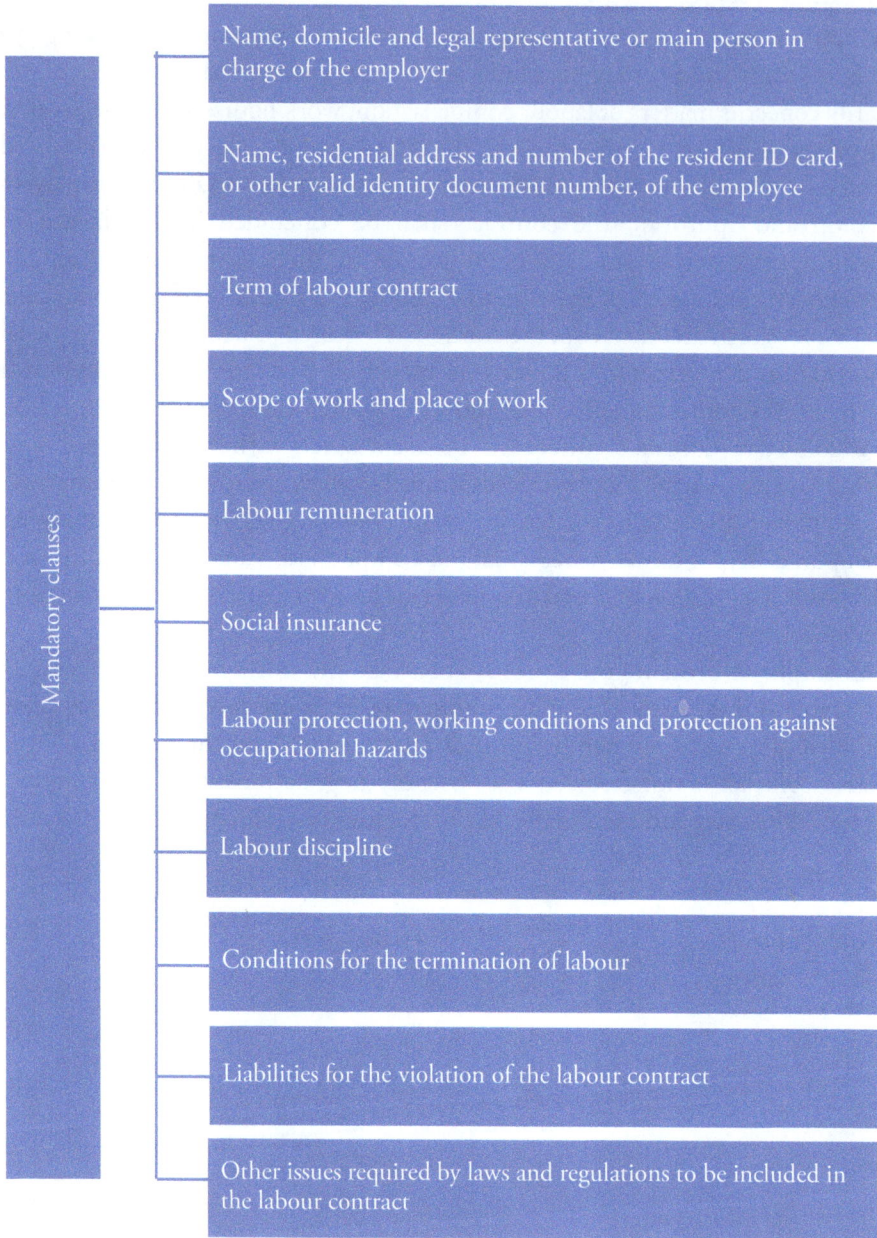

The labour contract may also contain other clauses agreed upon by the parties through consultation, such as probation period, training, confidentiality, supplementary insurance and welfare. However, the contractual terms shall not violate or counter against the provisions of laws, administrative rules and regulations.

The labour administration department shall order rectification of the labour contract if the employer fails to establish the mandatory clauses as prescribed in the Labour Contract Law or to deliver the text of the labour contract to the employee. As a result of such failures, the liability of any damages, harm or loss affecting the employee shall be borne by the employer.

> ## Practical Note: The Place of Work
>
> The place of work may differ from the registered place of the company. However, the place of work is required to be stated in the labour contract and the employer is required to establish a branch office as the place of work. The branch office shall assume social insurance and tax payment obligations in the city where the branch is registered.

The term of the labour contract may be classified into fixed term, non-fixed term (open-ended) and the completion of a specific assignment.

9.4.2.2.1 Fixed-term Contract

'Fixed-term contract' refers to a fixed term of employment with a termination date as agreed by the employee and the employer. Renewal of a fixed-term contract shall be conducted in the form of a new written contract.

9.4.2.2.2 Non-fixed-term (Open-ended) Contract

'Non-fixed-term (open-ended) contract' refers to employment with no definite termination date. An open-ended labour contract may be concluded between an employer and employee upon consultation.

If an employee proposes or agrees to renew and conclude a labour contract in any of the following circumstances, an open-ended labour contract shall be concluded unless the employee requests the conclusion of a fixed-term labour contract instead:

- The employee has been employed by the employer for ten consecutive years
- The labour contract is concluded consecutively for the third time
- The employer first introduces the labour contract system or the state-owned enterprise reconcludes its labour contracts as a consequence of restructuring and the employee has been working for the employer for ten consecutive years and is less than ten years away from legal retirement age

In addition, it shall be deemed that an open-ended labour contract has been concluded if there is no written contract concluded between the employer and the employee within one year of the work commencement date.

9.4.2.3 Completion of a Specific Assignment

The employee and employer may agree the conclusion of a labour contract with a term based on the completion of a specific task.

9.4.2.4 Non-compete Clauses

If an employee has an obligation of confidentiality to safeguard trade secrets and other intellectual property of the employer, the employer may include non-compete provisions in the labour contract or a confidentiality agreement, although personnel subject to such non-compete provisions are limited to senior management, senior technicians and other individuals with confidentiality obligations. The scope, geographical limitations and terms of the non-compete obligations shall be agreed upon by the employer and employee. The term of non-compete shall not exceed two years.

After the cancellation or termination of a labour contract, the employer shall financially compensate such non-compete obligations on a monthly basis during the non-compete period. In case of any breaches of the non-compete provisions by the employee, liquidated damages shall be paid to the employer in accordance with the stipulated terms of the non-compete agreement.

9.4.2.5 Contract Amendments

Any contract amendments shall be conducted through a consultation between the employer and employee and shall be made in writing. If there are any changes to the employer's name, legal representation, main person in charge or investor, the performance of the contract is not affected. Equally, the validation of the labour contract is not affected after an acquisition or division. The original contract shall remain valid and be performed by the employer who succeeds to the rights and obligations of the original employer.

9.4.2.6 When the Labour Contract is Deemed Invalid

A labour contract can be completely or partially invalidated by the labour dispute arbitration committee or the People's Court. The invalidity of the contract shall have no legal effect from the time of its conclusion (*ab initio*), and where the contract is partially invalid, the remaining part shall remain valid.

In the following circumstances, the contract may be deemed as invalid:

- The labour contract is in violation of laws, administrative rules and regulations
- The labour contract is concluded or amended by means of fraud, coercion or exploitation of the other party
- The labour contract acquits the employer from legal liability and denies the employee legal rights

Where the contract is determined to be invalid, the party at fault shall bear the liabilities of any damages of harm or loss caused to the other party. If the contract is invalid but the employee has fulfilled his obligations, the employer is obliged to pay the employee labour compensation. The amount of labour compensation shall be calculated in relation to a similar position within the same company.

9.4.3 Probation

The probation should be treated as a period to further assess whether both the employer and employee are suited. Specifically, the employer may utilise the period to assess the actual skills of the employee in comparison to his previous experience and job title. In some cases, the previous job title or experiences could be overstated by the employee for a better and more professional image, and the skills or competence of the employee may not match with the job description or qualify him for the current job title. Therefore, where the probation period is used in accordance with the Labour Law, the Labour Contract Law and related rules and regulations, an unqualified employee can be terminated without compensation during the probation period.

The probation period is stipulated by the employer and the employee on the basis of equality, free will and consensus according to the specific situation, and no party can force the other to agree to a clause. The two parties may either stipulate a probation period or stipulate no probation period after reaching a consensus through consultation.

The probation period shall form part of the employment term of the labour contract. If only a probation period is contained in a labour contract, such a probation period shall be deemed invalid and be recognised as the validity term of the labour contract. Only one period of probation is allowed to be set between the same employee and employer, and the terms of a probation period shall adhere to the following:

- Maximum one month for an employment term of no less than three months and less than one year

- Maximum two months for an employment term of no less than one year and less than three years
- Maximum six months for an employment term no less than three years (fixed-term contracts) or for any open-ended contracts
- No probation period for labour contracts with a term of less than three months or labour contracts that terminate upon the completion of a certain task

The minimum salary for employees during probation shall be no less than the minimum wage level for the same position with the employer or 80% of the salary agreed in the labour contract and shall not be less than the minimum wage of the place where the employer is located.

As a labour relationship is established between the employer and employee, probationary employees are entitled to the same level of social insurance benefits as other employees. The employer shall make social insurance contributions, such as pension and unemployment premiums, for the probationary employee.

9.4.3.1 Probation Assessment

If the employee fails to meet the requirements of employment during the probation period, the employer may cancel the employment. In practice, employment requirements are the standards based on which the employer hires an employee. Employers may specify such requirements in the corporate rules and regulations and inform the employee of such requirements in a comprehensive job description that matches such requirements. Such job descriptions may be attached to the labour contract. The employee can be evaluated on such employment requirements and evidently show in a performance assessment whether he met or failed the employment requirements, provided that such an evaluation procedure is fair and just, as stipulated by the law.

Where the employer terminates the probationary employee on the basis of failure to meet employment requirements, the employer must prove that the employee 'failed to meet the employment requirements'.

Generally, the employer is required to prove the following three terms:

- The employee is informed of the employment requirements at the time of hiring
- The employer has conducted a just and fair evaluation of the employee during the probationary period
- The evaluation result shows the employee to be unqualified

9.5 Management

9.5.1 Employee Handbook

The Labour Law requires employers to formulate and improve labour rules and regulations in accordance with the law in order to ensure that employees enjoy their labour rights and perform their labour obligations. In practice, corporate rules and regulations are commonly referred to as an 'employee handbook'.

The employee handbook should establish clear, legitimate and consistent internal company policies and act as an employee management tool. Essential fundamental provisions to manage the daily routine of employees related to overtime, code of conduct, performance and promotion standards, reimbursement, business travel, special leave, vacation days, rest and working time, disciplinary actions, terminations, and so forth, should be stipulated in the employee handbook and company procedures.

The employee handbook, whether formulated or amended, is required to be presented to the workers' congress for a discussion and vote, and the company shall further solicit opinions from the workers' representatives. If there is no workers' congress, a staff conference shall be called. Equally, if the implementation of a provision is deemed inappropriate, the employer reserves the right to raise an issue. For foreign companies operating in China, a well-translated Chinese version of the employee handbook is advisable, since internal policies and procedures must be clearly understood by all employees, and any labour suit brought to the arbitral tribunal shall require the Chinese translation of the employee handbook.

Once the employee handbook is formulated, it is required to be disclosed to all current and new onboarding employees. Keeping records of employee-handbook training or disclosure is encouraged. This can be recorded via employees signing a training form, retaining notice of publicising the employee handbook for opinion and consent, or signing a commitment of compliance to the handbook when entering into a labour contract.

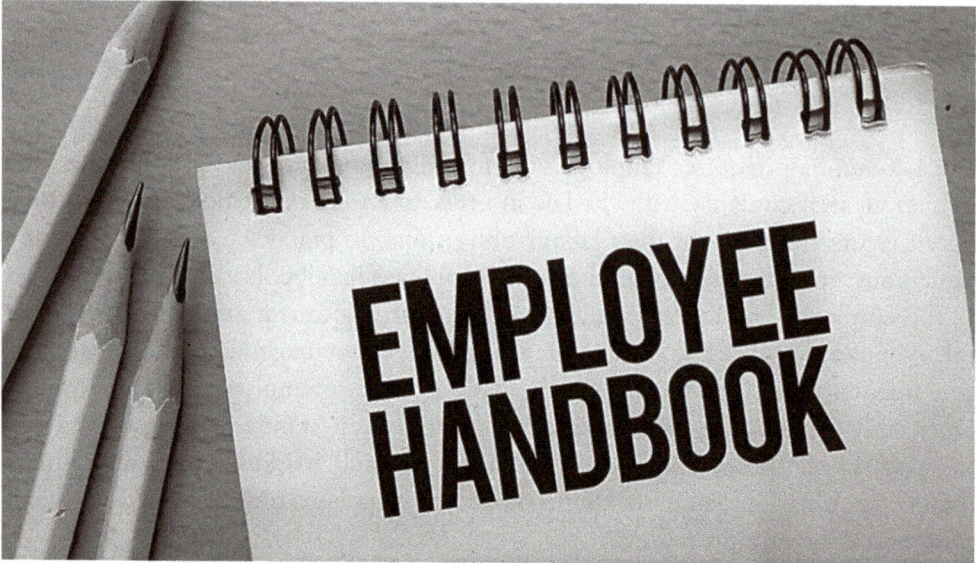

Internal company policies in China can serve as a basis for judicial organs to handle labour dispute cases. For example, a well-written employee handbook can stipulate breaches of minor and major misconduct, as well as appropriate disciplinary measures. Therefore, if an employee is terminated and a well-written employee handbook is implemented, there is a documented procedure and supporting evidence demonstrating the process of the termination (such as first – warning, second – disciplinary action, and third – termination) or the ground for an immediate termination if there is a serious misconduct in breach of the policies in the employee handbook.

9.5.2 Working Hours

Employers are normally obliged to utilise the standard working hours as prescribed by the Labour Law. In cases where the constraints of the work characteristics or production features limit the implementation of the standard working hours, the employer may apply the flexible-working-time or cumulative-working-time system. Such alternative working hours are subject to case-by-case approval by the labour administration department.

9.5.2.1 Standard Working Hours

Standard working hours are restricted to eight hours per day and 44 hours per week on average. Employers are obliged to guarantee at least one day off per week.

Working hours may be extended after consultation with the trade union and employees but are restricted to one hour maximum per day. Under special circumstances, and if the health of employees is unaffected, the working hours may be extended to three hours maximum per day, and the cumulated total extension of hours shall not exceed 36 hours per month.

Extended-hours limitations do not apply in the extraordinary circumstances as defined below:

- In the event of a natural disaster or an accident and the life and health of employees or the safety of property is in peril and urgent attention is required
- In the event of a breakdown of production equipment, transportation lines or public facilities, and production and public interests are affected, and rush repairs must be done without delay
- Other circumstances stipulated by the laws, administrative rules and the regulations

Any extension of working hours according to the prescribed extension provisions shall be remunerated accordingly using the below calculation:

- If the extension of working hours falls within normal working hours, 150% of the normal working wage shall be remunerated
- If the extension of working hours falls on an arranged day off and no off-day is compensated, 200% of the normal working wage shall be remunerated
- If the extension of working hours falls on a statutory holiday, 300% of the normal working wage shall be remunerated

9.5.2.2 Alternative Working Hours

9.5.2.2.1 Flexible-working-time System

'Flexible-working-time system' refers to irregular working hours or working hours that cannot be fixed under the standard due to a particular business activity, special requirements of work or duties of a particular post. The following employees may apply for the flexible-working-time system:

- Senior management personnel, personnel who work outside the office, sales personnel and other enterprise employees whose work cannot be properly measured with the standard working hours
- Long-distance transportation personnel, taxi drivers, certain railway, port or warehouse employees who carry out loading and off-loading, and other personnel whose work must be flexible due to the special nature of their job
- Other employees for whom – due to special characteristics of the business,

special demands of the job or the scope of duties – the application of the flexible-working-time system is appropriate

Employees with flexible working hours shall enjoy at least one day off per week, and employers shall take employees' opinions into account and apply proper methods of work and rest to ensure their right to enjoy rest and holidays at the completion of production and work tasks.

9.5.2.2.2 Cumulative-working-time System

'Cumulative-working-time system' refers to a working time system adopted by an enterprise for certain personnel due to the special nature of their posts, the continuous nature of a business activity, or seasonal or other natural restrictions. The working time is comprehensively calculated on the basis of a weekly, monthly, seasonal or yearly period, provided that the average working time per day and per month respectively are generally the same as the statutory standard working time.

The following employees may apply for implementation of the comprehensive-working-time system:

- Personnel in industries such as communications, railway, postal service, marine conveyance, airlines or fishing, who, due to the special nature of their work, must work continuously
- Certain personnel in industries such as geological and resource surveying, construction, salt production, sugar production, tourism, etc., which are restricted by season and natural conditions
- Other suitable personnel

The total working time of one day can be longer than eight hours, and the total working time of one month can be longer than 40 hours, but the total working time of a comprehensively calculated period shall not exceed the total statutory working time. Any work exceeding the statutory working time shall be deemed as extended working time and be subject to overtime pay.

9.5.3 Benefits and Entitlements

9.5.3.1 Statutory Paid Annual Leave

Employees who have worked for one full year or more are entitled to statutory annual leave with pay. The duration of leave for each employee is determined by reference to the accumulated years of work (with all employers, not just the current employer).

9.5.3.1.1 Calculations of Statutory Annual Leave

Employment Duration	Amount of Annual Leave
1 year or more but less than 10 years	5 days of paid annual leave
10 years or more but less than 20 years	10 days of paid annual leave
20 years or more	15 days of paid annual leave

The statutory holidays and rest days stipulated by the State are not included in the calculation of annual leave. Generally, annual leave should be taken during the current calendar year. However, if the employer cannot grant annual leave due to operational needs, prior consent from the employee shall be obtained and 300% of the employee's daily wage for each day of untaken annual leave shall be paid.

In addition to statutory annual leave, the employer may, according to the internal policy of the employer, grant additional days of annual leave as employee welfare, and such additional annual leave is not legally obliged to be paid 300% of the salary if not taken.

9.5.3.2 Statutory Holidays

Employers shall arrange paid holidays in accordance with the law. Holidays include New Year's Day, Spring Festival, International Labour Day, National Day, and other holidays provided by the laws, rules and regulations. Specific holiday arrangements are published by the State Council every year.

9.5.3.3 Sick Leave

'Sick leave' refers to the time period when an employee who suffers from an illness or a non-work-related injury ceases working or accepts treatment and needs to take leave according to the doctor's advice. The period of sick leave is normally determined by the doctor's advice and medical certificate. This depends on the severity of the employee's illness or injury and the professional advice given by the doctor.

'Medical-treatment period' refers to the time period when an employee takes leave due to illness or non-work-related injury, and the employer is forbidden from terminating the employment contract. Generally, the medical-treatment period is accumulated from the first day of sick leave, and the maximum days are based on the employee's length of service. The actual calculation of the medical-treatment period may vary according to local regulations.

During a period of sick leave, the employer shall pay a sick-leave wage to the employee. The employer is not required to pay the full wage but a certain proportion of the wage following national or local legislations, yet the sick-leave pay shall in no way be lower than 80% of the minimum wage.

9.5.3.4 Maternity Leave

The national standard for maternity leave is that female employees are entitled to 98 days of maternity leave. For female employees who have experienced a difficult childbirth, 15 extra days may be added. If the female employee gives birth to more than one child in a single instance (twins, triplets, etc.), 15 extra days may be added for each child. In fact, many provinces and municipalities have formulated more favourable local policies based on local population, economics, and other developmental situations.

9.5.3.5 Other Leave

Other types of leave granted to employees include wedding leave, paternity leave, funeral leave, and public leave.

9.5.4 Wages

The Labour Law states that wages shall follow the principle of distribution according to the work, and equal pay for equal work. 'Distribution according to the work' refers to the quantity and quality of work provided by the employee. 'Equal pay for equal work' refers to the equal remuneration for labour regardless of gender, age, nationality and race.

9.5.4.1 Minimum Wage

The system of guaranteed minimum wages is implemented by the State, although the specific standards of minimum wages are determined by the People's Governments of provinces, autonomous regions or municipalities directly under the Central Government and are submitted to the State Council for the record. Determination and readjustment of the standards of minimum wages are made with reference to the following factors in a comprehensive manner:

- Lowest living expenses of employees themselves plus the average number of financially reliant family members
- Average wage level of the society as a whole
- Labour productivity
- Situation of employment
- Regional differences in economic development

The responsibility for the formulation of wage distribution and wage level falls upon the employers. Any wage formulation shall be made according to the production and business operation, as well as economic results, and shall be according to the law. Wages shall not be lower than the minimum wage of the local standards and shall be remunerated on a monthly basis. The date of payment shall be agreed between employers and employees. In the case of holidays or rest days, wages shall be paid in advance, on the nearest working day.

Wages shall be paid in the statutory currency and shall not be substituted by material objects and negotiable securities. Therefore, the wages in China shall be paid in the form of renminbi and shall not be paid in other currencies, material objects or negotiable securities instead.

9.5.4.2 Failure to Pay Wages

If an employer fails to pay wages, the employee may apply for an order to pay at the local court. Equally, the labour administration authorities at all levels shall have the right to supervise and inspect the payment of wages by all employers. If an employer commits any infringement of the legitimate rights and interests of employees, the labour administration department can order him to pay employees remuneration of wages or compensation.

Infringements of labour remuneration include but are not limited to the following:

- Embezzling wages or delaying the payment of wages to employees without reason
- Paying wages lower than the local lowest wage standard
- Failing to pay overtime payment after working overtime
- Failing to pay economic compensation to the employee in accordance with the provisions for the dissolution or termination of labour contracts

9.5.5 Social Insurance

Social insurance is an important aspect of the social security system and is a compulsory insurance system implemented by the State. Funds for social insurance are raised and established by the government, employers, employees and other social forces to enable assistance and compensation from the State in old age, unemployment, disease or work-related injuries, as well as maternity.

Employers and employees are required to contribute to mandatory social insurance and housing-fund schemes in China. Social insurance includes pension, medical insurance, unemployment insurance, work-related injury insurance and maternity insurance. Since the economic development varies from region to region, the minimum contributions required by employers and employees and social insurance standards are determined by the local labour and social security bureaus.

9.5.6 Vocational Training

In a broad sense, any acts relating to the work of obtaining knowledge and skills in a planned and gradual way falls into the scope of vocational training. Providing vocational training is stipulated under the Labour Law as a duty for the State, the People's Government at all levels, and enterprises. Specifically, enterprises are required to set up a system of vocational training and to retain and use vocational training funds in accordance with the provisions of the State. Equally, employers shall provide employees with vocational training in a planned way and in light of the actual conditions of the employment.

In practice, vocational training can be categorised into (1) training sessions for newly recruited employees and (2) special technical training funded by the enterprise through the conclusion of a training agreement specifying a term of service with such an employee. The training agreement between an employer and an employee on a term of service shall not affect the increment of the worker's labour compensation during the term of service, in accordance with the normal wage-adjustment mechanism.

If the employee breaches the agreed term of service, the employee shall pay the liquidated damages to the employer in accordance with the terms of the agreement, although the liquidated damages shall not exceed the amount of the training fees or the training allowance allocated for the part of the employment period that is not performed.

9.5.7 Occupational Health and Safety

Health and safety standards and rules are established by the State. All employers are obliged to set up and continuously perfect the occupational health and safety system within the workplace, including training staff, ensuring relevant workplace standards, preventing accidents and lessening occupational hazards according to the relevant rules and regulations.

Occupational health and safety facilities must meet the standards set by the State. Any facilities in newly built, renovated or expanded projects must be designed, constructed and operated or utilised simultaneously with the main part of the project. Workers engaged in occupational hazards shall be provided with the necessary labour protection and receive regular health examinations. Workers engaged in specialised operations must receive specialised training and acquire qualifications for such special operations. Safe operation of machinery is mandatory, and workers are provisioned with the right to refuse any commands from managerial personnel that run contrary to established rules and compel employees to operate under unsafe conditions. Additionally, workers have the right to criticise, report or file charges against any acts endangering the safety of their life or their health.

Companies in violation of occupational health and safety rules and regulations shall be ordered by the labour administration department to correct actions, and a fine may be imposed. If the circumstances are serious, the above-said departments shall refer the matter to the People's Government at or above the county level to issue a decision to halt business operations. If companies fail to prevent hidden dangers and cause loss of life and property to employees, the personnel responsible shall be investigated for criminal responsibility by applying *mutatis mutandis* (having made the necessary changes) to the relevant provisions of the Criminal Law.

9.5.8 Scope of Work for Female Staff and Juvenile Workers

Specific limits to the scope of work are stipulated for female staff and juvenile workers. These provisions protect the vulnerable from occupational health and safety hazards.

Employers are prohibited from arranging the following work for female staff:

- Work in the pit of mines, work with Grade IV physical labour intensity as prescribed by the State, or other work forbidden to women
- During menstrual periods, work high above the ground, under low temperatures or in cold water, or work with Grade III physical labour intensity as prescribed by the State
- During pregnancy, work with Grade III physical labour intensity as stipulated by the State, or other work forbidden to pregnant women
- During pregnancy of seven months or more, extended working hours or night-shift work
- During breastfeeding of babies less than one year old, work with Grade III physical labour intensity as prescribed by the State, extended working hours, night-shift work, or other labour forbidden to women during the breastfeeding period

'Juvenile workers' refers to employees at least 16 years of age but not older than 18 years of age. Employers are required to provide regular physical examinations and are prohibited from allowing juveniles to work in the pit of mines, work with Grade IV physical labour intensity as prescribed by the State or conduct other work forbidden to juvenile workers.

Any violation of the provisions for female staff and workers and juvenile workers infringes upon their legitimate rights and interests and shall result in corrections and fines. Where female staff and workers and juvenile workers are harmed as a result of negligence, the employer shall be liable for compensation.

9.5.9 Temporary Work

Temporary work can be categorised into Part-time Work or Labour Dispatch where workers are dispatched to work placements by employment agencies.

9.5.9.1 Part-time Work

'Part-time work' refers to labour where remuneration is calculated on an hourly basis and does not exceed four hours per day or an accumulated 24 hours per week. Parties to a part-time labour contract may conclude an oral contract, and the probation period is not required. An employee who engages in part-time labour may conclude a labour contract with one or more employers, but a subsequently concluded labour contract shall not affect the performance of the previous concluded contract.

9.5.9.2 Labour Dispatch

'Labour dispatch' refers to dispatched workers placed by employment agencies in receiving entities. Labour dispatch is defined as supplementary employment only to be adopted for the following circumstances:

- Temporary work for a maximum term of six months
- Auxiliary position that supports a main employee position
- Substitution of an employee who cannot work in a given period

9.5.9.2.1 Employment Agencies

Employment agencies dispatching workers into entities shall not engage in a labour dispatch operation without obtaining all of the following conditions:

- Registered capital of no less than CNY 2 million
- Proper business premises and facilities
- Established a work-placement management system according to the laws and regulations
- Acquired a business licence with the labour administration department, proceeded in the business registration formalities and obtained required licences
- Other requirements stipulated by the laws and regulations

The employment agency is required to enter into staffing agreements with entities into which dispatched workers are placed (hereon referred to as 'receiving entities'). The staffing agreement shall define the job positions, the number of persons dispatched, the term of the placement, the amount and method of labour remuneration, social insurance premiums and the liability of breach of agreement.

9.5.9.2.2 Receiving Entities

Receiving entities are prohibited from transferring the dispatched worker to another employer and shall perform the following obligations:

- Implement state labour standards and provide corresponding labour protection and working conditions
- Notify the dispatched employees of the job requirements and salary
- Pay overtime wages and performance bonuses and provide welfare benefits appropriate for the position
- Provide the necessary training for the job
- Implement a normal wage-adjustment mechanism for continuous labour dispatching

9.5.9.2.3 Dispatched Workers

The dispatched worker is recognised under the Labour Contract Law as an employee of the employment agent. Therefore, a labour relationship is established between the employment agent and the dispatched worker, and a labour contract with the same contractual terms as a normal labour contract shall be concluded, although the fixed term of employment shall be no less than two years.

Workers dispatched to a receiving entity are entitled to receive the same amount of remuneration as the employees in the same position or work in the receiving entity. The same remuneration system based on the principle of 'equal pay for equal work' shall be extended to the workers dispatched to the receiving entity. The employment agency cannot retain any part of the remuneration, and wages are required to be paid on a monthly basis. In periods where employees are not dispatched to a receiving entity, the employment agency shall pay the minimum wage established in the location of the employment agency.

Workers have the right to join the labour union, either through the employment agency or the receiving entities. In accordance with the law, workers may also organise unions to protect their lawful rights and interests.

Dispatched workers may cancel their labour contract with the employment agency according to same relevant employee termination provisions of the Labour Contract Law. Equally, the receiving entity may cancel the work and return the dispatched worker according to employer termination provisions of the Labour Contract Law. Once the receiving entity cancels the work and returns the dispatched worker, the employment agency can terminate the labour contract according to the relevant provisions.

9.5.10 Supervision and Inspection

9.5.10.1 Labour Administration and Inspection

The system of labour administration is structured in the following manner:

- The labour administration department of the State Council shall supervise and manage the implementation of the employment contract system throughout the country
- The labour administration departments of the local governments at the county level or above shall supervise and manage the implementation of the labour contract system in their respective administrative jurisdictions
- The labour administration departments of the local governments at the county level or above shall solicit the opinions of the labour unions, enterprise representatives and the authorities in charge of the industries concerned in the course of supervision and management of the implementation of the labour contract system

Labour administration departments are ordained with the power to stop any acts that violate laws, rules and regulations on labour and to order rectification. Inspectors from the labour administration departments have the right to enter into the employing units to investigate, consult necessary data and inspect labour sites in the following matters:

- Employers' formulation of rules and regulations directly related to the immediate interests of workers, and the implementation thereof
- Conclusion and termination of labour contracts between employers and employees
- Compliance with relevant regulations regarding work placement by employment agencies and receiving entities
- Employers' compliance with relevant regulations regarding employees' working hours, rest and leave
- Payment of labour remuneration as specified in the labour contracts, and implementation of minimum wage by employers

- Employers' participation in various types of social insurance and payment of social insurance premiums
- Other labour matters as prescribed by the laws and regulations

During the supervision and inspection process, the employer and employees shall provide and answer to the authorities truthfully. As a result of any unjustifiable obstruction or retaliation against informers, the relevant administration shall impose fines, and where the case constitutes a crime, persons who are held responsible shall be investigated for criminal responsibility according to the law. If the employer is found to be in violation of the relevant rules and regulations, the general penalty imposed by the labour administration department is recertification and fines according to the corresponding provisions. In specific circumstances, criminal liability may be pursued.

9.5.10.2 Trade Unions

Employees shall have the right to participate in and organise trade unions in accordance with the law. In practice, trade unions can operate within the parameters provisioned by the State, and never against the State, although they are permitted to be against the employers.

Trade unions represent and safeguard the legitimate rights and interests of employees and independently carry out their activities in accordance with the law. The Duties and rights of trade unions may be summarised as follows:

- The right of supervision (for example, where an enterprise intends to unilaterally cancel an employee's employment contract, it shall give prior notice to the trade union)
- The right of representation (for example, where employees conduct collective negotiations with an employer or go on strike, the trade union shall conduct negotiations, talks and other relevant activities on behalf of the employees)
- The right of support (for example, where the employees sign labour contracts with the employing entity, or where there are labour conflicts, the trade union shall give direction, assistance and other relevant support)
- The right of a legal person (for example, the trade union has its own name, premises, property, reputation, and so forth)

9.6 Employment Termination

Terminating employees is a sensitive and tricky issue in China. After the probation period, employers could find the employee to lack the necessary skills or negatively perform and influence the working environment. Without awareness of how to terminate the employee in a culturally sensitive manner, the employer may find difficulties in managing the rest of the workforce and could face a potential lawsuit.

Direct termination without solid ground and proof will cause risk of law disputes for employers. Even if the employee violates the internal rules, the employer should not arbitrarily dismiss an employee at will, but strictly follow the laws and regulations, the company policies and other by-laws and keep evidence of such violation. Direct termination may result in a lawsuit between the employer and employee at the arbitral tribunal or the court. In a case where unlawful termination is recognised, employees can be entitled to compensation of restoration of the full employment term or double the mandatory compensation pay as liquidated damages.

9.6.1 When the Labour Contract is Terminated by the Employer

Employers who intend to unilaterally terminate labour contracts shall have statutory reasons. Any termination of employment is required to adhere to statutory procedures, and corresponding economic compensation in line with the provisioned circumstances of economic compensation shall be paid. The termination of a labour contract shall be supported by a certificate certifying the termination. Failure to issue the certificate shall result in a rectification order and compensation to the employee for any damages caused.

9.6.1.1 Reasons for Termination

The employer may terminate the employee under the following circumstances:

- The employee fails to meet the employment conditions during the probation period
- The employee seriously violates the rules and regulations of the employer
- The employee seriously derelicts duty or engages in activity for personal gain and causes significant losses to the employer
- The employee establishes labour relationships with another employer simultaneously, which results in a major impact on the completion of tasks of the current employer, or the employee fails to rectify the issue after being cautioned by the employer

- The labour contract is made invalid by the fraud, coercion or exploitation of the other party's disadvantaged position, or a party causes the other party to conclude or amend the labour contract against the latter's true intent
- Criminal liability is pursued against the employee in accordance with the law

9.6.1.1.1 Note on Determining Incompetency

Employers cannot subjectively evaluate the competence of employees. Instead, such a conclusion is required to be evaluated through an appraisal system of democratic and open procedures. In practice, a dedicated appraisal institution and mechanism with transparent examination and approval standards may be implemented. Equally, employees shall be allowed to raise objections or a re-evaluation of the appraisal results. Any appraisal systems should easily be recognised by the labour dispute arbitration committees and the People's Courts.

9.6.1.2 Termination Procedures

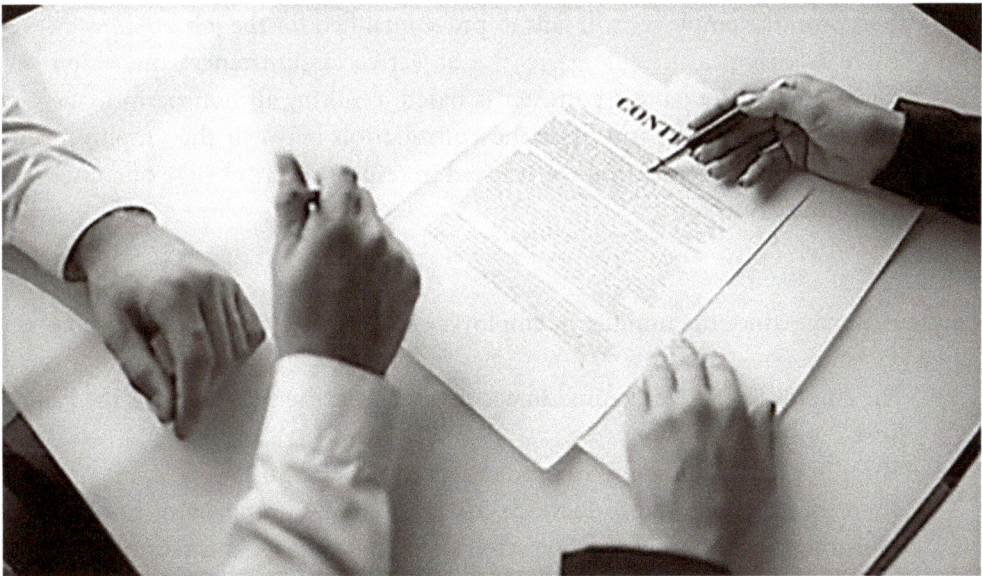

9.6.1.2.1 Termination Without Compensation

Serious statutory violation can result in immediate cancellation without compensation, although trade unions are entitled to be notified of the reasons for termination in advance and may demand that the employer make adjustments. The employing unit shall take into consideration the opinions of the trade union and inform the trade union of the results in writing. If the employer is deemed to violate the provisions of laws and administrative regulations or the stipulations of the labour contract, the trade union shall have the right to require the employing unit to make rectifications. Where the trade union is not notified of the labour contract termination, it may be considered as a violation, and the People's Court shall support the employee's request for compensation. However, the employer is allowed to make remedies or corrections before the employee brings the lawsuit if it fails to comply with procedures for trade union notification.

9.6.1.2.2 Termination with Compensation

An employer may cancel the labour contract under any of the following circumstances by giving the employee 30 days' prior written notice or one month's wages in lieu of notice, and compensation shall be paid as well:

- The employee is sick or injured due to reasons unrelated to work and fails to perform the original work after the expiration of the prescribed treatment period or fails to perform other work arranged by the employer
- The employee is not qualified for the job, and after training or adjustment of their post, the employee still fails to prove qualified for the job
- There is a significant change to the objective circumstances on which the conclusion of the labour contract is based, resulting in non-performance of the labour contract, and after the consultation between the employer and employee, no agreement can be reached in respect to the change of content of the labour contract

9.6.1.2.3 Redundancy

Employers may reduce the number of employees under the following circumstances:

- The employer has restructured in accordance with the provisions of the Enterprise Bankruptcy Law
- There is a serious difficulty in production and operation
- There is a change of production, innovation of significant technology, or adjustment of the mode of operation of the enterprise, and redundancy will still be made after the change of labour contracts
- There is a significant change to the objective circumstances on which the conclusion of the labour contract is based, and this causes the non-performance of the labour contract

In reducing staff, employers are required to observe the following priority:

- Employees who have concluded a fixed-term labour contract of a long period with the employer

- Employees who have concluded an open-ended labour contract with the employer
- Employees who are the sole income supporting either the elderly or minors

If the employer recruits new employees within six months from the date of redundancy, the employment offer shall first be made to the redundant employees.

9.6.1.2.3.1 Redundancy Procedures

The number of redundancies may be subject to the opinion of the trade unions. Specifically, if the number totals 20 employees or the number of employees is less than 20 but accounts for more than 10% of the total employees, the employer shall, 30 days prior to redundancy, submit an explanation detailing the situation to the trade union or all employees and listen to the opinions of the trade union or all employees. The employing unit may then lay off employees after reporting the employee lay-off plan to the labour administration authority.

9.6.1.2.3.2 Compensation (Severance) Calculation

Compensation (severance) to employees is calculated based on the length of service of the employee for the employer at the rate of one month's wages for each full year worked. Any term of no less than six months but less than one year shall be considered as one year, and any term of less than six months shall be considered as half a year and paid with one half of the monthly salary.

If the average wage of the employee within 12 months prior to the termination of the labour contract is three times higher than the average monthly wage of employees established in the previous years by the local government in the location of the employer, the compensation shall be three times the average monthly wage. However, the maximum years of compensation shall not exceed 12 years (i.e. 12 months of salary).

If the average wage of the employee within the 12 months prior to the cancellation or termination of the labour contract is lower than the local lowest wage standard, reference shall be made to the local lowest wage standard.

9.6.1.2.3.3 Other Circumstances for Termination with Compensation

The following termination circumstances are subject to compensation (severance) according to the above compensation calculations:

- The employee proposes to cancel the labour contract due to the employer's fault, such as failure to pay salary

- The employer proposes to cancel the labour contract through reaching an agreement after consultation
- The labour contract is a fixed labour contract and expires, save where the employee refuses to renew the labour contract even though the conditions offered by the employer are the same as or better than those stipulated in the current contract
- The employer is declared bankrupt according to the law
- The business licence of the employer is revoked
- The employer is ordered to close or is closed down, or the employer decides on early dissolution
- Other circumstances stipulated by laws or administrative regulations apply

9.6.1.2.3.4 Prohibited Termination of Labour

If the employees fall under any of the following circumstances, the employer shall not cancel the labour contract:

- The employee engages in operations that would expose him to occupational hazards and has not undergone an occupational health examination before leaving work or is suspected of occupational disease and is being diagnosed or is under medical observation
- The worker is confirmed to have lost labour capacity, completely or partially, due to occupational disease or is injured due to work-related reasons
- The employee has contracted an illness or sustained a non-work-related injury and the prescribed period of medical treatment has not expired
- The female employee is pregnant or in the maternity or nursing period
- The employee has 15 years of consecutive employment and his statutory retirement age is in less than five years
- Other circumstances prescribed by the laws and administrative regulations apply

If the labour contract has expired in any of the circumstances prescribed above, the labour contract shall be extended until the relevant circumstance ceases to exist and the contract can be terminated. However, in the circumstance of loss of capacity to work, wholly or partially, the termination of a labour contract shall be handled in accordance with relevant state regulations on work-related injury insurance.

9.6.2 When the Labour Contract is Terminated by the Employee

9.6.2.1 Advance Notification of Termination

The employee may cancel the labour contract in writing 30 days in advance, and during the probation period the labour contract may be cancelled in writing three days in advance. After 30 days from the date of the resignation, the labour contract shall be automatically cancelled and no economic compensation is required.

9.6.2.2 Immediate Resignation

Employees may dissolve the labour contact without prior notification if:

- the employer fails to provide labour protection or labour conditions in accordance with the agreements of the labour contract
- the employer fails to pay labour remuneration in full in a timely manner
- the employer fails to pay social insurance premiums for the employee in accordance with the law
- the rules and systems of the employing unit violate laws and regulations, and the rights of the employees are harmed
- the labour contract is invalid according to the rules and regulations
- other circumstances provisioned by laws and administrative regulations apply

The employer shall be subject to compensation to the employee under the above circumstances.

9.6.3 Liabilities of Illegally Terminating a Labour Contract

If the labour contract is terminated in violation of the law and the employee demands the performance of the contract, the employer is subject to fulfil its obligations. If there is no request to fulfil the performance of the contract or the contract cannot be performed, the employer shall pay damages that are double the amount of compensation.

9.6.4 Labour Disputes

'Labour dispute' refers to a dispute arising from the exercise of labour rights and the fulfilment of labour obligations between the parties within labour relationships. Labour disputes based on labour relationships are specific to the employer and employee. The employer includes enterprises, individual economic organisations, private non-enterprise entities and state organs, public institutions and social organisations, as well as partnerships, such as accounting firms, law firms, foundations, and so forth, within the territory of the People's Republic of China. The employee is a natural person of a legal age to work who signs a labour contract with the employer.

There are several methods available to solve labour disputes – including mediation, arbitration and litigation – that may appeal to three types of labour dispute resolution bodies: labour dispute mediation institutes, labour dispute arbitration committees and People's Courts. The law provisions labour disputes to proceed either through mediation and labour dispute arbitration or directly to the labour dispute arbitration before pursuing litigation in the People's Courts. Any settlement of a labour dispute shall follow the principle of legality, fairness and promptness, so as to safeguard the legitimate rights and interests of the parties involved in accordance with the law.

9.6.4.1 Meditation

A labour dispute mediation committee may be established within the employing unit. The committee shall be composed of representatives of the staff and workers, the employing unit and the trade union, and the chairmanship of the committee shall be assumed by a representative of the trade union. Parties may apply to the labour dispute mediation committee of their unit for mediation. If an agreement is reached through mediation in the case of a labour dispute, it shall be implemented by the parties. If mediation fails and one of the parties requests arbitration, that party may apply to the labour dispute arbitration committee for arbitration.

9.6.4.2 Arbitration

The committee shall be composed of representatives of the labour administration department, representatives from the trade union at the corresponding level and representatives from the employment unit. The chairmanship of the committee shall be assumed by a representative of the labour administration department. The party that requests arbitration shall file a written application with a labour dispute arbitration committee within 60 days of the date of the occurrence of the labour dispute. The arbitration committee shall generally make an arbitration decision within 60 days of the date of receiving the application. If no objections have been raised, the parties must execute the arbitration decision. If the party to a labour dispute is not satisfied with the arbitration decision, the party may bring a lawsuit to the People's Court within 15 days of the date of receiving the award of arbitration. Where the parties do not initiate litigation in a People's Court within 15 days of the date of receipt of the arbitral award, the arbitral award shall become effective on the sixteenth day of receiving it, and the parties should perform the arbitral award. If one of the parties fails to do so, the other party may apply for enforcement in the People's Court.

9.6.4.3 Litigation

'Labour litigation' refers to situations where the parties to a labour dispute are not satisfied with an arbitral award made by a labour dispute arbitration committee. Therefore, within a prescribed time limit, they file a lawsuit with a People's Court, and the People's Court conducts hearings and adjudication according to procedures prescribed by law.

10 Current: Employment of Foreigners

10.1 Introduction

Foreign employment in China is governed by the Administrative Regulation on the Management of Employment of Foreigners in China (Regulations). The Regulations were jointly promulgated on 22 January 1996 by the Ministry of Labour, the Ministry of Public Security, the Minister of Foreign Affairs and the Ministry of Human Resources and Social Security. The latest revision of the Regulations was in 2017, and all foreigners employed in China and entities employing foreigners are subject to the Regulations. The Regulations mainly stipulates the provisions of foreign employment in China, including eligibility to work in China, application procedures and labour administration.

10.1.1 Definition

Foreigners are referred to as 'persons not of Chinese nationality', as defined in the Nationality Law of the People's Republic of China, although persons of Hong Kong, Macau and Taiwan are excluded from the Regulations and subject to the Administration Provisions on the Employment of Taiwan, Hong Kong and Macau Residents in Mainland China.

'Foreign employees working in China' refers to foreigners without the right of permanent residency engaging in social labour and receiving remunerations in accordance with the law.

10.1.2 Work Permit

All foreign employees working in China are required to obtain a work permit before working in China; otherwise, it shall be deemed as illegal work in China. In such a violation, both the foreign employee and the employer in China are subject to legal liability.

10.1.2.1 Exemptions

Foreigners are only exempt from the work permit and certificates of permission if any of the following conditions apply:

The foreigner is entitled to diplomatic privileges and immunity.

The foreigner is a foreign technical professional or a foreign managing officer who is directly engaged by the Chinese government, or is engaged by government authorities or public institutions with senior professional titles or certificates of special skills as acknowledged by authoritative technical management departments or trade associations of their home countries or international organisations, and holds a Foreign Expert Certificate issued by the relevant authority in charge of administration of foreign-expert affairs.

The foreigner is a foreign worker who holds a Permit for Foreigners Undertaking Offshore Petroleum Operation in China and engages in offshore petroleum operation.

The foreigner has been approved by the Ministry of Culture to conduct art performances of a business character with a Permit for Temporary Performances of a Business Character.

Foreigners meeting one of the aforementioned conditions shall apply for the work visa at Chinese embassies, consulates and offices, along with documentation or certification issued by the relevant ministry or administration department.

10.1.3 Conditions of Foreign Employment

10.1.3.1 Validity of Employment Licences

Entities may only employ foreigners after obtaining the Certificates of the People's Republic of China Permitting the Employment of Foreigners (hereinafter referred to as the "Licence"). Individual economic organisations and individuals shall not employ foreigners.

Employers without the violation of relevant regulations of the State shall employ foreigners only for positions requiring special skills that cannot be fulfilled by domestic candidates. No foreigners can be engaged in cultural performances with business character, except those holding permits for temporary performances of a business character as approved by the Ministry of Culture.

10.1.3.2 Requirements for Foreigners

Foreigners seeking employment in China shall meet the following requirements:

Requirements

At least 18 years of age and in good health

Necessary professional skills and job experience required for the intended position

No criminal record

A confirmed employer

A valid passport, or an alternative international travel document in lieu of a passport

Foreigners seeking employment in China must enter China with a Z visa (or in line with the agreements on mutual exemption of visas if such agreements have been reached) and may be employed only after obtaining work permits for foreigners (hereinafter referred to as 'work permits') and residential documents for foreigners.

Foreigners who fail to obtain a residence certificate (i.e. those holding an F, L, C or G visa), or study or work as interns in China, and the accompanying family members of foreigners holding a Z visa, shall not seek employment in China. In special circumstances, employers may apply for licences according to the examination and approval procedures, and the employed foreigners shall, on the strength of the licences, change their identity with public security authorities and obtain a work permit and a residence certificate before taking the post.

The employment of spouses of personnel employed in foreign embassies and consulates, in UN organisations and in representative offices of other international organisations in China shall be handled according to the Regulations of the Ministry of Foreign Affairs of the People's Republic of China on the Employment of Spouses of the Persons Working in Foreign Embassies, Foreign Consulates, and UN Organisations in China.

Certificates of permission and work permits shall be prepared by the Ministry of Labour in a unified way.

10.2 Procedure

10.2.1 Application and Approval

Employers employing foreigners must complete an Application Form for the Employment for Foreigners (the Application Form) and submit it, together with the valid documents below, to the relevant industry supervisory department at the same level as the labour administration department in charge (hereinafter referred to as 'departments in charge of respective trades').

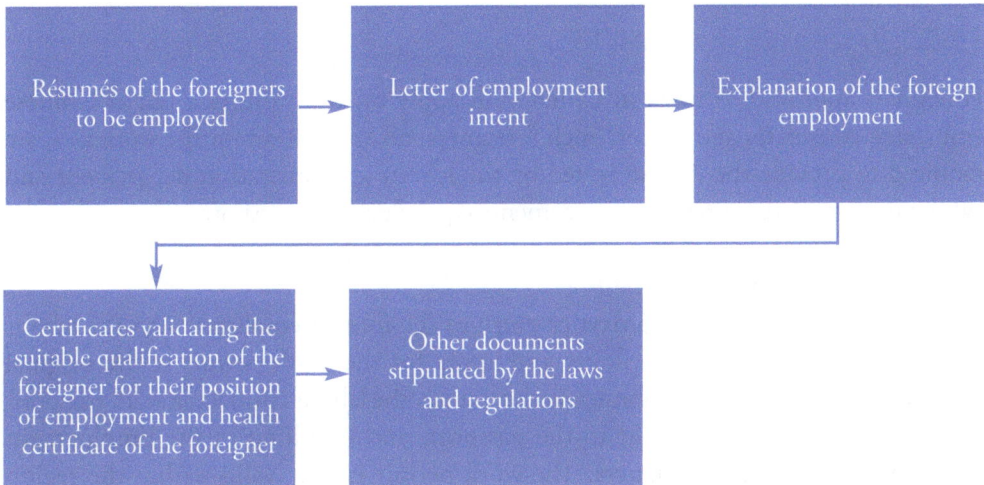

Résumés of the foreigners to be employed	Letter of employment intent	Explanation of the foreign employment
Certificates validating the suitable qualification of the foreigner for their position of employment and health certificate of the foreigner	Other documents stipulated by the laws and regulations	

Following examination and approval of the application by the relevant industry supervisory department, the employer must submit the Application Form for approval by either the labour administration department of the province, autonomous region or directly administered municipality in which it is located, or the prefectural or municipal-level labour administration department authorised by one of the aforementioned departments. The said labour administration department shall then specify the agency (the 'issuing agency') responsible for the issuance of the licence. The issuing agency shall review and approve the application according to the opinions of the relevant industry supervisory department and the demand in the labour market and shall issue the Licence upon approval.

Any employers who make up, illegally change, falsely use, transfer or trade the employment licence or work permit shall result in the confiscation of illegal proceeds and a fine of between CNY 10,000 and CNY 100,000.

Where employers of central government level or employers from industries that do not have a supervisory department wish to employ foreigners, such employers may directly submit the Application for issuance of an employment licence to the issuing agency of the relevant labour administration department.

Foreign-funded joint ventures wishing to employ foreigners do not require the approval of their respective industry supervisory departments. Instead, they may apply directly to the issuing agency of the relevant labour administration department for the issuance of an employment licence by submitting the contract, articles of association, approval certificates, business licences and those documents specified in the items above.

10.2.2 Processing the Work Visa

Foreigners approved to work in China shall apply for the work visa (Z) at Chinese embassies, consulates and offices. Such foreigners, on application for the work visa, are required to provide the license issued by the labour administration department and valid passports or documents, or documents equivalent to a passport.

10.2.2.1 Processing Work Permits

The employer shall, within 15 days of entry of the foreign employee, sign the labour contract with the foreign employee and apply for the work permit at the original certificate-issuing agency by submitting the license, the labour contract, a valid passport, or other documents equivalent to the passport, and by filling in the Employment Registration Form for Foreigners. The work permit is only valid within the region stipulated by the issuing agency.

10.2.2.2 Processing Residence Permits

Foreigners who have obtained a work permit shall apply for a residence permit at the public security authorities by producing their work permit within 30 days of entering China. The residence permit shall be valid for the same period as the work permit.

10.3 Labour Management

In accordance with the Regulations, the following rules and regulations shall apply after a foreigner has obtained approval for employment in China:

- The employer and the foreign employee shall, in accordance with the law, sign an employment contract, the term of which shall not exceed five years. Upon its expiry, the employment contract shall be terminated and the work permit rendered invalid
- If an extension of the employment contract is required, the employer must apply to the relevant labour administration department for approval within 30 days prior to the expiry of the original contract. Once the application has been approved, procedures for extension of the work permit shall be completed
- Foreign employees who have received approval to extend their employment term

in China or to change their employment location or employer must complete procedures for the extension or amendment of their residence permit with the local public security authority within ten days of receiving such approval

- Foreign employees who have received approval to extend their employment term in China or to change their employment location or employer must complete procedures for the extension or amendment of their residence permit with the local public security authority within ten days of receiving such approval
- The employer of a foreign employee in China must be the same unit as that specified on his work permit. Where a foreigner changes employers within the region designated by the original permit-issuing authority but continues to work in the same profession, such a change must be approved by the original permit-issuing authority and the work permit must be amended accordingly. However, where a foreigner seeks employment outside of the region designated by the original permit-issuing authority, or changes employers within the originally designated region to engage in a different profession, he must undertake procedures to secure a new work permit
- When the employment contract between an employer and a foreign employee is terminated, the employer shall promptly notify the labour and public security departments, arrange for the return of the foreign employee's work permit and residence permit and complete procedures with the public security department regarding that employee's departure from the country
- Where a foreigner's residence permit is revoked by the public security department due to their violation of Chinese law, the employer shall terminate that employee's labour contract and the local labour administration department shall revoke his work permit
- Labour disputes that arise between employers and foreign employees shall be handled in accordance with Chinese laws and regulations concerning the resolution of labour disputes
- Labour administration departments shall conduct an annual inspection of foreigners' work permits. The employer shall visit the relevant certificate-issuing office of the labour administration department to carry out procedures for the annual inspection of the work permit within 30 days prior to the completion of each year of employment. Permits that have not undergone inspection prior to the deadline shall automatically become invalid
- If a foreigner loses or damages his work permit during the term of his employment in China, he shall promptly report its loss or damage to the original certificate-issuing office and undertake the relevant procedures for the issuance of a new work permit

Foreigners in violation of any of the situations below shall have their work permit withdrawn by the labour department, and the labour department shall recommend that the public security bureau cancel their residence status:

- Refusal to allow a work permit to be inspected by the labour administration authorities
- Change of employer or profession without permission
- Extension of employment term without permission

10.4 Illegal Employment

The Law on Entry and Exit Control, revised in 2012, stipulates three situations of illegal employment of foreigners:

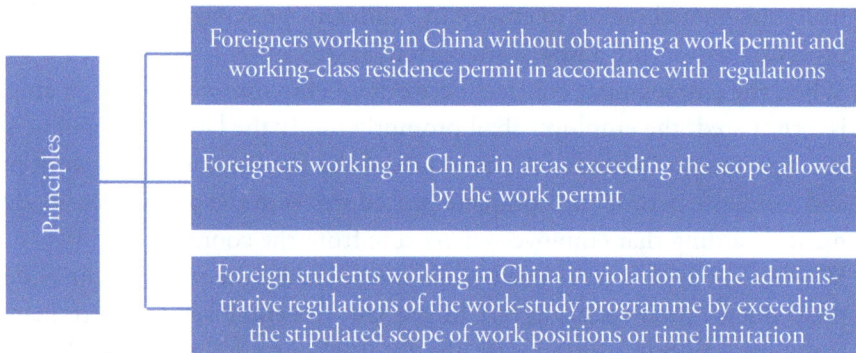

Under the Law of Entry and Exit Control, the corresponding penalties are provisioned for illegal employment:

- Foreigners working illegally in China shall be fined an amount of more than CNY 5,000 but less than CNY 20,000. In severe cases, the offenders shall be sentenced to detention of more than five days but less than 15 days and are subject to a fine of more than CNY 5,000 but less than CNY 20,000
- Individuals who introduce illegal employment to foreigners shall be fined CNY 5,000 for every introduction of illegal employment, with the total fine not exceeding CNY 50,000. Entities that commit such acts shall be fined CNY 5,000 for every introduction of illegal employment, with the total fine not exceeding CNY 100,000. All illegal income, if any, shall be confiscated
- Employers who hire foreigners illegally shall be fined CNY 10,000 for every illegal employment, with the total fine not exceeding CNY 100,000. All illegal income, if any, shall be confiscated

11 Basic Accounting

11.1 Introduction

The Accounting Law of the People's Republic of China (Accounting Law), revised in 2017, forms the overriding framework for administrative accounting rules and regulations. The Accounting Law is supplemented with the Accounting System for Business Enterprises and the Accounting Standards for Business Enterprises. Together, these laws unify a system of accounting practice, accounting procedures and accounting supervision in China.

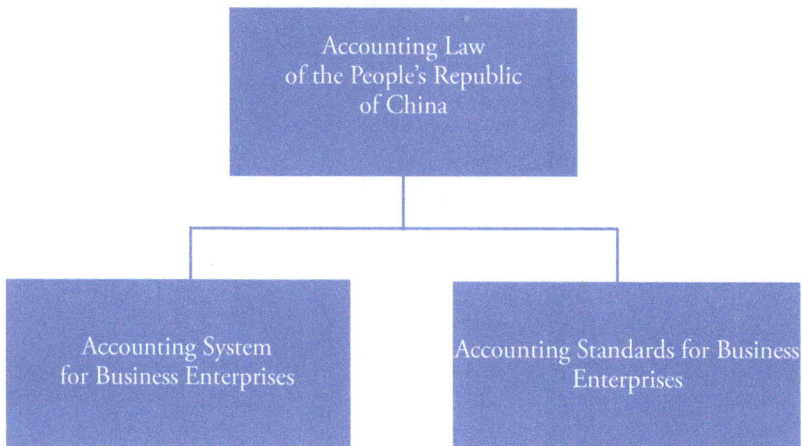

All accounting documents, books and financial statements must be written in Chinese. A foreign language can also be used concurrently. Companies are required to maintain accounting records, financial statements and supplementary memoranda for at least 15 years.

11.1.1 The Accounting System for Business Enterprises 2000 (ASBE) 企业制度 2000 年版

The ASBE, effective from 1 January 2001, is applicable to all types of companies, although with the adoption the Accounting Standards for Business Enterprises in 2006 (CAS 2006), certain companies were required to adopt the CAS 2006.

The ASBE comprises of 16 specific accounting standards and other related accounting regulations.

1.	Inventories	2.	Fixed assets
3.	Intangible assets	4.	Investments
5.	Borrowing costs	6.	Debt restructuring
7.	Revenue	8.	Construction contracts
9.	Leases	10.	Exchange of non-monetary assets
11.	Contingencies	12.	Accounting policies, changes of accounting estimates and correction of errors
13.	Cash flow statements	14.	Events after the balance sheet date
15.	Interim financial reporting	16.	Related party disclosures

11.1.2 The Accounting Standards for Business Enterprises (CAS 2006) 新企业会计准则体系

On 15 February 2006 the CAS 2006 was adopted by the MOFCOM. From 1 January 2007 all listed companies, and companies such as financial institutions and large- and medium-sized state-owned enterprises, were required to adopt the CAS 2006.

Eventually, the CAS 2006 became the only financial reporting for all types of business enterprises, except those small enterprises that are qualified to adopt the Accounting Standards for Small Enterprises.

11.2 Accounting Basics

11.2.1 Accounting Year and Tax Year

The accounting year starts on 1 January and ends on 31 December. Annual income tax returns and statutory audited financial statements are required to be filed with the local tax authorities within five months from the end of the tax year.

11.2.2 Recording Currency/Functional Currency

Under the Chinese Accounting Law, **renminbi (CNY)** is the mandatory recording currency (functional currency) for bookkeeping and financial statements, while foreign currency can be used for enterprises heavily engaged in foreign-currency transactions. However, all foreign-currency transactions shall be converted into renminbi when financial statements are prepared and submitted.

11.2.3 Accounts Receivables

Accounts Receivable	Calculation Subsidiary Accounts
Items, including notes receivable, accounts receivable and other receivables, shall be accounted for at the amounts occurred.	These are set up according to the names of corresponding customers and suppliers.

11.2.4 Liability

Enterprise liability shall be divided into current liabilities and long-term liabilities according to its liquidity.

Current Liabilities	Long-term Liabilities
'Current liabilities' refers to debts that shall be paid off within a year (inclusive) or an operating cycle longer than a year, including short-term loans, notes payable, accounts payable, advances from customers, employee remuneration payable, dividends payable, taxes and fees payable, other temporary receipts and payables, accrued expenses, and long-term borrowings due within a year.	'Long-term liabilities' refers to debts that shall be redeemed over a year or an operating cycle longer than a year, including long-term borrowings, bonds payable, long-term payables, and so forth.

11.2.5 Inventories

Inventories are materials or supplies that are held for sale or are in the process of production, or that are to be consumed in the production process or in the rendering of services. Inventories are recorded using the method below.

First-in-first-out	Ensures that the oldest goods purchases are sold first and the remaining inventories are the newest
Weighted average cost	Considers assigning a weighted average cost to all goods sold and goods stored in inventory
Last-in-first-out method	Ensures that the most recent goods purchased are sold first and those stored in the inventory are the oldest
Specific-identification	Specifically keeps track of each specific item in the inventory and assigns costs individually

Under the CAS 2006, the last-in-first-out method is forbidden.

11.2.6 Assets

An asset is a resource owned or controlled by an enterprise generated from past transactions or events and is expected to generate economic benefits to the enterprise.

Fixed Assets	Intangible Assets
A fixed asset is a non-monetary asset with a useful life of over 12 months and is used in the production of goods or rendering of services, for rental to others, or for administrative purposes, such as buildings and structures, machinery and equipment, vehicles and other equipment, and apparatus and tools relating to the production and operations of an enterprise.	An intangible asset is an identifiable non-monetary asset without physical substance that is owned or controlled by the enterprise. Recognition of intangible assets shall meet the following two conditions: 1) the future economic benefits expected to flow to the enterprise, and 2) the cost of intangible assets can be measured reliably.

11.2.7 Revenue Recognition

Companies shall only recognise revenue from the sale of goods when:

- the significant risks and rewards of ownership have been transferred to the buyer
- the company retains no continuing managerial involvement to the degree usually associated with ownership or effective control over the goods sold
- the economic benefit associated with the transaction will likely flow to the enterprise
- the amount of revenue and associated costs can be measured reliably

Companies shall only recognise revenue from the rendering of services and use the percentage of completion method when:

- the outcome of a transaction involving the provision of services can be estimated reliably
- the total amount of service revenue and the total costs can be measured reliably
- the economic benefit associated with the transaction will likely flow to the enterprise
- the degree of completion of the services provided can be recognised reliably

11.2.8 Owners' Equity

Owners' equity on the balance sheet includes paid-in capital, capital reserves, capital surplus reserve and undistributed profits.

Paid-in Capital	Actual amount of capital contributed by the investors in a company in accordance with the company's articles of association, investment contracts or agreements
Capital Reserves	Capital that is contributed by an investor more than its share of the registered capital
Capital Surplus	Premium on capital (or stock), reserve of donated non-cash assets, receipt of cash donation, reserve of equity investment, transfer-ins of appropriations, foreign currency capital translation difference, and other capital surplus
Surplus Reserve	Statutory surplus reserve amount that is specified in the relevant laws or regulations and the discretionary surplus reserve amount appropriated at the discretion of enterprises
Undistributed Profit	Accumulated balance of the distribution of profits (or recovery for losses) and the distribution (or recovery) over the years

11.2.9 Consolidation (for investments in subsidiaries)

The ASBE provisions that the accounting of company subsidiaries that meet one of the following conditions shall be consolidated

- Investee entities over which the parent company holds more than 50% of the registered capital of the investee
- Investee entities over which the parent company holds 50% or less of the registered capital of the investee, but in substance has control

'Control' refers to the parent company's ability to govern the financial and operating policies of a subsidiary, and benefits from the subsidiary's activities.

The CAS 2006 determines 'control' as the parent company's power of control of the subsidiary. Where such control exists, there is a parent–subsidiary relationship, and the parent company shall include all subsidiaries within the scope of consolidation.

State-owned enterprises are not regarded as related parties because they are controlled by the State.

11.3 Financial reports

11.3.1 Financial Accounting Reports

Financial accounting reports include financial statements, notes to financial statements, and other related information that shall be disclosed in the financial accounting reports. Contents of such financial accounting reports shall conform to the uniform requirements stipulated in the related laws.

Financial statements should at least include the following:

Items

- Balance sheet
- Income statement
- Cash-flow statement
- Statement of changes in owners' equity (or shareholders' equity), and notes

Notes to financial statements should at least include the following:

- Basic situation of the enterprise
- Basis of preparation of the financial statement
- Statement of compliance with accounting standards
- Significant accounting policies and estimates
- Description of changes in accounting policies and estimates and a correction of errors
- Other important items requiring description (mainly including contingencies and commitments, and non-adjusting events after the balance sheet date)
- Disclosure of related party relationships and transactions
- Description of the transfer and sale of significant assets
- Description of business merger and split-up

11.3.2 Audited Financial Statements

Audits are required under the Company Law, financial reporting regulations and income tax laws in China, and audited financial statements should be filed with the tax authorities together with the annual income tax returns. Foreign-invested enterprises are required to provide auditors with all their documents, books and reports. The financial statements to be submitted for an annual audit include the balance sheet, income statement, statement of changes in owners' equity, statement of cash flow, and relevant supporting notes.

Audited financial statements must be submitted to a number of government authorities, primarily

- the local offices of the State Administration for Market Regulation
- the State Administration of Taxation
- the local finance bureau
- the State Administration of Foreign Exchange

Audited financial statements must be submitted to the relevant authorities within four to six months of the year-end, depending on local government requirements.

11.4 General CAS 2006 and International Financial Reporting Standards (IFRS) Comparison

Definition and Measurement Differences

Category	CAS 2006	IFRS
Fixed assets	Measured by using the historical cost of the fixed asset. No revaluation of assets is allowed.	Measured by using the historical cost of the fixed asset. Subsequent measurements are made by using fair value.
Investment real estate	When the real estate is transferred from the classification of inventory to investment property, the difference between the historical cost and the fair value on the transfer date is recognised as a loss or profit. If there is a profit, it is recognised as other comprehensive income and transferred to owner's equity when the investment property is disposed of. If there is a loss, it is accounted in the income statement and is reflected in the cost.	Investment real estate can be measured at the historical cost or fair value. On the transfer date, the difference between the historical value and the fair value is recognised in the income statement for the period.
Reversal of impairment losses	Reversal of impairment of long-term assets is not allowed (i.e. fixed assets, intangible assets, investment property). Reversal of impairment of current assets is allowed.	Impairment of non-current assets, such as fixed assets and intangible assets, is allowed to be reversed and recognised in profit or loss for the current period. However, reversal of impairment losses for goodwill is forbidden.

Category	CAS 2006	IFRS
Related party	Related parties refer to: two parties between which one party fully or jointly controls the other party or exerts significant influence on the other party; or two or more parties are fully or jointly controlled or are subject to significant influence by the same party. However, in the case of state-owned enterprises, enterprises that are merely both under the control by the state but have no other elements of related-party relationship do not constitute related parties.	All state-owned companies are recognised as related parties, and transactions between the related parties are recognised as related transactions. Therefore, all state-owned companies are subject to disclosure.
Income statements	Expenses are required to be classified by their function.	Expenses may be classified either by the nature of expenses or their function. The enterprise is free to choose which method provides the most reliable and most relevant information.
Cash flow statements	• Requires the use of the direct method accompanied by a note showing the reconciliation of profit-to-net cash flow from operating activities using the indirect method. • Bank overdraft amounts are required to be deducted from cash or cash equivalents. • Received dividends and interest income are accounted as investing activity. Interest paid is accounted as financing activities.	• May choose to use either the direct or indirect method. • Bank overdraft amounts are included in cash or cash equivalents. Received dividends and interest income. • Paid interest can be accounted as business activities or investment activities.

Audit Disclosure Differences

Category	CAS 2006	IFRS
Disclosure of monetary funds, loans and bank long-term loans.		In the notes of the monetary funds, it is required to disclose the bank deposit floating rates (current, regular); for example, the maximum and the minimum of the regular interest rate within the current year, the maximum and the minimum of the floating interest rate (current rate) within the current year. To disclose the interest rate risks of long-term bank loans, the maximum and minimum interest rate of the current year is required to be disclosed.
Related parties	Disclosure of related parties shall include all exchanges and transactions between the related parties.	Disclosure of related parties is subdivided into two groups: • *Related companie* *Companies* directly related to the audited entity, including the parent company, subsidiaries and affiliated companies. • *Related parties* Parties belonging to the same group as the audited entity (i.e. associated parties under the same control) and other indirectly related parties (i.e the holding company of the audited entity).

Category	CAS 2006	IFRS
Details of financial instruments	From 2018, Chinese companies listed abroad are required to disclose the same financial instruments in line with the IFRS. Currently, except for listed companies abroad, there is no requirement for companies to disclose financial instruments. From 2020, all companies in China shall follow the IFRS financial instruments disclosure.	Financial instruments in detail are required to be disclosed, including the following: • Financial assets and disclosure of financial liabilities • Credit-risk disclosure of financial assets • Disclosure of fair value of financial instruments • Disclosure of liquidity risk • Disclosure of interest-rate risk • Disclosure of foreign-exchange risk

12 Current: China Tax 2022

12.1 Introduction

Tax laws are enacted by the People's Congress and the Standing Committee, while the implementation regulations are formulated by the State Council.

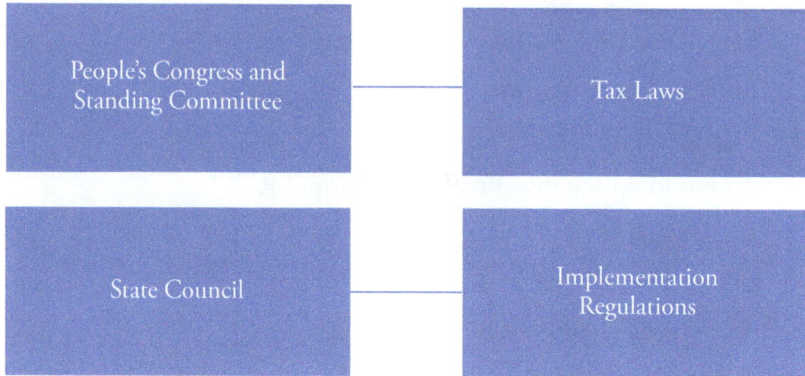

The Ministry of Finance (MOF) and the State Taxation Administration (STA) are delegated to provide interpretation and implementation of the tax laws and regulations. Meanwhile, the STA is also responsible for supervising the enforcement of tax collection at the local level.

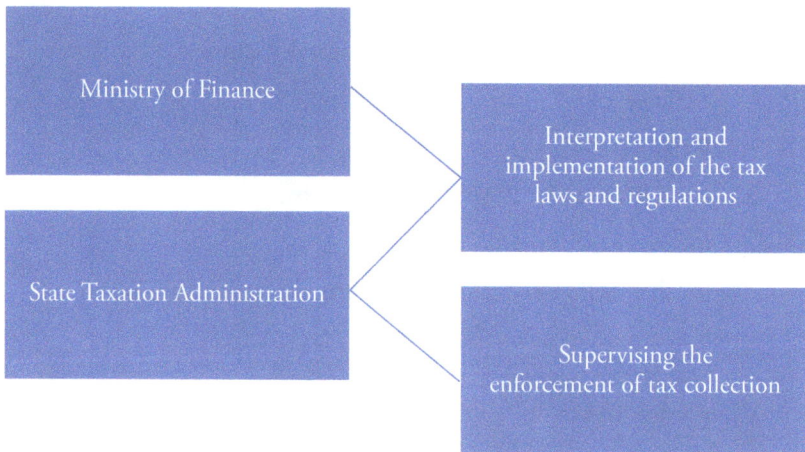

The tax year commences on 1 January and ends on 31 December.

12.2 Enterprise Income Tax

12.2.1 Tax Resident Enterprise

Tax resident enterprise (TRE) is defined in the Enterprise Income Tax Law of the People's Republic of China as:

An enterprise established according to Chinese law or an enterprise established according to foreign laws but with its effective management located in China

12.2.1.1 TRE Tax Rate

Normal enterprise	25%
Small and micro enterprise • Engaged in industries not restricted or prohibited by the State • Annual taxable income does not exceed CNY 3 million • The number of employees does not exceed 300 • Total assets do not exceed CNY 50 million	5%

12.2.1.2 Withholding Income Tax Rate for Non-TREs

Non-resident enterprises (non-TREs) without institutions or establishments in China, or established institutions or establishments whose income obtained by the said enterprises has no actual connection with the institutions or establishments, are subject to enterprise income tax (EIT).

'Withholding tax (WHT)' refers to the tax paid at source when making payments to non-resident enterprises. In other words, the tax is paid to the Chinese tax bureau by the payer of the income rather than by the recipient of the income. The tax is thus withheld or deducted from the income due to the recipient.

WHT rates are usually 10%.

Renminbi (CNY) currency is the currency for EIT. Foreign currency income is converted into CNY for tax-payment purposes.

12.2.2 Tax Deduction and Other Treatments

12.2.2.1 Depreciation Calculated

For fixed assets used during the production, wear and tear is permitted. Generally, the straight-line method of depreciation is allowed.

Minimum depreciation periods for different kinds of assets are specified as follows unless otherwise stated:

Item	Duration
Buildings and structures	20 years
Aircrafts, trains, vessels, machinery, mechanisms, and other production equipment	10 years
Appliances, tools, furniture, etc.	5 years
Means of transport other than aircraft, trains and vessels	4 years
Electronic equipment	3 years
Production-nature biological assets in the nature of forestry	10 years
Production-nature biological assets in the nature of livestock	3 years

12.2.2.3 Accelerated Depreciation Calculations

Item	Calculation
Certain types of fixed assets	Shorter tax depreciation life or accelerated depreciation
New fixed assets for manufacturing industries or new fixed assets and equipment acquired specifically for research-and-development purposes	Shorter appreciation life or under-accelerated depreciation method

12.2.2.4 Intangible-assets Calculations

Intangible assets, such as patents, copyrights, trademarks and land use rights, are amortised utilising the straight-line method over a period of not less than ten years or the limit set out in the contract or agreement.

Item	Calculation
Intangible assets, such as patents, copyrights, trademarks and land use rights	Shorter tax depreciation life or accelerated depreciation
New fixed assets for manufacturing industries or new fixed assets and equipment acquired specifically for research-and-development purposes	Shorter appreciation life or under-accelerated depreciation method

12.2.2.5 Other Non-deductible Expenses

Interest on loans	Interest on loans is deductible. Interest expenses shall not exceed the following proportions of debt investment and related equity investment: 1. Financial companies 5:1 (debt:equity) 2. Non-financial companies 2:1 (debt:equity) The deduction shall be permitted in the tax year, but the excess amount cannot be deducted in subsequent years.
Entertainment	Business entertainment expenses incurred in connection with preparation activities may account for 60% of the total amount incurred.
Advertising and business promotion expenses	Advertising expenses and business promotion expenses are deductible within 15% of the portion of sales (business) income earned in the current tax year; expenses exceeding the amount can be carried forward to the following tax years. Sectors such as cosmetics, pharmaceutical, and beverage (excluding alcoholic beverage manufacturers) can deduct up to 30%.
Asset loss	Asset loss (including bad-debt loss) may be deductible in the tax year during which such loss is incurred, provided that supporting documents are submitted to the in-charge tax bureau before or during the annual income tax reconciliation filing.
Charitable donations	Charitable donations can be deducted if they do not exceed 12% of the total profits in the same year.

12.2.2.6 Dividends and Interests

Dividends and interests paid to foreign shareholders abroad are subject to withholding tax at 10% rate.

12.2.2.6.1 Filing and Payment

12.2.2.6.1.1 How is tax filed?

- Annual tax returns shall be filed on or before 31 May after the end of a tax year (subject to local variation)
- Provisional reporting and payments shall be made on a monthly or quarterly basis, dependent on the in-charge tax authorities
- Provisional payments shall be settled within 15 days from the end of each month/quarter
- TRE with one or more branches shall combine the taxable income of its branches and file EIT returns. Two or more TREs cannot consolidate EIT returns unless provided by the State

12.3 Individuals

12.3.1 How is individual income tax calculated?

Resides in China for 183 days or more	Resides in China for less than 183 days	Resides in China for less than 90 days
An individual who is domiciled in China or a non-domiciled individual who resides in the PRC for 183 days or more (total accumulated days) is considered a tax resident of China. Tax residents are subject to both incomes derived within and outside the territory of China.	Non-tax residents who reside in China for less than 183 days (total accumulated days) and are not domiciled in China are subject to individual income tax on the income derived from China.	Remuneration from foreign employers to individuals working in the PRC is exempt from tax if the individual resides in the PRC for less than 90 days in a calendar year, provided that the remuneration is not borne or paid by an establishment in the PRC.

12.3.2 Individual Income Tax Rates for General Income

Comprehensive Income	Wages and salaries
	Provision of labour services
	Authors' remuneration
	Royalties

Individual income tax (IIT) is withheld on comprehensive income of tax residents and is made on a consolidated basis and calculated utilising an annual cumulative income method. For non-tax residents, IIT is withheld on an item-by-item basis and by month or by time. The general standard deduction for general income is CNY 60,000 per tax year or CNY 5,000 per month for a non-tax resident.

Income from comprehensive income is taxed according to the following progressive rates, ranging from 3% to 45%:

Annual Taxable Income (CNY)[1]	Tax Rate (%)
36,000 or less	3
The part >36,000 < 144,000	10
The part > 144,000 < 300,000	20
The part > 300,000 < 420,000	25
The part > 420,000 < 660,000	30
The part > 660,000 < 960,000	35
The part > 960,000	45

[1] The annual taxable income in the table refers to the amount remaining after deducting the CNY 60,000 standard general deduction, special deductions, special extra deductions, and other deductions under the law, from the annual general income received by a resident individual in a single tax year.

12.3.2.1 Deductions

Special Deductions	Special Additional Deductions	Other Deductions
'Special deductions' refers to social contributions, including basic pension insurance, basic medical insurance, unemployment insurance, and other social security contributions, such as housing provident funds.	'Special additional deductions' refers to expenses for children's education, continuing education, medical treatment for major illness, home loan interest or house rentals, support for the elderly, and so forth.	Other deductions specified according to the law include the expenses incurred by an individual for the payment of enterprise annuities and occupational annuities in compliance with state regulations, the purchase of commercial health insurance and tax-deferred commercial pension insurance in compliance with state regulations, and other items that may be deducted as specified by the State Council.

12.3.2.2 Foreigners

Until January 2024, foreigners in China may still deduct certain items from IIT or claim special additional deductions.

Deductible items for foreigners include the following:

- Employee housing costs borne by an employer (with supporting invoices)
- Reasonable home-leave fares of two trips per annum for the employee (with supporting invoices)
- Reasonable employee relocation and moving costs (with supporting invoices)
- Reasonable reimbursement of certain meals, laundry, language training costs and children's educational expenses in the PRC (with supporting invoices)

12.3.2.3 Income Other Than Employment Income

12.3.2.3.1 Private-owned Businesses, Sole-proprietorship Enterprises, and Businesses on a Contract or Lease Basis

Income earned by individuals from privately owned businesses, sole-proprietorship enterprises or from the operation of a business on a contract or lease basis is generally subject to IIT at progressive rates from 5% to 35%. The 35% marginal rate applies to annual taxable income (gross revenue less allowable costs, expenses and losses) over CNY 500,000.

12.3.2.3.2 Income from Interest, Dividends, Transfer of Property, Royalty Income, Rental Income and Other Income

Such income is normally taxed at a flat rate of 20%. However, IIT may be reduced or exempted for certain income meeting certain prescribed conditions.

12.3.3 Tax Filing and Payment

IIT shall be withheld by the payer.

Employers should withhold IIT from resident individuals' employment income and pay it to the tax authorities with a cumulative withholding method on a monthly basis.

If the annual cumulative tax amount withheld and the final tax payable amount are inconsistent, resident individuals should perform annual IIT reconciliation filing with the in-charge tax authorities from 1 March to 30 June in the following year. For the tax years 2019 and 2020, resident individuals can be exempted from the annual IIT reconciliation filing if certain prescribed criteria are met.

For non-resident individuals' employment income, employers should withhold IIT on a monthly basis. IIT returns must be filed within 15 days of the end of each month.

12.3.4 Annual IIT Self-declaration Requirement

A taxpayer under any of the following six circumstances is required to perform IIT self-declaration with the tax authorities according to the law, including; where it is necessary to process final settlement for the consolidated income, where there is no withholding agent for taxable income, where the withholding agent does not withhold tax in respect of taxable income, where the taxpayer obtains overseas income, where the taxpayer cancels Chinese household registration due to immigration and where non-resident individuals are obtaining employment income from two or more places within the PRC.

12.4 Other Taxes

12.4.1 Value-added Tax

In May 2016 value-added tax (VAT) was reformed and expanded to several key sectors including real estate and construction, financial services, and insurance and lifestyle services. The reforms serve to unify all sectors within a disruptive VAT system, providing incentives to distribute the tax burden down the VAT chain. In practice, VAT unification stands to decrease the payable VAT and improve cash flow for registered taxpayers.

VAT is offset by a special VAT invoice, which acts as VAT credit to offset input VAT from output VAT. Above is a simplified version of the VAT chain.

VAT taxpayers are classified into 'general VAT taxpayers' with annual turnover exceeding CNY 5 million and 'small-scale VAT taxpayers'. General VAT taxpayers are required to be registered as general VAT taxpayers and may offset VAT with special VAT invoices, while small-scale VAT taxpayers may either offset VAT with special VAT invoices or enjoy VAT exemptions, provided the monthly sales revenues are below CNY 100,000 or the quarterly sales are below CNY 300,000.

12.4.1.1 VAT Rates

Sale or importation of goods	13%
Tangible, movable property leasing services	
Transportation services, postal services, basic telecommunications services, construction services, immovable property leasing services, sale of immovable properties, transfer of land use rights	9%
Value-added telecommunications services, financial services, modern services (except for leasing services), consumer services, sales of intangible properties (except for land use rights). Sale of intangible assets	6%
Exportation of goods Exportation of repair, replacement and processing services	0%

12.4.2 Consumption Tax

Consumption tax is levied on manufacturers and importers of specific consumer goods, including tobacco, alcohol, high-end cosmetics, jewellery, fireworks, gasoline and diesel and certain petroleum products, motorcycles, automobiles, golf equipment, yachts, luxury watches, and so forth. The payable tax is calculated on the sales amount and/or the sales volume, depending on the tax item.

12.4.3 Urban Construction and Maintenance Tax and Educational Surcharge

Urban construction and maintenance tax and educational surcharges (surtaxes) are imposed with VAT, the taxpayers of indirect taxes also being the taxpayers of urban construction and maintenance tax. Urban construction tax rate is dependent on the taxpayer's location: 7% for urban areas, 5% for county areas and 1% for other areas. Educational surcharge is imposed at 3%.

12.4.4 Rate of Customs Duties

Customs duty is levied on imported goods and collected by the customs authorities during the importation time. Customs duties are computed either on an *ad valorem* basis or a quantity basis. Generally, the applicable rate is based on the origin of the goods. The product origin also determines the number of applicable policies, such as quotas, preferential tariffs, anti-dumping actions, countervailing duty, and so forth.

Most-favoured-nation (MFN) tariff rate is adopted for goods originating from World Trade Organization member countries or those that have concluded bilateral trade agreements with China that contain clauses referring to most-favoured-nation treatment, and the import of goods where the place of origin is within the territory of China.

The conventional tariff rate is adopted for import goods where the place of origin is a country or region that has concluded a trade agreement with China that contains clauses of preferential duty.

Preferential tariff is adopted for import goods where the place of origin is a country or region that has concluded a trade agreement that contains clauses of special preferential tariff with the People's Republic of China.

Goods may be imported into and exported out of designated free-trade zones without liability to customs duty or VAT.

12.4.5 Stamp Duty

All enterprises and individuals executing taxable vouchers or conduct securities transactions within the territory of China are subject to stamp tax, as well as entities and individuals generating taxable vouchers outside the territory of China and used within China. For tax declaration and payment, a withholding agent shall withhold, declare and pay the taxable amount to the authorities. Rates vary between 0.005% on loan contracts and 0.1% for property leasing and property insurance contracts.

13 Current: Intellectual Property Rights

13.1 Introduction

Protecting trademarks is a crucial first step for any foreign company looking to do business in China.

Foreign companies often fail to protect their trademarks, holding on to the misconception that there's a lack of intellectual property (IP) enforcement in China. However, the People's Republic of China has been a member of the World Intellectual Property Organization (WIPO) since 1980. There are three national laws, which form the national legal framework for IP protection in China: the Trademark Law, promulgated in 1982 and last revised in 2019; the Copyright Law, promulgated in 1984 and last revised in 2020; and the Patent Law, promulgated in 1984 and last revised in 2020.

The latest revisions to the Trademark Law and the Patent Law reflect China's commitment to strengthen the protection of intellectual property. The revised Trademark Law was part of the Three-year Plan for Trademark Registration Facilitation Reform 2018–2021, commonly referred to as 'The Three-year Plan' (published in March 2018). The Three-year Plan (formed under the mandate for advocating innovative culture), strengthening IP innovation and protecting and utilising IP – all highlighted in the New Era of President Xi Jinping, initiated at the 19th National Congress of the Communist Party of China – outlines the blueprint for the establishment of high-quality, convenient and efficient trademark application channels. It also endeavours to simplify trademark registration and management, as well as trademark review collaboration.

13.2 Trademark

In China, trademarks are registered according to the first-to-file rule rather than the first-to-use rule utilised in many Western jurisdictions.

In other words, whoever is first to file the application to register the trademark is granted approval. As a result, many foreign companies fail to understand the first-to-file rule and fail to protect their trademark in China.

China uses the Classification of Similar Goods and Services, which is composed based on the International Classification of Goods and Services (Nice Classification) system for classifying goods and services for trademark registration. The government body responsible for administering the trademark registration system is the Trademark Office under the China National Intellectual Property Administration, to which the applications for trademark registration shall be made. There is also the Trademark Review and Adjudication Board (TRAB), which is responsible for handling trademark disputes.

13.2.1 The Trademark System

'Registered trademarks' refers to trademarks approved by and registered with the Trademark Office, including goods marks, service marks, collective marks and certification marks. The registrant of a trademark enjoys the exclusive right to use the trademark protected by law.

'Collective trademarks' refers to marks registered in the name of a group or any other organisation. These marks are used in business activities by the members to indicate their membership.

'Certification trademarks' refers to marks owned and controlled by organisations that exercise supervision over particular goods or services. These marks are used to indicate that the goods or services of the third party meet certain standards in relation to the place of origin, raw materials, mode of manufacture, quality, or other specific characteristics.

Special provisions for the registration and administration of collective and certification marks are issued separately by the State Administration for Market Regulation.

When registering a trademark, the applicant should ensure that the mark holds distinctive characters and does not conflict with prior registered trademarks. Marks only bearing generic names, devices or model numbers of the goods cannot be registered as trademarks. Applicants should therefore consider firstly conducting a preliminary search to ensure no similar trademark is registered, and secondly adopting distinctive characters in the trademark that distinguish it from others. Applicants also need to specify the class of goods or services to which it is to apply.

Under most circumstances it is not compulsory to register a trademark for goods sold on the Chinese domestic market, except for tobacco products, which may not be sold in the market before the registration thereof is approved.

Registered marks receive certain protections under the law. Using a mark that is identical with or similar to a registered mark for the same or a similar category of goods or services to which the registered mark applies is prohibited. Unregistered marks are not generally protected by the law.

13.2.2 Types of Marks that Can Be Registered

Any natural person, legal person or other organisation may apply for trademark registration at the Trademark Office. Two or more natural persons, legal persons or other organisations may jointly file for the same trademark and jointly enjoy and exercise the exclusive right to use the trademark.

Any symbol – including word, device, alphabet, number, three-dimensional sign, colour combination, sound, or combination of all of the aforesaid – that distinguishes the goods or services may be registered. The following are forbidden:

- Marks identical with or similar to the country name, national flag, national emblem, national anthem, military flag, military emblem or military medal of China, or marks identical with the name and logo of central government agencies, the name of a specific location where a central government agency is located or the name or the device of a landmark building

- Marks identical with or similar to the state name, national flag, national emblem, or military flag of another country, except where there is the permission from the government concerned

- Marks identical with or similar to the flags, emblems or names of international intergovernmental organisations unless with the permission of the organisation concerned or if the use is unlikely to cause confusion to the public

- Marks identical with or similar to official authentic symbols or inspection marks that indicate official control or guarantee, except with authorisation

- Marks identical with or similar to the symbols or names of the Red Cross or the Red Crescent

- Marks that are discriminatory against any nationality

- Fraudulent marks and those that might be deceptive and misleading in advertising goods

- Marks detrimental to socialist morals or customs, or that have other unhealthy influences

- Geographical names of administrative regions at county level or above and commonly known foreign place names unless those place names have other meanings or the place name is an integral part of a collective trademark or certification trademark (any trademarks bearing any of the above geographical names that have already been registered shall continue to be valid)

- Marks containing only the generic name, devices or model numbers of the goods

- Marks indicating only the quality, main raw materials, functions, use, weight, quantity, or other features of the goods

- Marks lacking distinctive characters unless the mark has already required distinctiveness through use and is readily distinguishable

- Three-dimensional marks only indicating the shape inherent in the nature of the related goods or only dictated by the need to achieve technical effects or the need to give substantive value to related goods

13.2.3 Well-known Trademarks

Trademark owners may seek the protection of well-known trademarks when there is an infringement to their trademark rights. Well-known trademarks shall be determined as one of the necessary facts when handling trademark-related cases as required by the trademark owner and with consideration of the following factors:

- The degree of popularity the trademark in its trading areas
- The duration the trademark has been in use
- The duration, extent and geographical range of the advertising and publicity of the trademark
- The records on the protection of the trademark as a well-known trademark
- Other reasons for the reputation of the trademark

Where a trademark applied for registration is copied, imitated or translated from other well-known trademarks of the same or similar goods that are not registered in China and it is easy to cause confusion, or from other well-known trademarks of different or dissimilar goods that have been registered in China, which causes confusion and possible damage to the interests of the owner, it shall not be used or registered.

Well-known trademarks shall only be determined during the process of registered trademark review or the investigation of law violations, trademark disputes and civil or administrative cases. Manufacturers and business operators shall not use characters such as 'Well-known Trademark' on goods, related packaging or advertising, or other commercial activities.

13.2.4 Trademark Applications

Applications for trademark registration shall be submitted to the Trademark Office either independently or through a qualified trademark agency.

13.2.4.1 Trademark Agencies

Trademark agencies shall be appointed by the registrar based on the principle of integrity, honesty and credibility and in accordance with the laws and administrative rules and regulations. The Trademark Law requires a written statement of the appointment, with clear limits to the agent's authority. Trademark agencies shall bear confidentiality obligations for any obtained trade secrets.

Trademark agencies shall clearly inform the client if there is a possibility that the trademark they have applied for registration for is not in accordance with the legal provisions.

Trademark agencies are prohibited from accepting appointments under the following circumstances:

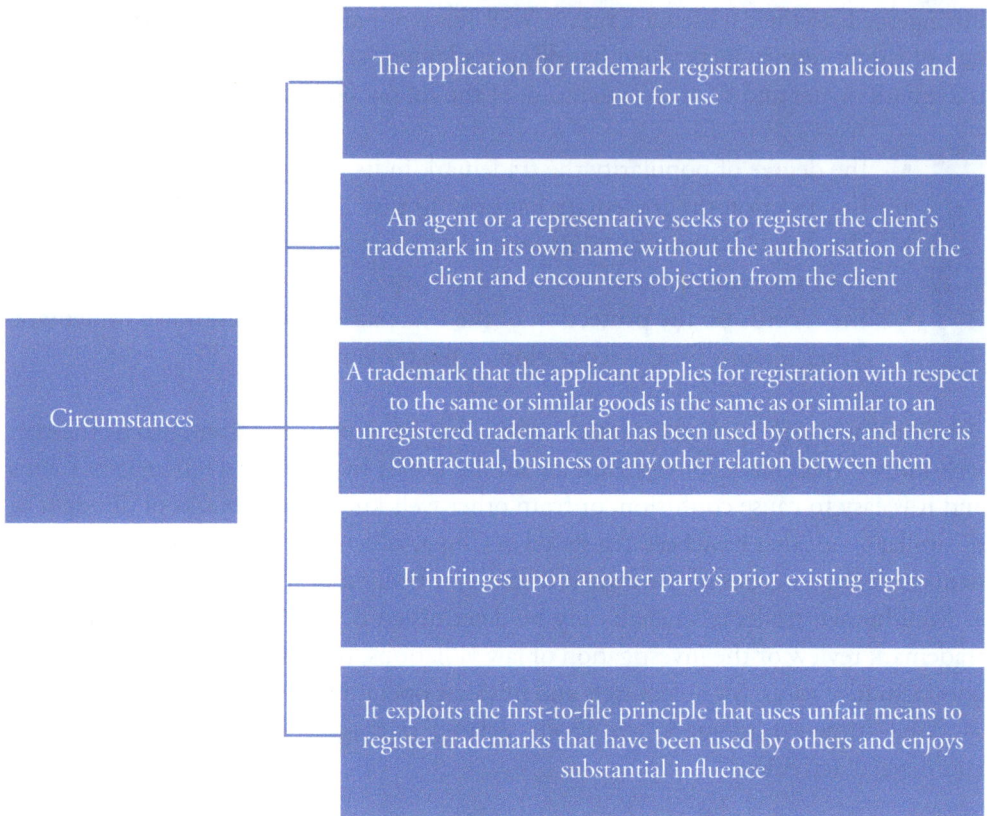

Circumstances	
	The application for trademark registration is malicious and not for use
	An agent or a representative seeks to register the client's trademark in its own name without the authorisation of the client and encounters objection from the client
	A trademark that the applicant applies for registration with respect to the same or similar goods is the same as or similar to an unregistered trademark that has been used by others, and there is contractual, business or any other relation between them
	It infringes upon another party's prior existing rights
	It exploits the first-to-file principle that uses unfair means to register trademarks that have been used by others and enjoys substantial influence

A trademark agency shall only apply for the registration of trademarks on behalf of a client and shall not apply for the registration of any other trademarks.

13.2.5 Applications of Foreigners and Foreign Enterprises

Foreigners and foreign enterprises shall authorise a qualified trademark agency in China to apply for the registration of a trademark or handle any other trademark matters and are subject to agreements signed between the foreigner's home country and China – or treaties to which both countries have acceded – and are based on the principle of reciprocity.

All application materials, and materials relating to trademarks, must be in the Chinese language.

13.2.6 Categories of Products

An application for trademark registration shall indicate the class and the goods of the trademark based on the prescribed classification of goods. An application can apply for registering the same trademark for several classes.

13.2.7 Trademark Law Revision 2019

In the amended Trademark Law 2019, Article 4 stipulates that an application for trademark registration that is malicious and not filed for the purpose of use shall be refused registration. Equally, where a registered trademark violates Article 4, an invalidation may be raised by entities or individuals through the China National Intellectual Property Administration (CNIPA). Furthermore, according to the amended Trademark Law, when determining the maliciousness of the trademark registration, the criteria for invalidation are more flexible than during the registration phase; namely, if a trademark filed in bad faith is approved for registration, the legitimate owner of the trademark may still be able to rebut the registration by raising legitimate reasons for invalidation.

Trademark registrations made in bad faith can be subject to administrative warnings and/or penalties. In this manner, stricter regulation of trademark registration provides strong protection for legitimate trademark owners in the Chinese market. Specifically for those who have found that their trademark has already been registered by a trademark squatter, the amended Trademark Law provisions a solution to pursue such trademark squatters directly through CNIPA without having to purchase the trademark from the squatter or engage litigation, which saves valuable time and money.

13.2.8 Priority Trademarks

Trademark registration in China follows the first-to-file principle. Under the Trademark Law, the following provisions apply:

- Where there are two or more applicants applying for registration of an identical or similar trademark for the same type of commodities or similar commodities, the preliminary approval and announcement shall be made for the earlier one
- Where such applications are submitted on the same day, the preliminary approval and announcement shall be made for the one used earlier, and other applications shall be rejected

The date of the official filing receipt issued by the Trademark Office is the official date of the application.

The first-to-file rule does not apply to an applicant entitled to priority, which may include the following:

- One who applies for trademark registration in China for the same goods with the same trademark within six months from the date of the first application in a foreign country, and there is an agreement signed between the foreign country and China or there is an international treaty to which both countries are parties or there is the principle of reciprocity between the foreign country and China that recognises priority
- One who uses a trademark for the first time on exhibited goods in an international exhibition sponsored or recognised by the Chinese government and files an application for trademark registration within six months from the date of exhibition of the commodity

An applicant claiming priority shall state in writing at the time of application and submit, within three months, a copy of the first application for trademark registration or the name of the exhibition and evidencing materials to prove the use of the trademark in the exhibition and the date of the exhibition, etc.

13.2.9 Examination and Approval

Examination shall be completed within nine months of the date of the trademark registration receipt. Applicants shall be preliminarily approved and announced if compliant with the Trademark Law.

During the process of examination, the application contents may be required to be explained or revised if the Trademark Office considers it necessary. Failure to provide an explanation or correction shall not affect the Trademark Office's decision.

The Trademark Office shall grant preliminary approval to a trademark if the examiner considers that it is registerable under the Trademark Law and the Trademark Regulations, and if there are no conflicting applications or registrations.

Where a trademark application is found compliant for a certain part of the designated goods, the application shall be granted preliminary approval and gazetted on such part of the goods only. The remaining other unapproved part shall be rejected, and the applicant shall receive written notification of the reasons.

13.2.10 Trademark Licences and Assignments

13.2.10.1 Licensing

Trademark registrants may license trademarks to other parties by concluding a licensing agreement. The licensor shall file the licence of trademark with the Trademark Office for records, and the licensing arrangement shall be publicly announced. The trademark licence shall not be used to defend the bona fide third party if it has not been filed for record.

The licensee of a trademark licence shall indicate the name of the licensee and the place of origin on the goods that bear the registered trademark.

13.2.10.2 Assignment

Registrants may transfer their trademarks to other parties. Both the transferer and transferee are required to jointly file an assignment application at the Trademark Office, with a written transfer agreement, a completed application in the form required by the Trademark Office, and the original trademark registration certificate. The trademark registrant shall assign similar trademarks on the same goods or the same or similar trademarks on similar goods.

Upon the approval of the transfer, the assignment shall be published and the transferee shall enjoy the exclusive right to use the trademark upon the date of the announcement. For registered trademarks that may easily lead to confusion or other adverse effects, the Trademark Office shall not approve assignment.

13.2.11 Invalidation

13.2.11.1 Violation

The Trademark Office shall invalidate any registered trademark if it:

- contains elements not allowed to be used as a trademark
- contains elements not allowed to be registered as a trademark
- as a three-dimensional sign, merely indicates the shape inherent in the nature of the goods or is only dictated by the need to achieve technical effects or the need to give the goods substantive value
- is registered by the trademark agency, except for the registration of trademarks on behalf of a client
- is acquired by deceptive or improper means

Individuals and organisations may also apply to the TRAB to invalidate such registered trademarks.

The prior rights owner or interested party may apply to the TRAB for the invalidation of a trademark within five years of the registration of such a trademark if it is in violation of the law. In the event of malicious registration, owners of well-known trademarks may be exempt from the aforesaid five-year duration.

If the TRAB accepts the case, parties shall be notified and required to submit arguments within a specified time. The TRAB shall rule whether to maintain or invalidate the trademark within 12 months of receipt of such an application and notify the parties in writing. In the event that the party concerned is dissatisfied with the ruling, it may appeal to the People's Court within 30 days of receipt of the notice. The People's Court shall notify the counterparty of the trademark ruling procedures of participation in the proceedings as a third party.

Registered trademarks deemed as invalid shall cause the exclusive right to use such registered trademarks as deemed inexistent *ab initio*.

13.2.11.2 Revocation

If a trademark registrant changes the registered trademark, the name or address of the registrant or other registered items at its discretion in the process of using the registered trademark, the local administrative department shall order it to make corrections within a time limit. If no correction is made within the time limit, the Trademark Office shall revoke its registered trademark.

Any person may apply to the Trademark Office for revocation of the registered trademark if it becomes the generic name of the goods approved for use or it is not used for three consecutive years without proper reasons. The Trademark Office shall decide within nine months of the date of receiving the application.

If a trademark is revoked, invalidated or not renewed upon expiration of the period of validity, the Trademark Office shall not approve any application for the registration of a trademark identical with or similar to the said trademark within one year of revocation, invalidation or cancellation.

13.2.12 Appealing Cancellation

A party that's had its trademark cancelled by the Trademark Office may appeal to the TRAB within 15 days of receiving the notice of a cancellation. If dissatisfied with the TRAB's decision, it may initiate legal action with the court within 30 days of receiving the decision.

13.2.13 Remedies Protecting the Exclusive Right to Use

The exclusive right to use the registered trademark is limited to the goods for which the trademark has been approved. Infringements of the exclusive right to use a registered trademark are:

- Using a trademark that is identical with a registered trademark on the same kind of goods without the licensing of the trademark registrant
- Using a trademark that is similar to a registered trademark on the same goods, or using a trademark that is identical with or similar to a registered trademark on similar goods in a confusing way, without the licensing of the trademark registrant
- Selling products that violate the right to exclusive use of a trademark
- Counterfeiting or arbitrarily forging another's registered trademark or selling counterfeited or arbitrarily forged trademarks
- Altering the registered trademark without authorisation from the trademark registrant and selling such products with the altered trademark
- Providing convenience, or even assisting others, to infringe the exclusive right to use a registered trademark on purpose
- Other conducts causing prejudice to others' exclusive rights to use their registered trademark

13.2.13.1 Trademark Infringement Investigation

The State Administration for Market Regulation of county level and above may exercise the following powers in the investigation of an alleged infringement violation based on the available evidence of illegal conduct or information supplied by a member of the public:

- Question the parties concerned and investigate the circumstances in connection with the infringement of another's exclusive right to use a registered trademark
- Look up and copy the contracts, invoices, books, and other materials pertaining to the trademark-infringing activities of the parties concerned
- Conduct an on-site inspection of the premises where the party concerned is suspected of carrying out activities that have infringed upon another's exclusive right to use a registered trademark
- Inspect the articles involved in trademark-infringing activities (articles that are proven to have infringed upon another's exclusive right to use a registered trademark may be sealed and taken into custody)

The parties concerned shall assist or render cooperation and shall not refuse or hinder the investigation.

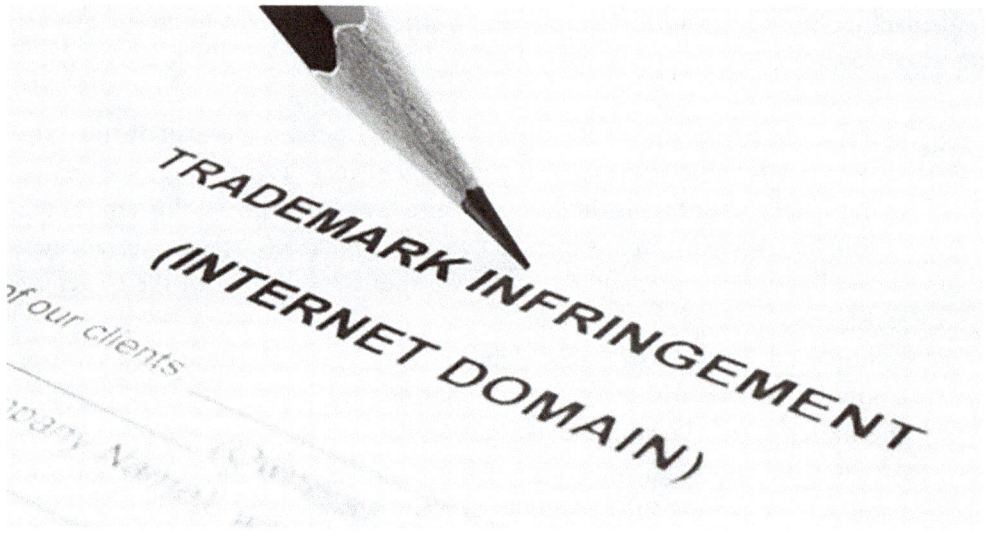

In the course of investigation of a trademark-infringement case, where there is dispute over the ownership of trademark rights, or the rights holder has simultaneously filed a trademark-infringement lawsuit with a People's Court, the State Administration for Market Regulation may suspend investigation of the case. Upon elimination of the reason(s) for suspension, the investigation procedures shall be resumed or terminated.

If infringement is found by the State Administration for Market Regulation, the infringer shall be ordered to stop the infringing act and the infringing commodities and the tools mainly used for manufacturing of the infringing commodities and the forgery of registered trademark labels shall be confiscated and destroyed. If the infringer's illegal turnover is CNY 50,000 or more, a fine up to the five times the amount of illegal turnover may be imposed. If there is no illegal turnover or the illegal turnover is below CNY 50,000, a fine up to CNY 250,000 may be imposed. Any two or more occasions of infringements within five years, as well as other serious offences, shall be subject to severe punishment.

13.2.13.2 Dispute Settlement

In the event of a dispute arising from any of the acts of infringement of exclusive rights to use registered trademarks according to the Trademark law, the parties concerned shall negotiate for resolution. Where the parties concerned are unwilling to negotiate or where negotiation is unsuccessful, the trademark registrant or a stakeholder may file a lawsuit with a People's Court or request that the State Administration for Market Regulation handle the dispute.

13.2.13.3 Preservation Measures

A trademark registrant or a stakeholder may apply to the People's Court for taking preservation measures prior to filing a lawsuit pursuant to the law under the following situations:

- Where it can be proven that the infringement in process or to be conducted on the exclusive right to use the registered trademark will cause irreparable damage to its legal interests if it is not stopped promptly, a trademark registrant or stakeholder may apply to the People's Court to take preservation measures, such as to cease relevant behaviours and carry out property preservation prior to filing a lawsuit.
- The evidence may be lost or destroyed or difficult to obtain in the future.

13.2.13.4 Compensation

The compensation amount for infringement of trademarks shall be determined in accordance with the actual losses suffered by the rights holder due to the infringement. Where it is difficult to determine the actual losses, the compensation amount may be determined in accordance with the gains derived by the infringer from the infringement. If the losses of the rights holder or the gains derived by the infringer are difficult to determine, the compensation amount shall be determined reasonably with reference to the multiples of the licensing fee of the said trademark.

For malicious infringement of trademarks, in serious cases the compensation amount shall be determined in accordance with the aforesaid method based on one to five times the determined amount.

Where it is difficult to determine the actual losses suffered by the rights holder due to the infringement or the gains derived by the infringer from the infringement or the licensing fee of the registered trademark, the People's Court shall rule on a compensation amount of not more than CNY 5 million, based on the extent of the infringement.

The amount of compensation shall include reasonable expenses of the rights owner to prevent the infringement.

Where there is a dispute over the compensation amount for infringement of exclusive rights to use trademarks, the party concerned may request mediation by the State Administration for Market Regulation and may file a lawsuit with a People's Court pursuant to the Civil Procedural Law of the People's Republic of China. Upon mediation by the State Administration for Market Regulation, where the parties concerned are unable to conclude an agreement or the mediation letter in effect is not performed, the parties concerned may file a lawsuit with a People's Court pursuant to the Civil Procedural Law of the People's Republic of China.

In the determination of the compensation amount by the People's Court, the following measures may be undertaken:

- Where the rights holder has provided proof to his best effort, and the accounts books and materials relating to the infringement are held by the infringer, the People's Court may order the infringer to provide accounts books and materials relating to the infringement
- Where the infringer does not provide accounts books and materials, or where the accounts books and materials provided are false, the People's Court may determine the compensation amount with reference to the assertion of the rights holder and the evidence provided

13.2.13.5 Non-compensation

Where the holder of a registered trademark claims for compensation and the infringer pleads a defence that such a holder has never used the registered trademark, the People's Court may request such a holder to provide proof of using the trademark over the past three years. If the holder can neither prove such usage nor evidence that it has suffered other losses due to infringement, the so-called infringer shall not be liable for compensation.

Where a seller selling goods is ignorant of infringing others' registered trademarks and can prove the legality of acquiring such goods and name the provider, such a seller shall be exempted from liabilities for compensations.

13.2.13.6 Criminal Offences

Criminal liability shall be pursued in accordance with the law if the offence constitutes a criminal offence, such as:

- the use of a trademark identical with a registered trademark on the same type of goods without licensing by the trademark registrant, and such use has constituted a criminal offence
- the forgery or unauthorised manufacturing of others' registered trademarks or sale of forged or unauthorised registered trademarks, and such activity has constituted a criminal offence
- the sale of goods bearing a counterfeited registered trademark when the seller is aware of the counterfeit, and such activity has constituted a criminal offence

13.3 Patent

The Patent Law was enacted in 1984 and revised on 17 October 2020 by the Standing Committee of National People's Congress. The revised Patent Law became effective from 1 June 2021.

13.3.1 Scope

'Invention creations' refers to inventions, utility models and designs.

'Invention' refers to any new technical solution pertaining to any or all of a product or process or the improvement thereof.

'Utility model' refers to any practical, new technical solution relating to the shape or structure, or their combination, of a product that is fit for practical use.

'Design' refers to any new design relating to the shape or pattern of a product, or a combination thereof, or a combination of colours and shapes or pattern that has a sense of aesthetics and is suitable for industrial application.

Once a patent right for an invention or utility model has been granted, unless otherwise provided by the law, no organisation or individual may, without authorisation from the patentee, exploit the patent – namely, produce, use, offer for sale, sell or import the patented product thereof for production and commercial purposes, or use the patented process, or use, offer for sale, sell or import the product directly obtained through the said patented process.

Once a patent right for design has been granted, no organisation or individual may, without authorisation from the patentee, exploit the patent – namely, produce, offer for sale, sell or import any product containing the patented design for production and commercial purposes.

13.3.2 Patentability Criteria for Inventions and Utility Models

Any invention or utility model for which a patent right is to be granted is required to meet these three criteria: novelty, creativity and practical applicability.

Novelty	Creativity	Practical Applicability
An invention or a utility model cannot be attributed to any existing technologies. No prior application to the Patent Office was filed by an organisation or individual for an identical invention or utility model before the date of the patent application, and no such application has been recorded in application documents or patent documents announced by the Patent Office after the date of the patent application.	Compared with existing technology, an invention shall possess prominent substantial features and represent notable progress. A utility model shall possess substantial features and represent any progress.	'Practical applicability' refers to an invention or a utility model that can be used or manufactured and is capable of producing positive results.

13.3.3 Patentability Criteria for Designs

Designs are only subject to the novelty criterion, as defined above, to enjoy patent protection, although a design shall possess a clear distinction from existing designs or combination of features of existing designs (any design made public in China or abroad) and shall not conflict with the legitimate rights obtained by others prior to the date of application.

13.3.3.1 Novelty Preservation

Within six months before the application date, an invention creation shall not lose its novelty in the following situations:

- It is made public for the first time for the purpose of public interest when the State is in a state of emergency or an extraordinary situation
- It is exhibited for the first time at an international exhibition sponsored or recognised by the Chinese government
- It is published for the first time at the prescribed academic or technical meeting
- It was disclosed by others without the consent of the applicant

13.3.3.2 Non-patentable Invention Creations

The following items are excluded from patentability:

- Scientific discoveries
- Rules and methods for intellectual activities
- Methods for the diagnosis or treatment of diseases
- Animal and plant varieties (but production methods for products are patentable)
- Nuclear transformation methods and substances obtained by means of nuclear transformation
- Designs used principally to identify the patterns or colours of graphic print products or on a combination of both patterns and colours
- Invention creations that violate social ethics, public morality or harm public interest
- Invention creations accomplished by reliance on genetic resources obtained or used in violation of laws and regulations

In addition to the above are any inventions filed that relate to national security or other vital interests of the State and confidentiality are required to be maintained and handled in accordance with the relevant provisions of the State.

13.3.4 Applicants

Entities established in China or PRC individuals may either directly file a patent application or entrust an agency to handle the formalities on their behalf. Applications for patents of foreign individuals, enterprises and other organisations without any habitual residence or business address in China are required to entrust a patent agent to handle the patent application and, subject to bilateral and multilateral agreements signed between the PRC and applicant's home country, where there is no agreement, the principle of reciprocity applies.

An invention creation created by an employee while performing his job duty or mainly using materials and technical resources of the entity is a service invention creation, and the right to apply for a patent therefore is vested in the entity, while the right to apply for a patent for a non-service invention creation is vested in the inventor or designer. Where inventions are made using the material or technical resources of an entity, and the entity has reached an agreement with the inventor employee on the right to apply for a patent and the ownership of the patent right for the invention, the provisions in such an agreement shall prevail.

For an invention creation made by two or more individuals or entities in collaboration, or made by an individual or entity under the entrustment of another individual or entity, the right to apply for a patent shall be vested in the individual or entity that accomplished the invention creation in collaboration, or the individual or entity that accomplished it under entrustment unless otherwise agreed by the parties concerned.

If two or more applicants apply for a patent for the same invention creation, the patent right shall be granted to the first applicant. An applicant may withdraw his application for a patent at any time before the patent right is granted.

13.3.5 Methods of Application

In general, patent applicants may submit their patent application (whether for inventions, utility models or designs) in a written form or via Internet electronic transmission.

When a patent application is filed for an invention or a utility model, the following documents shall be submitted:

- Written request specifying the name of the invention or utility model, the name of the inventor, the name or title and address of the relevant applicant and information regarding others in relation to the application
- Written description setting forth the invention or the utility model in a manner sufficiently clear and complete, so that a technician of the relevant field may carry it out (where necessary, drawings are required to be attached)
- Abstract of the invention or utility model to briefly state the main technical points
- Written claim of a description defining the extent of the patent protection in a clear and concise manner

When a patent application is filed for design, the following documents shall be submitted:

- Written request
- Pictures or photographs of the design clearly displaying the design of the product
- Brief statement of the design
- Other relevant documents

13.3.6 Date of Document Submission

The receipt date of the patent application documents by the patent administrative department is the filing date. Where the documents are sent by mail, the date when the application was mailed as indicated by the postmark shall be the filing date. All notices, decisions or other documents issued in electronic form by the Patent Office to patent applicants shall be deemed as having been delivered to the applicant upon lapse of a 15-day period from the date of issuance of the documents.

13.3.7 Right to Priority

In the event that an applicant files an application in China for a patent pertaining to the same subject within 12 months of the date it filed an application for a utility model or invention in a foreign country or within six months of the date it filed an application for a design, the applicant may enjoy the right of priority based upon any agreements concluded between the foreign country of the original application and China, international treaties that both countries are party to, or upon the principle of reciprocity. The applicant is required to submit a written declaration of the right of priority in the application process and to submit a copy of the original patent application within 16 months (in the case of invention or utility model) or three months (in the case of design) of the date of application.

Equally, the revised Patent Law 2020 permits the right of priority where an applicant files an application for a patent on the same subject within 12 months of the date the application for the invention or utility model is filed for the first time in China or within six months of the date the application for the design is filed for the first time in China. The applicant may claim the right of priority (i.e. a subsequent patent application solving the same technical problem but that may not be exactly the same as the prior patent application in the way the patent is written or described) with the China National Intellectual Property Administration (CNIPA).

13.3.8 Application in Other Countries and International Application

Chinese entities and individuals wishing to apply to foreign countries for a patent of an invention or a utility model accomplished in China are required to report to the patent administrative department for confidentiality examination.

Any Chinese individual or entity may file an international application for patent in accordance with any relevant international treaty to which China is a party. Where an applicant files an international application for a patent, he shall observe the provisions of the preceding paragraph as well, and the patent administrative department shall handle any international application in accordance with relevant international treaties to which China is a party.

Where the patent application for any invention or utility model has already been filed in a foreign country in violation of the law, the application filed for the patent in China shall not be granted.

13.3.9 Examination and Approval of Patent Applications

13.3.9.1 Examination of Utility Models and Designs

The patent administrative office shall conduct a preliminary examination of substance of the application. If there is no cause to reject the application, the patent administrative department shall grant the patent right, issue the relevant patent certificate, register the patent and make a public announcement. The patent right for the utility model or design shall be effective as of the date of announcement.

13.3.9.2 Examination of Inventions

The Patent Office shall conduct a preliminary examination to examine the application according to the relevant laws. Applications that conform to the requirements of the law shall be publicly announced within 18 months of the filing date (earlier announcement may be made upon the request of the applicant). An applicant may request an examination for the substance of the application and provide the reference materials in relation to the invention. Such a request shall be made within three years of the date of the application. Failure to request a substantive examination within the prescribed period shall result in the application being considered withdrawn. Also, the Patent Office may, at its sole discretion and when it deems necessary, proceed to examine the substance of any application for a patent for an invention.

Where the applicant has filed an application for the same patent abroad, the Patent Office may require the applicant to provide any documents supporting the application abroad or the results of any prior examination of the application. Where the applicant is unable to provide such materials without valid reason within the specified time, the application shall be deemed to have been withdrawn.

Upon completion of a substantive examination, the Patent Office shall either approve the application, grant the patent right, issue the patent certificate and make a public announcement thereof, or instruct the applicant to request a statement or amendment to the application within a specified time limit if it finds the application does not conform to the law. If the applicant concerned fails to give a response within the specified time limit without justifiable reason, the application shall be deemed to have been withdrawn, and if the Patent Office still finds that the application does not comply with the law after statement or amendment, the application shall be rejected.

13.3.9.3 Re-examination

A patent applicant who is dissatisfied with the decision of rejection by the Trademark Office may request re-examination with the Patent Re-examination Board within three months of the date of the notification of rejection. Where the applicant is dissatisfied with the decision of the Patent Re-examination Board, he may initiate proceedings in the People's Court within three months of the date of the notification of the Board's decision.

13.3.10 Term of Patent Right

The term of the patent right commences from the date of application, and different terms are applied to inventions, utility models and designs.

Inventions	Utility Models	Design
Valid for 20 years	Valid for 10 years	Valid for 15 years

Where the patent right for an invention is granted after four full years from the date of application and after three full years from the date of request for substantive examination, the Patent Office shall, at the request of the relevant patentee, grant compensatory right duration in case of any unreasonable delay in granting the patent right, except for unreasonable delay caused by the applicant.

13.3.11 Special Provisions for Pharmaceuticals

In order to make up for the time spent on review and approval of new pharmaceuticals going into the market, the patentee may request a compensatory patent term for the patents for inventions related to new pharmaceuticals that have been approved on the market in China. Such a term shall not exceed five years, and the total valid patent term after the new pharmaceutical is approved shall not exceed 14 years.

13.3.12 Annual Fee

The patentee shall pay an annual fee commencing from the year in which the patent right is granted.

13.3.13 Early Termination

The patent right can be terminated before the expiration date under the following circumstances:

- The annual fee is unpaid
- A patentee issues a written declaration waiving the patent right

13.3.14 Invalidation

Where an individual or organisation deems that a patent granted does not adhere to the law, they may request that the Patent Re-examination Board declare a patent right invalid. The Patent Re-examination Board is required to examine such a request promptly. Any decisions of the Patent Re-examination Board shall be notified to both parties, and where the patent right is declared invalid, the declaration shall be registered and announced. Either party may initiate proceedings in the People's Court within three months of the date of receipt of the notification of the decision if they are dissatisfied with the decision.

13.3.14.1 Effect of Invalidation

A patent declared invalid shall be deemed as if it never existed.

The decision on invalidating a patent right has no retroactive effect on judgments, decisions or rulings regarding patent infringements made and enforced by the People's Court or patent authorities prior to the declaration of invalidity. Therefore, where a patent infringement action has been brought in the People's Court, the invalid patent right does not affect the validity of the court ruling.

Any patent-licensing contracts or patent-transfer contracts performed prior to the declaration shall also not be affected. However, compensation shall be made for any damages caused by the patentee in bad faith, and if it constitutes blatant violation of the principle of equity, should the patent infringement damages, patent royalties or the assignment fees for patent rights not be refunded, refund shall be made fully or partly.

13.3.15 Licensing

13.3.15.1 Voluntary Licensing

Patent holders or other rights holders are permitted to voluntarily license their patent rights to others. However, before any individual or entity other than the patent holder is permitted to 'use' or 'work' a patent, they are required to enter into a written licensing agreement with the patent holder.

13.3.15.2 Compulsory Licensing

The patent administrative office may grant a compulsory licence to an individual or entity based on the application of the individual or entity that is also qualified to develop the invention or utility model. A compulsory licence can be granted under the following circumstances:

- A patentee has not implemented or fully implemented the patent without a valid reason after the patent has been granted for more than three years and after the patent application has been filed for four years
- The exercising patent rights by a patentee are determined as monopolistic acts pursuant to the law, and mandatory licensing will eliminate or reduce the negative impact
- The patent right of an invention or utility model is granted and represents major technological improvement and economic significance compared with the previous invention or utility model and its exploitation is dependent on the previous one. In such circumstances, the Patent Office may, upon request from the patentee of the later invention or utility model, grant a compulsory licence to exploit the earlier invention or utility model. If such a licence is granted to the later patentee, the earlier patentee may also apply for a compulsory licence of the later patent
- Where there is a state of national emergency or other extraordinary circumstance, or for the public interest, the Patent Office may grant a compulsory licence to exploit the patent for an invention or utility model

For the purpose of public health, a compulsory licence may be granted for manufacturing patented drugs and having them exported to countries or regions that comply with the provisions of the relevant international treaties to which the People's Republic of China has acceded.

Applications for compulsory licences must be submitted to the Patent Office together with supporting documents demonstrating that the applicant was unable to obtain a voluntary licence from the patent owner with fair terms and conditions and within a reasonable time period.

Any compulsory licence granted shall be notified to the relevant patentee and shall be registered and announced accordingly. The compulsory licence shall determine the scope and duration of exploitation based upon the reason submitted in the application for the compulsory licence. Where the reasons to grant the compulsory licence cease to exist and are unlikely to recur, the patentee may request to terminate the compulsory licence.

No individual or entity that is granted a compulsory licence is entitled to the exclusive right to exploit or the right to authorise third parties. Any individual or entity that obtains a compulsory licence shall pay reasonable royalties to the relevant patentee or in accordance with the provisions of the relevant treaties to which the PRC accedes to. Payment shall be determined by and between the two parties. Failure to reach an agreement shall result in a ruling from the Patent Office.

13.3.16 Infringement

13.3.16.1 Effect of a Patent Grant

The effect of a grant of patent rights is to vest in the patent holder the exclusive right to use the patent. As a consequence, no unit or individual may manufacture, use or sell for any production or business purpose any patented products, processes or designs without the prior permission of the patent holder. Where any of these provisions are violated, an infringement of the patent holder's rights shall be deemed to have occurred.

13.3.16.2 Scope of Protection

In determining whether conduct constituting infringement has occurred, the standard to be applied is whether or not the conduct has invaded the scope of protection of the patent holder's rights. With respect to patents for inventions and utility models, the scope of protection is that which is specified in the request for patent rights submitted by the patent holder in his application. The scope of protection for a design patent shall be confined to the design as shown in the pictures or photographs accompanying the application.

13.3.16.3 Exclusions

The following circumstances are not deemed as infringement:

- Scientific discoveries
- Where, after the sale of a patented product or products directly obtained by the patenting process by a patentee or any individual or entity permitted by the patentee, any other person uses, offers for sale, sells or imports the product
- Where, before the date of the application for a patent, an identical product has been manufactured, an identical process has been used or any necessary preparation for the manufacture or the use has been made, and the product or process shall continue to be manufactured or used within the original scope only
- Where any foreign means of transport that temporarily passes through the territory of China uses the patent concerned for its own needs in its devices and equipment, and the use is based on an agreement concluded between the country to which the foreign means of transport belongs and China, or in accordance with any international treaty to which both countries are party, or on the basis of the principle of mutual benefit
- Where the use of the patent concerned is solely for the purposes of scientific research and experimentation
- Where, for the purpose of providing information necessary for administrative approval, any party manufactures, uses or imports patent medicines or medical devices, or such items are manufactured or imported for such a party

Additionally, if for production or commercial purposes a patent-infringing product is used or sold without knowing that it was made and sold without the patentee's authorisation, the user or seller shall not be liable for compensation if it is able to prove the legal source of the product.

13.3.16.4 Actions Against Infringement

The Patent Law provides that when an alleged infringement of a party's patent rights has occurred it shall be resolved through consultation between the parties. If a party is unwilling to partake in consultation or if the consultation fails, the patent holder or any other interested party may choose to pursue a remedy through either administrative or judicial channels.

An administrative action may be brought by bringing the case before the administrative authority for patent affairs. A judicial remedy may be sought by lodging a suit directly with the People's Court.

Proceedings to seek relief against alleged infringement must be initiated within two years of the date on which the patent holder or interested party became aware of – or should have become aware of – the alleged infringing conduct.

Where an administrative remedy is sought, the administrative agency may order the infringing party to cease the infringing conduct. Parties to the case may also request that the administrative agency conduct mediation over the compensation amount for the infringed patent. Parties that are dissatisfied may appeal the administrative orders by bringing an action before the People's Court within 15 days of the date on which the order is issued. Where an infringing party does not institute proceedings, nor stops the infringement act within the time limit, the administrative agency may apply to the People's Court for compulsory enforcement.

In cases where patent holders or interested parties prove that another party is exploiting or is about to exploit or infringe upon its patent, and where, if the situation is not rectified in time, irreparable damage to its legal right cannot be avoided, the patent holders or interested parties may, before instituting legal proceedings, apply to a People's Court to adopt measures to cease such conduct and to preserve property.

Decisions of administrative and judicial authorities regarding infringement may be enforced on application to the People's Court in accordance with the provisions of the Civil Procedure Law of the People's Republic of China.

Where there is an infringement of a patent right, the amount of compensation shall be determined based on the actual loss suffered by the relevant rights holder. If it is difficult to determine the loss, the compensation shall be determined based on a multiple of the patent royalty. Where there is a deliberate infringement with serious circumstances, the amount of compensation shall be determined as between one and five times the amount of loss suffered, or where the loss cannot be determined, the multiple of the patent royalty. Where it is difficult to determine the loss or the benefit or the patent royalty, the People's Court shall – regarding factors such as type of patent right, as well as infringement nature and circumstances – determine what compensation is appropriate between CNY 30,000 and CNY 5,000,000. The amount of compensation shall further include reasonable expenses paid by the rights holder to stop the infringement.

13.3.17 Special Provisions for Pharmaceutical Patents

The revised Patent Law 2020 permits further protection for pharmaceutical patents. Both the applicant for generic drug-marketing approval and the relevant patentee or interested party are entitled to initiate an action through an early resolution mechanism to deal with patent disputes during the drug-marketing approval procedure. Specifically, the relevant parties may request that the court make a decision on whether the technical solutions for related generic drugs applied for marketing approval, fall within the protection scope of others' patented drugs, or request the China National Intellectual Property Administration (CNIPA) for an administrative ruling. The National Medical Products Administration may make a decision on whether to suspend the approval of the related generic drugs based on an effective judgment rendered by the court or the decision made by the CNIPA.

The pharmaceutical patents linkage system includes a series of systems connecting the drug-marketing approval process with the patent-right-granting-and-confirmation procedure and the patent-dispute resolution, and involves a complex collaborative system, with drug regulatory departments, patent administration departments and judicial departments involved. The purpose of the pharmaceutical patents linkage system is to set up an early resolution mechanism for pharmaceutical patent disputes in order to resolve possible patent-infringement disputes prior to the marketing of generic drugs by confirming the validity of patents for originator drugs and/or whether the technical solutions for related generic drugs fall within the scope of patent protection for the originator drugs. Thus, on the one hand, the system can avoid generic drugs infringing upon the commercial interests of the holders of the patented originator drugs after the generic drugs go to the market, which combats the long-term research-and-development enthusiasm of the original pharmaceutical companies, and on the other hand, it can prevent a situation where the supply to patients of generic drugs that go to the market cannot continue if involved in infringement disputes, which results in damage to public interest.

13.4 Copyright

The Copyright Law vests power to control copyright matters at the national level in the State Copyright Administration. The copyright administrative departments at provincial level (including in autonomous regions and directly administered municipalities) are vested with the power to administer copyright matters in their respective jurisdictions.

13.4.1 Eligibility

13.4.1.1 Chinese Persons

The Copyright Law provides protection to works of 'Chinese citizens, legal persons and other organisations of China, whether published or not'.

13.4.1.2 Foreigners and Persons Without Nationality

The Copyright Law provides protection to works by foreigners and persons without nationality that are 'first published' in the territory of the PRC, while the works of 'foreign persons' and 'persons without nationality' published outside China enjoy protection under bilateral agreements signed between China and the country, or usual country of domicile of the author, or under international conventions to which both China and the aforesaid country are participants.

13.4.2 Protected Subject Matter

13.4.2.1 Works

Works protected under the Copyright Law shall refer to intellectual creations with originality in the realm of literature, art or science that can be represented in a certain form, such as:

- writings
- oral works
- musical, dramatic and folk art, and dance and acrobatic artistic works
- works of fine art and architectural works
- photographic works
- film works and other similar works
- engineering designs, product designs, maps, schematic diagrams and other graphic works and model works
- computer software
- other works stipulated by laws and administrative regulations

When exercising copyright, copyright holders shall not violate the Constitution and the laws, or harm public interest. The State shall supervise and regulate the publication and dissemination of works pursuant to the law.

The Copyright Law explicitly excludes the following subject matter from copyright:

- Laws, regulations and administrative or judicial documents, and their official translations
- Pure factual information
- Calendars, numerical tables, forms in common use and formulas

Copyright of a work is stipulated to be vested in the person who created the work (i.e. the author).

Where a work is created according to the will or under the charge and responsibility of a legal person or other organisation, the copyright shall belong to the legal person or other organisation. Exceptions to these rules include (but are not limited to) the following:

- Cinematographic, television, video and sound recordings, the copyrights of which are vested in the producers of such works; but screenwriters, directors, cinematographers, lyricists, composers and other authors shall have the right of authorship to the said work and have the right to obtain remuneration there-from
- Adaption, translation annotation or arrangement of pre-existing work shall be owned by the adaptor, provided the exercise of such copyright does not prejudice the original work
- Collections of several works, portions of works or data or other materials by reason of the selection and arrangement of their contents that reflect original-ity shall be works of collections. The copyright in a work of collection shall be owned by the maker of such a collection, provided that such a collection does not prejudice the copyright in each of the collected works
- The ownership of copyright in commissioned works is to be governed by the contract between the parties. Failing the conclusion of a contract, the copy-right vests in the commissioned party

13.4.2.2 Occupational Works

'Occupational work', which is a distinct category of work, is defined as a 'work created by a citizen in order to accomplish a task assigned to him' by a legal person or a non-legal person.

Subject to the exceptions discussed in the next paragraph, copyright of occupational works vests in the author, although the employer enjoys 'priority in using such works within his scope of business'. For two years after the completion of a work made during employment, the author may not permit any third party to use the work in the same manner it is used by the employer without the consent of the employer. For any of the following works made during employment, the author shall enjoy the right of authorship, and the employer shall enjoy other rights and may pay renumeration to the author:

- Engineering design plans, product design drawings, maps, schematic diagrams, computer software and other works made during employment that were created mainly by using the material and technical conditions provided by the employer, and for which the employer assumes responsibility
- Works created by a staff member of a newspaper office, periodicals office, news agency, radio station or television station
- Other works of which the copyright belongs to the employer as per the laws and administrative regulations or a contract

13.4.3 Moral Rights and Economic Rights

Copyright refers to the following moral rights and economic rights held by a copyright owner:

a) The right of publication (decide whether or not to publish a work)
b) The right of authorship (claim authorship of a work by indicating their own name as the author)
c) The right of modification (modify or authorise others to modify a work)
d) The right of integrity (protect a work against misrepresentation and distortion)
e) The right of reproduction (reproduce a work by means of printing, photocopying, rubbing, sound-recording, videotaping, or photographic reproduction, etc.)
f) The right of distribution (provide the original or reproduction of a work by selling, giving, etc.)
g) The right of leasing (lease a work – namely, permitting another party to pay for the temporary use of a film work or other similar works and computer software (excluding computer software specifically marked as not for lease))

h) The right of exhibition (exhibit the original or copies of an artwork or photographic work)

i) The right of performance (publicly perform a work and use various mediums to publicly broadcast the performance of a work)

j) The right of projection (publicly represent an art, photographic or film work, or other similar work, by means of technical equipment, such as a film projector or slide projector, etc.)

k) The right of broadcasting (communicate or relay a work to the public by wired or wireless channels, excluding the right of communication by information networks)

l) The right of communication via information networks (make a work available to the public by wired or wireless channels so that the public can access it at a place and time of their choice)

m) The right of cinematisation (fix a work on a medium by the method of producing an audiovisual work)

n) The right of adaptation (adapt a work so as to create a new and creative work)

o) The right of translation (convert a written work from one language to another)

p) The right of compilation (select or arrange works or extracts of works to be compiled into a new work)

q) Other rights that shall be enjoyed by the copyright holder

13.4.4 Duration of Protection

There is no limit on the term of protection of an author's rights of authorship, modification and integrity of his work.

The right of publication and rights listed in the above items e) to q) for works of a natural person are protected for the duration of the author's lifetime and 50 years afterwards, ending on 31 December of the fiftieth year after the author's death. Where there is a joint ownership, the protection period shall continue for 50 years from the death of the last surviving author.

Regarding works of legal persons or other organisations and audiovisual works, the right of publication shall be protected for a term of 50 years after completion of such works (ending on 31 December of the fiftieth year). The rights in the above items e) to q) shall be protected for 50 years from first publication (ending on 31 December of the fiftieth year). If such work is not published within 50 years after its completion, it shall no longer be protected.

13.4.5 Restriction of Rights

In the following circumstances, a work may be used without permission or remuneration, provided that the name of the author and/or title of the work is indicated. The normal use of such a work shall not be affected and the legitimate rights and interests of the copyright owner shall not be unreasonably harmed.

- Use of a work that is published by others for personal learning, research or appreciation
- Appropriate citation of a work published by others in a work for the purpose of introduction or commentary of a certain work or explanation of a certain issue
- Inevitable representation or citation of a published work on media (such as newspapers, periodicals, radio stations, television stations, etc.) for the reporting of current-affairs news
- Publication by media (such as newspapers or periodicals) or broadcasting by media (such as radio stations, television stations, etc.) of articles on current affairs pertaining to politics, economics and religious issues published by other media (such as newspapers, periodicals, radio stations, television stations, etc.), except where the author has stated that publication or broadcasting is not permitted
- Publication or broadcasting by media (such as newspapers, periodicals, radio stations, television stations, etc.) of speeches made to the public, except where the author has stated that publication or broadcasting is not permitted
- Translation or replication of small quantities of published works for use by teaching or scientific research personnel in classroom teaching or scientific research at schools, provided that publication and distribution shall be prohibited
- Use of published works by state agencies, within a reasonable scope for execution of official duties
- Replication by libraries, archives, memorials, museums, art galleries, etc. of works collected by them for the purpose of display or preservation
- Gratis performance of published works to the public for free, and no remuneration is paid to the performers, with no profiting purpose
- Copying, drawing, photographing and video-recording of artworks installed or displayed at outdoor public premises
- Translation of Chinese language works published by Chinese citizens, legal persons or any other organisations into minority language works for publication and distribution in China
- Translation of published works into Braille for publication

Use of others' works by publishers, performers, producers of audiovisual recordings, radio stations, television stations, etc., pursuant to the relevant provisions of the law, shall not infringe the author's right of authorship, right of revision, right to preserve the integrity of the work and right to receive remuneration.

13.4.6 Copyright Licensing and Transfer

A licensing contract shall be concluded with the copyright holder for use of the work of others unless otherwise stipulated by the law. A contract licensing usage shall include the following main contents:

- Type of rights licensed for usage
- Whether the rights licensed for usage are exclusive or non-exclusive rights
- Geographical scope and period of licensing usage
- Standards and method for payment of remuneration
- Default liability
- Any other contents deemed necessary by both parties

A written contract shall be concluded for the transfer of rights stipulated in item (e) to item (q) of the copyright owner list. A rights transfer contract shall include the following main contents:

- Name of the work
- Types of rights transferred and geographical scope
- Transfer price
- Date and method for payment of transfer price
- Default liability
- Any other contents deemed necessary by both parties

In the event of pledge of copyright, the pledgor and the pledgee shall complete pledge registration formalities with the copyright administrative authorities of the State Council. Rights not specified by the copyright holder for licensing, and transfer in a contract thereof shall not be exercised by the counterparty without the consent of the copyright holder.

The standards for payment of remuneration for use of the work may be agreed by the parties concerned, or the parties concerned may pay remuneration pursuant to the standards for payment of remuneration formulated by the copyright administrative authorities of the State Council jointly with the relevant authorities. Where there is no specific agreement between the parties concerned, remuneration shall be paid pursuant to the standards for payment of remuneration formulated by the copyright administrative authorities of the State Council jointly with the relevant authorities.

13.4.7 Publication of Books, Newspapers and Periodicals

Books	Newspapers and Periodicals
A book publisher proposing to publish a book is required to enter a publishing contract with the copyright holder and pay remuneration. The publication right of the book publisher, pursuant to contractual agreement with the copyright holder, shall be protected by the law, and others are prohibited to publish the work. The copyright holder shall deliver the work within the period stipulated in the contract, and the book publisher shall publish the books pursuant to the publication quality and deadline stipulated in the contract. Where the book publisher fails to publish the books within the period stipulated in the contract, it shall bear civil liability due to breach of contract. The book publisher shall notify the copyright holder of reprint or publication of a new edition of the work and pay remuneration. Where the book publisher refuses to reprint or publish a new edition after the books are sold out, the copyright holder shall have the right to terminate the contract.	The copyright holder may submit the same manuscript to another newspaper publisher or periodical publisher under the following circumstances unless otherwise agreed between both parties: • The newspaper publisher fails to notify the copyright holder of the decision to publish the manuscript within 15 days of the date of submission of the manuscript • The periodical publisher fails to notify the copyright holder of the decision to publish the manuscript within 30 days of the date of submission of the manuscript

13.4.7.1 Rights of Publishers

Book publishers may modify a work with the consent of the author.

Newspapers and periodicals may modify the wordings of a work, but any content modification shall be subject to the author's consent. For a published work, other newspaper or periodical publishers may reprint the work or publish the work in the form of digest or material, provided that remuneration shall be paid to the copyright holder unless the copyright holder states that the work cannot be reprinted or extracted.

A publisher shall have the right to license or prohibit others' use of layout designs of books and periodicals published by the publisher. The period of protection of such rights shall be ten years and shall expire on 31 December of the tenth year following the first publication of the book or periodical that uses the said layout design.

13.4.7.2 Special Provisions

Publication of a work created from adaptation, translation, annotation, collation or compilation of an existing work; the consent of the copyright holder of the adapted, translated, annotated, collated or compiled work; and the consent of the copyright holder of the original work shall be obtained, and remuneration shall be paid.

Except where the author has stated prohibited prior use, compilation and publication of textbooks for nine-year compulsory education and national educational planning, compilation of parts of published works or short literary works, musical works, or single artwork or photographic works in textbooks shall not require licensing by the copyright holder. Although remuneration shall be paid pursuant to the provisions, the name of the author and the title of the work shall be stated, and other rights enjoyed by the copyright holder pursuant to this law shall not be infringed.

13.4.8 Public Performance

13.4.8.1 Consent

Consent of the copyright holder shall be obtained and remuneration paid for the performance of another's work. In terms of an organised performance, the organiser shall be responsible for such duties.

Performers shall enjoy the following rights in their performance:

1) State the identity of the performers.
2) Protect the image of the performance from distortion.
3) License others to make live broadcast and public transmission of a live performance, and receive remuneration.
4) License others to make audiovisual recordings, and receive remuneration.

5) License others to replicate or distribute audiovisual recordings that contain the performance, and receive remuneration.

6) License others to transmit the performance to the public through an information network, and receive remuneration.

A licensee who uses a work in a manner stipulated in points 3 to 6 of the preceding list shall also obtain the consent of the copyright holder and pay remuneration.

13.4.9 Sound and Visual Recordings

Creators of sound and/or visual recordings are required to obtain permission and pay remuneration to the copyright holder. Any work created from the adaption, translation, annotation or arrangement of a pre-existing work, shall obtain permission and pay remuneration to both the copyright holder for the adaption, translation, annotation or arrangement and the copyright holder of the original work.

The conclusion of a contract is required for sound and/or visual recordings of a performance between the performer and recorder. The maker can license any reproduction, distribution or lease of recordings of sound and/or visual to the public and obtain remuneration therefrom. Such a licensee who copies, distributes or disseminates audio and video recordings to the public through an information network shall obtain the permission of both the copyright owner and the performer and pay remuneration. A licensee who leases audio and video recordings shall also obtain permission from the performer and pay remuneration.

13.4.10 Broadcasts by Radio and Television Broadcasting Stations

Any radio or television broadcast of an author's unpublished work, cinematographic work or work created by an analogous process shall obtain permission and pay remuneration to the copyright holder, although only the remuneration is required for the radio or television broadcast of a published work or sound recording.

A radio or television broadcast shall have the right to prohibit the following acts carried out without its permission:

- Any rebroadcast of its radio or television broadcasts
- Any recordings of its radio or television broadcasts onto a sound and/or visual medium and the reproduction thereof
- Any distribution of its radio or television broadcasts via information networks

13.4.11 Infringement Liability

The Copyright Law lists acts of infringement that can result in civil liability, including injunctions, compensation and the compulsory offering of public apologies by infringers. Such acts include the following:

Violations

- Unauthorised publication of a work
- Publication of a joint work by an author without attribution to the other joint author(s)
- Affixing one's name to another's work in pursuit of personal gains
- Misrepresentation or distortion of a work
- Plagiarism of another's work: Adapting, compiling, broadcasting or performing a work without authorisation from the copyright owner (except as otherwise provided in the law)
- Use of a work without payment of remuneration required under regulations
- Renting films, computer software or audiovisual recordings without the consent of the copyright holder (except as otherwise provided in the law)
- Using the format design of a published book or periodical without the consent of the publisher
- Broadcasting directly from a performance site, broadcasting a live performance to the public or recording a performance without the consent of the performers
- Other infringements of copyright and neighbouring rights

Specific violations shall also result in fines issued by the copyright administration department, as well as confiscation of unlawful income. In case of a serious offence, main materials, tools, equipment, and so forth may also be confiscated. These acts include the following:

Violations

- Copying, distributing, performing, screening, broadcasting or compiling works or broadcasting works to the public over an information network without the consent of the copyright holder
- Publishing a book over which another party holds the exclusive right of publication
- Copying or distributing audiovisual recordings of performances or broadcasting performances to the public over an information network without the consent of the performers

Violations

- Copying or distributing recorded audiovisual recordings or broadcasting such to the pubic over an information network without the consent of the producer
- Copying or distributing radio or television programmes without the permission of the producer
- Deliberately ignoring or disrupting the technical measures taken by the rights holder to protect the copyright or related rights of his works or audio-visual recordings without the consent of the rights holder
- Deliberately deleting or altering the electronic copyright management data of works or audiovisual recordings without the consent of the copyright holder
- Producing and selling fake works that use another's name

14 Current: Technology Transfer

14.1 Introduction

Technology transfer is primarily governed by the Civil Code of the People's Republic of China (Civil Code), adopted on 1 January 2021, and the Foreign Trade Law of the People's Republic of China (Foreign Trade Law), adopted by the Standing Committee of the NPC on 12 May 1994 and last revised on 7 November 2016.

Apart from the national laws, there are also regulations and administrative measures stipulating the implementation of technology transfer to and from China.

14.1.1 Scope

'Technology import and export' refers to the acts of transferring technology from outside the territory of China into the territory of China, or vice versa. Transfer can be conducted through trade, investment, or economic and technical cooperation, and the mode of acquisition of the technology may include any of the following:

- Assignment of patent rights
- Assignment of the rights to apply for patents
- Licensing of patent exploitation
- Assignment of technical secrets
- Provision of technical services
- Other forms of transfer of technology

14.1.2 Qualified Technology Transfer

Technology transfer is required to fulfil the following criteria:

- Conform with state industry policies
- Conform with science and technology policies and social development policies
- Benefit the promotion of China's scientific and technological advancement and the development of foreign economic and technological cooperation and independence
- Benefit the safeguard of China's economic and technological rights and interests

14.1.2.1 Categories of Technologies

Technology transfers are classified into three categories: prohibited import and export technologies, restricted import and export technologies, and free import and export technologies, which may be imported and exported without restriction. Import and export of restricted technology is subject to licence control. Free import and export technology may be imported or exported without licence, but the import or export contract must be registered. As in many other countries, import of advanced and appropriate technology is encouraged.

Technology transfer may be prohibited or restricted for any of the following reasons:

- To safeguard national security, public interest or public morals
- To protect human health and safety, the lives and health of animals and plants, or the environment
- To implement gold and silver import/export measures
- Where there is a shortfall in the domestic supply of natural resources, or to effectively protect important natural resources that are in danger of depletion
- Where there is limited market capacity in the importing country or region
- Where there are serious disruptions to the order of export operations
- To establish or speed up the establishment of specific domestic industries
- Where there is an involvement of agricultural, livestock or fishery products
- To secure China's international financial status and a balance of payment
- To comply with international treaties and agreements to which China is a signatory or participant
- Other reasons in accordance with the relevant laws and administrative regulations

14.1.3 Technology Transfer Contracts

Transfer contracts must be in writing and generally contain clauses specifying the name of the project; the content, scope and requirements of the object; the plan, place and manner of performance; the confidentiality of technological information and materials; the ownership over the technological achievements and the method of proceed distribution; the criteria and method of inspection for acceptance; interpretation of terminologies; and the like.

A technology contract that illegally monopolises technologies or infringes upon others' technological work products is invalid. Such illegal monopoly includes:

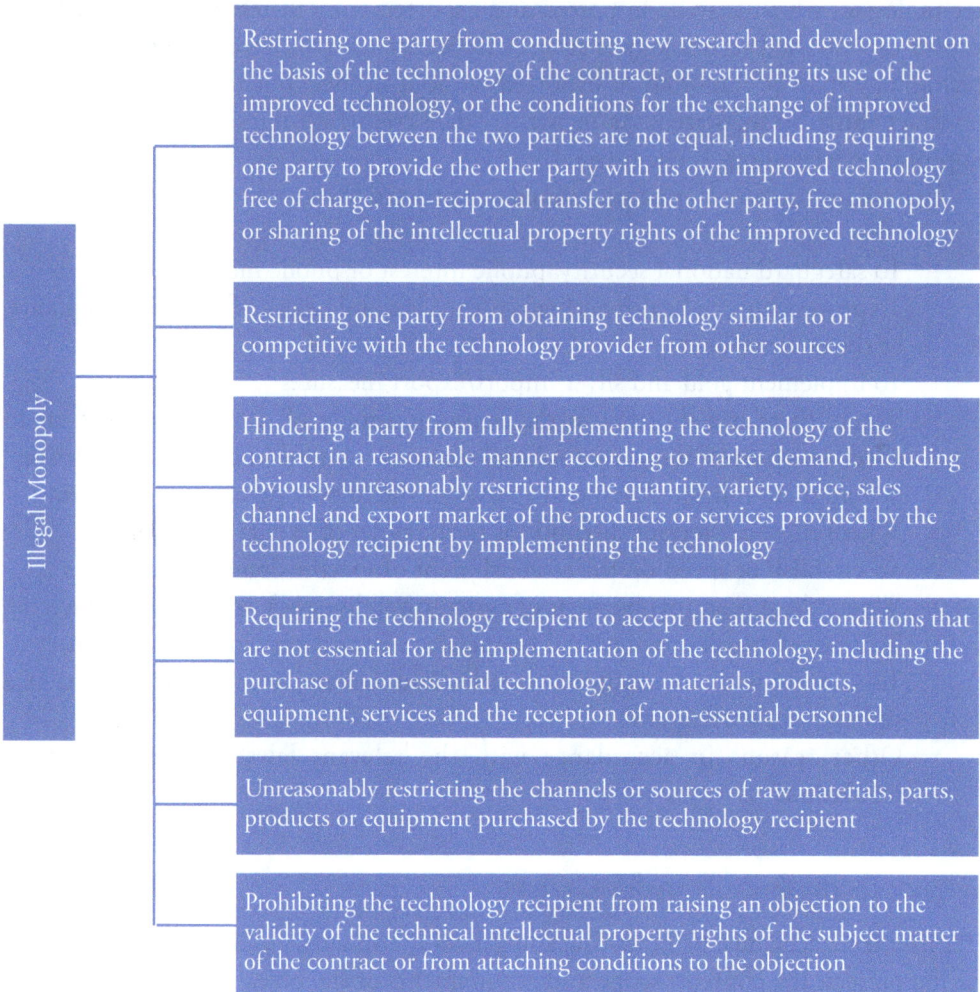

Illegal Monopoly

- Restricting one party from conducting new research and development on the basis of the technology of the contract, or restricting its use of the improved technology, or the conditions for the exchange of improved technology between the two parties are not equal, including requiring one party to provide the other party with its own improved technology free of charge, non-reciprocal transfer to the other party, free monopoly, or sharing of the intellectual property rights of the improved technology

- Restricting one party from obtaining technology similar to or competitive with the technology provider from other sources

- Hindering a party from fully implementing the technology of the contract in a reasonable manner according to market demand, including obviously unreasonably restricting the quantity, variety, price, sales channel and export market of the products or services provided by the technology recipient by implementing the technology

- Requiring the technology recipient to accept the attached conditions that are not essential for the implementation of the technology, including the purchase of non-essential technology, raw materials, products, equipment, services and the reception of non-essential personnel

- Unreasonably restricting the channels or sources of raw materials, parts, products or equipment purchased by the technology recipient

- Prohibiting the technology recipient from raising an objection to the validity of the technical intellectual property rights of the subject matter of the contract or from attaching conditions to the objection

14.1.3.1 Registration of Contracts

All technology import/export contracts are required to be registered with the Ministry of Commerce or the competent authorities in charge of commerce at provincial level or cities with independent planning, dependent on the types of contracts involved. Contracts of free import and export technology can be delegated to departments of commerce at lower levels.

14.1.3.1.1 Lawful-owner Requirement

The assignor of the technology must guarantee it is the 'lawful owner' of the technology, or the one with the right to transfer or authorise the use of the technology. In the event that an assignee is accused of an infringement by a third party when using technology provided by the assignor in accordance with their contract, the assignor is obliged to assist the assignee in removing any obstacles. If the assignee's use of the technology constitutes an infringement of the third party's legal rights and interests, the assignor must bear responsibility.

14.1.3.1.2 Technology Requirement

The technology provided by the assignor must be complete, accurate, effective and able to fulfil the technical objectives specified in the contract.

14.1.3.1.3 Technology Improvement

Improvements made to technology during the term of the contract belong to the improving party. Thereafter, the assignor and assignee may negotiate the continued use of the technology in accordance with the principles of fairness and equity.

14.1.4 Confidentiality

The Technology Transfer Regulations impose an obligation on the technology recipient to keep the technology confidential. However, this obligation is conditional on the requirement that the technology has not been made public. Moreover, the confidentiality obligation is limited to the 'scope and duration' agreed upon in the contract.

14.2 Technology Export

China encourages the exporting of 'mature industrial technology'. As in cases of technology import, no prohibited technology may be exported, and the export of restricted technologies is subject to licensing controls. The export of technologies that are subject to state control – such as nuclear technology, technology related to dual-purpose nuclear products, technology for monitoring the production of chemicals, and military technology, etc. – is regulated by separate administrative regulations.

Export of Restricted Technologies

Export of restricted technologies and their related products is subject to licensing controls. Technologies that fall within the Catalogue of Technologies Prohibited and Restricted from Export (the Catalogue), as adjusted on 28 August 2020, may not be exported or are subject to restriction and licence.

According to the joint announcement of the Ministry of Commerce and the Ministry of Science and Technology, the amendment of the Catalogue involves 53 entries.

Prohibited Entries (deleted)

- Microbial fertiliser technology (050302J)
- Chemical synthesis and semi-synthetic caffeine production technology (052701J)
- Riboflavin (VB2) production process (052702J)
- Chemical synthesis and semi-synthetic medicine production technology (052705J)

Restricted

- Veterinary drug production technology (050501X) control points 3, 4, 7, 8, 10, 12, 13, 15 and 16
- Newcastle disease vaccine technology (050508X)
- Chemical synthesis and semi-synthetic medicine production technology (052703X). Natural medicine production technology (052704X)
- Functional polymer material preparation and processing technology (052706X)
- Criminal technology (053603X) control point 4
- Medical diagnostic equipment and equipment manufacturing technology (053604X) control point 4
- Space data transmission technology (056003X) control points 1 and 3
- Information security firewall software technology (056202X)

- Silkworm species, breeding and cocoon collection and processing technology (050304J)
- Spacecraft measurement and control technology (053701J)
- Cartographic technology (054101J)
- Space data-transmission technology (056002J)
- Satellite application technology (056003J)

- Crop (including pasture) germplasm resources and their breeding technology (050101X)
- Aquatic germplasm breeding technology (050401X)
- Chemical raw material production technology (052601X)
- Biological pesticide production technology (052603X)
- Biotechnology drug production technology (052702X)
- Tissue engineering medical device product preparation and processing technology (052707X)
- Artificial crystal growth and processing technology (053104X)
- Space instrument and equipment manufacturing technology (054011X)
- Cartographic technology (054107X)
- Satellite application technology (056004X)
- Information processing technology (056101X)
- Vacuum technology (057604X)

- Artificial breeding technology of agricultural wild plants (180103X)
- Genetic engineering (genes and vectors) (180104X)
- Cashmere goat breeding technology (180302X)
- Cashmere goat breed nurturing technology (180303X)
- 3D printing technology (183506X)
- Application technology of construction machinery (183507X)
- Basic common technology of machine tool industry (183508X)
- Large-scale high-speed wind tunnel design and construction technology (183605X)
- Large-scale vibration platform design and construction technology (183606X)

- Petroleum equipment core component design and manufacturing technology (183607X)
- Large-scale petrochemical equipment basic process technology (183608X)
- Heavy machinery industry strategic new product design technology (183609X)
- Offshore island reef utilisation and safety assurance equipment technology (183708X)
- Aerospace bearing technology (183709X)
- Unmanned aerial vehicle technology (184012X)
- Laser technology (184013X)
- Large-scale power equipment design technology (184401X)
- Cryptography security technology (186103X)
- High-performance detection technology (186104X)
- Information defence technology (186105X)
- Information countermeasure technology (186106X)
- Basic software security enhancement technology (186203X)
- Space remote-sensing image-acquisition technology (187608X)

15 Current: Cyber, Data and Personal Information Protection Laws

15.1 Introduction

With the rapid development of the internet, data, and artificial intelligence, China has gradually improved relevant legislation in recent years, and a governance framework has been formed, which includes three basic laws: the Cybersecurity Law, the Data Security Law, and the Personal Information Protection Law.

The three laws have successively come into effect, jointly building and improving the fields of information protection and cybersecurity. The legal protection system is more complete, comprehensive and systematic, so as to form a standardised and orderly policy environment and create a good digital ecosystem.

15.2 Cybersecurity Law

Prior to the promulgation of the Cybersecurity Law of the People's Republic of China (Cybersecurity Law) on 1 June 2017, the provisions concerning cybersecurity were stipulated across separate laws and regulations. The Cybersecurity Law (CSL) establishes clear responsibilities of regulatory bodies and the management system framework. Under the CSL, the provisions are formulated to ensure cybersecurity through safeguarding cyberspace sovereignty, establishing responsibilities of regulatory departments and the management system framework.

15.2.1 Scope

The CSL applies to the construction, operation, maintenance and use of the network, as well as the supervision and administration of cybersecurity within the territory of the People's Republic of China. Therefore, foreign persons/entities providing services with network facilities located overseas are not subject to the CSL. However, the PRC authority may take technical measures and other necessary measures to block the transmission of any prohibited publication or transmission under the laws of the PRC from outside of the PRC.

15.2.2 Definition

'Cyber' refers to the system constituted by computers or other information terminals and relevant equipment to collect, save, transmit, exchange and process information.

'Cybersecurity' refers to taking necessary measures to prevent attacks, intrusions, interference, sabotage on the network, illicit use of the network and accidents, as well as maintaining network stability and reliable operational conditions, and the capabilities for ensuring the integrity, confidentiality and availability of the network data.

15.2.3 Cybersecurity Management Obligations

15.2.3.1 Regulatory Government Body

The Cyberspace Administration of China is established as the primary authority for the overall planning and coordination of cybersecurity work and relevant supervision and administration work. The competent telecommunication department of the State Council, public security department of the State Council, public security department and relevant authorities (determined by the relevant provisions of the State) shall protect, supervise and administrate cybersecurity within the scope of their respective responsibilities in accordance with the provisions of the CSL and other relevant laws and administrative regulations.

Overall, cybersecurity management is governed by the State and relevant government bodies under the State Council. Under the CSL the State and relevant government bodies are obligated to the following provisions:

Protect

- They must take measures to defend against and deal with cybersecurity risks and threats from both within and outside the territory of the PRC; protect key information infrastructure from attacks, intrusions, interference and damage; punish illegal criminal activities on the network in accordance with the law; and preserve cyberspace security and order
- They must protect the rights of citizens, legal persons and other organisations to use cyberspace according to the law. Specifically, a secure and healthy network environment is required for minors; any use of the network to harm the physical and psychological health of minors shall result in punitive measures according to the law
- Behaviours endangering cybersecurity can be reported to the cybersecurity administration authorities, telecommunication departments and public security departments, etc. Any department receiving a report is responsible for promptly handling such a report in accordance with the law and transferring the report to the department of the relevant jurisdiction if such a report is beyond its own responsibility

Network Security

- The State is responsible for the promotion of network access and raising the level of network service to provide the public with convenient network services and guarantee the orderly and free flow of network information in accordance with the law

Promote

- They must apply equal focus on cybersecurity and information-based development in the following: guidelines of positive use, scientific development, lawful management and security assurance; promoting the construction of cyber infrastructure and its interconnection; encouraging innovation in and application of cyber technologies; supporting the cultivation of talents in respect of cybersecurity guarantee system; and raising the ability to protect cybersecurity
- They must promote safe and reliable network products and services
- They must advocate honest, faithful, healthy and civilised cyber behaviours, advance the spreading of core socialist values and take measures to improve the awareness and level of cybersecurity of the whole of society, forming a sound environment for promoting cybersecurity with the participation of the public

Formulate Standards

- Relevant departments under the State Council shall organise the formulation of relevant national and industrial standards for cybersecurity administration and the security of network products, services and operations and make revisions at appropriate times
- They must conduct overall planning, increase the input and support key cybersecurity technology industries and projects
- They must support enterprises, research institutions, institutions of higher education and network-related industrial organisations to participate in the formulation of national and industrial cybersecurity standards

Training

- They must organise and provide regular publicity and education on cyber-security and guide, supervise and urge relevant entities to provide such publicity and education on cybersecurity in an effective way
- They must support enterprises, institutions of higher education, vocational schools and other educational training institutions to carry out cyber-security and promote the exchange of talents for cybersecurity

Development

- They must continuously improve cybersecurity strategies, specify the basic requirements and main objectives for cybersecurity protection and propose cybersecurity policies and working tasks and measures in key areas
- They must actively carry out international exchange and cooperation in the following: cyberspace governance, research and development of cyber technologies, establishment of the standards thereof and fighting against illegal crimes committed on the network and other aspects, promotion of the construction of a peaceful, safe, open and cooperative cyberspace, and establishment of a multilateral, democratic and transparent system for network governance
- They must encourage the development of technologies that protect and use network data
- They must promote the availability of public data resources and propel technological innovation and social and economic development. They must boost the construction of a socialised service system for cybersecurity and encourage enterprises and institutions concerned to provide security services such as the authentication, detection and risk evaluation of cybersecurity.

15.2.3.2 Liabilities

Where operators of government affairs for government departments fail to perform their obligations of cybersecurity protection as provisioned by the CSL, the administration at the next higher level, or relevant administration, shall order them to rectify the situation. Additionally, the governing administration shall impose sanctions on the person(s) directly in charge and other directly responsible persons.

Government departments are forbidden to abuse power or seek personal gains. Any individual in violation or neglect of duty, abuse of power or personal gains is subject to sanctions if it does not constitute a crime.

15.2.4 Network Operation Security

15.2.4.1 Definition

'Network operators' refers to owners, administrators of the network, and network service providers. In practice, network operators may also include enterprises and institutions providing services and conducting activities through networks. For example, in addition to traditional telecom operators and internet firms, network operators may also include the following:

- Financial institutions that collect citizens' personal information and provide online services, such as banking institutions, insurance companies, securities companies and foundations
- Providers of cybersecurity products and services
- Enterprises with websites and that provide network services

All network operators are required to provide technical support and assistance to the public security organs and to state security investigating crimes.

15.2.4.2 Construction and Operation

Any construction and operation of a network or provision of services through a network shall adhere to the following in accordance with the provisions of laws and administrative regulations and the mandatory national standards:

- Conduct technical measures and other necessary measures to ensure the secure and stable operation of the network
- Effectively respond to cybersecurity incidents
- Prevent illegal crimes committed on the network
- Maintain the integrity, confidentiality and availability of cyber data

15.2.4.3 Management

Network operators must ensure the network is free from interference, damage or unauthorised access and prevent network data from being divulged, stolen or falsified. Network operators are required to adhere to the following provisions in accordance with the classified protection system for cybersecurity stipulated by the State:

- Formulate internal security management systems and operating rules, determine persons responsible for network security and implement network security protection responsibility

- Adopt technological measures to prevent computer viruses, network attacks, network intrusions and other actions endangering network security
- Adopt technological measures for monitoring and recording network operational statuses and network security incidents, and follow relevant provisions to store network logs for at least six months
- Adopt measures such as data classification, backup of important data, and encryption
- Carry out other obligations as mandated by law or administrative regulations

15.2.4.4 Security

Contingency plans for cybersecurity incidents are required to be formulated by network operators. Plans shall promptly resolve system bugs, computer viruses, network attacks and intrusions, and other security risks. Where any incident endangering cybersecurity occurs, network operators shall immediately initiate contingency plans, take corresponding remedial measures and report to the relevant competent departments in accordance with the Provisions. Persons failing to implement contingency plans and prevent network data from being divulged, stolen or falsified shall be warned and ordered to rectify the violation by the relevant government department. Any refusal to rectify, or such failure endangers cybersecurity, shall result in a fine of between CNY 10,000 and CNY 100,000, and a fine of between CNY 5,000 and CNY 50,000 shall be imposed on any person(s) directly in charge and other directly responsible persons.

Any activities carried out in relation to cybersecurity testing are required to comply with the relevant regulations of the State; related activities include cybersecurity authentication, detection and risk evaluation and releasing cybersecurity information – such as system bugs, computer viruses, network attacks and intrusions – to society. Failure to carry out the above activities according to the relevant regulations of the State shall be ordered by the relevant government department to be rectified. If the circumstances are serious, a fine of between CNY 10,000 and CNY 100,000 shall be imposed and the authorities may suspend network operation, prohibit business for internal rectification, shut down the website or revoke relevant business permits or business licences. Additionally, a fine of between CNY 5,000 and CNY 50,000 shall be imposed on the person(s) directly in charge and other directly responsible persons.

Individuals and organisations are strictly forbidden to engage in activities endangering cybersecurity (including illegally invading others' networks, interfering with the normal functions of others' networks and stealing cyber data), provide programmes or tools (such as network intrusions, interference with the normal functions and protective measures of the network) and theft of cyber data. Equally, individuals and organisations are required to stop technical support, advertising promotion, payment and settlement services or other types of assistance to such persons or organisations engaged in endangering cybersecurity.

Engaging in such prohibited activities or providing support in the aforementioned manners shall result in the following if such violation does not constitute as a crime:

- Confiscation of illegal gains
- Detention of a maximum of five days (where the circumstances are considered serious, the detention period is provisioned as a minimum of five days and a maximum of 15 days)
- Possible fine of between CNY 50,000 and CNY 500,000 (where the circumstances are considered serious or the entity commits the violation, the fine imposed may be between CNY 100, 000 and CNY 1,000,000)
- Where the violation is committed by a person, the person shall be forbidden from practising cybersecurity management and taking key positions in the field of network operation either within five years for a public security offence or for life for a criminal offence
- Where the entity commits the violation, in addition to the penalties listed, the person(s) directly in charge and other directly responsible persons shall be subject to the same penalties

15.2.4.5 Cooperation

Relevant industrial organisations are required to establish and perfect cybersecurity protection regulations and coordination mechanisms for their own industry. The provisions of the law stipulate that industrial organisations shall strengthen the analysis and evaluation of cybersecurity risks, regularly provide risk warnings to their members and support and assist members in handling cybersecurity.

The State supports the cooperation among the network operators to improve their ability to safeguard security. Cooperation between network operators is encouraged in areas such as collection, analysis and reporting of cybersecurity information and emergency disposal.

In order to lawfully safeguard national security and assist crime investigation, network operators shall provide technical support and assistance to the public security organs and state security organs. Any information acquired by cyberspace administration authorities and relevant departments in the course of their fulfilment of responsibilities to protect cybersecurity shall be used exclusively for cybersecurity protection, and no other purpose. Failure to provide technical support and assistance to government departments shall be ordered to be rectified. Where the operator refuses to rectify or the circumstances are serious, a fine of between CNY 50,000 and CNY 500,000 shall be imposed, and a fine of between CNY 10,000 and CNY 100,000 shall be imposed on the person(s) directly in charge or other directly responsible persons.

Equally, where the cyberspace administration department uses the acquired information for any purposes other than cybersecurity protection, sanctions shall be imposed on the person(s) directly in charge and other directly responsible persons.

15.2.4.6 Special Provisions

15.2.4.6.1 Product Manufacturers, Security Service Suppliers and Other Service Providers

Under the CSL, products and services shall comply with compulsory national standards. In practice, cybersecurity products related to product manufacturers, security service suppliers and other organisations providing services through networks are required to respond to security flaws in products and provide security maintenance.

Cybersecurity products and services are required to abide by the following:

- Forbidden to install malwares
- Take immediate remedial measures in response to security risks, such as defects or bugs
- Provide security maintenance and shall not terminate the provision of security maintenance within the stipulated time limit or agreed time limit between the respective parties

Persons failing to implement and comply with the above provisions under the CSL shall be warned and ordered to rectify the violation by the relevant government department. Any refusal to rectify, or such failure endangers cybersecurity, shall result in a fine of between CNY 10,000 and CNY 100,000, and a fine of between CNY 5,000 and CNY 50,000 shall be imposed on any person(s) directly in charge and other directly responsible persons.

15.2.4.6.2 Critical Network Equipment

'Critical network equipment' refers to the catalogue of critical network equipment and specialised cybersecurity productions formulated and released by the Cyberspace Administration of China in concert with the relevant departments under the State Council.

Critical network equipment and specialised cybersecurity products are required, pursuant to the compulsory requirements of the relevant national standards, to pass the security certification by qualified institutions or to meet the requirements of security detection before being sold or provided.

15.2.4.6.3 Network Access and Domain Registration Providers

'Network access and domain registration providers' refers to the following:

> Network operators handling network access formalities for fixed-line or mobile phone users

> Network operators providing the user with information publication services, instant messaging services and other services

Such network operators are required to obtain the true identification of users at the time of concluding the agreement with users or at the time of confirming the provision of services. Where user operators do not provide true identification, the network operators are forbidden from providing the relevant services.

Failure to request the authentic identity information shall be ordered by the relevant government department to rectify. Where there is refusal to rectify or the circumstances are serious, a fine of between CNY 50,000 and CNY 500,000 shall be imposed and the authorities may suspend network operation, prohibit business for internal rectification, shut down the website or revoke relevant business permits or business licences. Additionally, a fine of between CNY 10,000 and CNY 100,000 shall be imposed on the person(s) directly in charge and other directly responsible persons.

15.2.5 Key Information Infrastructure

15.2.5.1 Definition

Information crucial to national security and economy is identified as key information infrastructure and is subject to specific security protection.

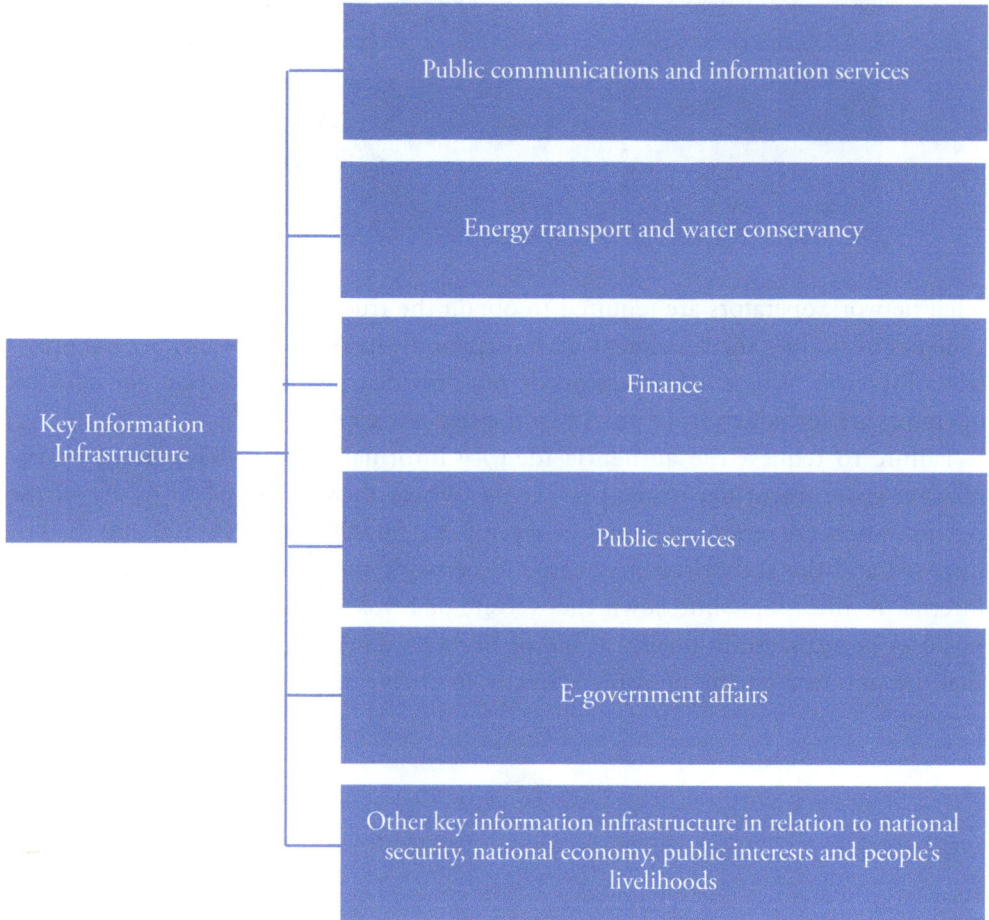

15.2.5.2 Obligations

15.2.5.2.1 Preliminary Obligations

Departments in charge of protecting the security of key information are required to respectively compile and organise the implementation of key information plans for their own industry and field. Equally, the related departments are required to guide and supervise the work related to the protection of operational security of key information infrastructure.

Any construction of key information infrastructure shall ensure there are properties to support stable and continuous operation of the business, and technical security measures are planned, established and used concurrently before the key information infrastructure is established.

15.2.5.2.2 Security Protection

In addition to the security protection provisions for network operators, key information infrastructure is required to adhere to the following:

- Set up independent security management institutions and designate persons responsible for security management whose security background, as well as that of personnel in key positions, is reviewed
- Periodically conduct cybersecurity education, technical training and skill assessment for practitioners
- Establish disaster recovery backups of important systems and databases
- Conduct by themselves, or entrust cybersecurity service institutions to conduct, the detection and assessment of cybersecurity service at least once a year
- Submit the detection and assessment situations, as well as improvement measures, to the relevant departments responsible for the security protection of key information infrastructure
- Formulate contingency plans for cybersecurity incidents and carry out drills periodically
- Other obligations stipulated by laws and administrative regulations

15.2.5.3 Third Parties

Key information infrastructures are, in accordance with the provisions, required to enter into confidential agreements with the providers when purchasing network products and services. Any confidential agreement shall clarify the obligations and responsibilities of security and confidentiality.

Where purchases of network products and services may influence national security, the purchase shall be reviewed by a security review organised by the Cyberspace Administration of China in concert with the relevant departments under the State Council. Utilisation of purchases without security examination or approval of the security examination shall be ordered by the relevant competent departments to stop using such products or services, and a fine of between one and ten times the purchase amount shall be imposed. Additionally, a fine of between CNY 10,000 and CNY 100,000 shall be imposed on the person(s) directly in charge and other directly responsible persons.

15.2.5.4 Data Storage

Personal and important data collected and produced during operations are required to be stored within the territory of the People's Republic of China. Any transfer of such information and data to an overseas party due to necessary business requirements shall pass a security assessment conducted by the Cyberspace Administration of China with the relevant departments under the State Council, although where the laws and regulations have other provisions, such provisions shall prevail.

Failure to store data or transfer data according to the provisions shall result in the following penalties from the relevant government department:

- Rectification of offence
- Warning
- Confiscation of illegal gains
- Fine of between CNY 50,000 and CNY 500,000

The relevant government authority may also impose the following penalties:

- Suspension of relevant business
- Prohibit business for internal rectification
- Shut down the website
- Revoke relevant business permits or business licences
- Fine of between CNY 10,000 and CNY 100,000 imposed on the person(s) directly in charge and other directly responsible persons

15.2.5.5 Compliance

Key information infrastructures are subject to the security protection measures conducted by the relevant departments and coordinated by the Cyberspace Administration of China. Security protection measures include the following:

- The random detection on security risks related to key information infrastructure, and the proposal of improvement measures (if necessary, entrusting professional cybersecurity service institutions to carry out detection and evaluation of any potential security risks related to the network)
- Periodically conducting emergency cybersecurity drills and enhancement to the level and ability of coordination and cooperation required to respond to cybersecurity
- Cybersecurity information-sharing among relevant government departments, key information infrastructure operators, relevant research institutions and cybersecurity institutions
- Technical support and assistance for emergency disposal of cybersecurity incidents and the recovery of network functions provided by relevant government departments

Failure to perform the obligations of cybersecurity protection shall result in a warning and an order to rectify the violation by the relevant government department. Any refusal to rectify, or such failure endangers cybersecurity, shall result in a fine of between CNY 100,000 and CNY 1,000,000, and a fine of between CNY 5,000 and CNY 50,000 shall be imposed on any person(s) directly in charge and other directly responsible persons.

15.2.6 Network Information Security

15.2.6.1 Published or Transmitted Information

The Cyberspace Administration of China and relevant departments are responsible for the supervision and management of cybersecurity information in accordance with the law. Information published or transmitted by individuals or organisations on networks are required to comply with the relevant laws and regulations.

Where prohibited information is sourced from outside the territory of the People's Republic of China, the Cyberspace Administration of China shall notify the relevant organisations to take technological measures and other necessary measures to the block the transmission. Where an overseas organisation, institution or individual engages in any activity endangering key information infrastructure of the People's Republic of China through attacks, invasions, interference or destruction resulting in serious consequences, it shall be investigated for its liabilities according to the law. The public security organ of the State Council and relevant departments may decide to freeze the assets of such an organisation, institution or individual, or take other necessary punitive measures.

15.2.6.2 Individual and Entity Obligations

Any individual or entity is responsible for the use of the network and is strictly forbidden from creating a website or establishing groups for communications of illegal and criminal activities including the following:

- Defrauding
- Passing criminal methods
- Producing or selling prohibited/controlled goods
- Disclosing information via utilising networks involving illegal and criminal activities, such as defrauding, producing or selling prohibited/controlled goods or other related illegal or criminal information

15.2.6.3 Network Operators' Obligations

Network operators are required to strengthen the management of the information published by users and establish complaint and reporting systems for network information security, disclose ways of complaint and reporting and other information, as well as promptly accept and handle complaints and reports.

Network operators are required to implement disposal measures to any violations committed by individuals or entities. Prohibited information published or transmitted is required to be stopped immediately upon discovery, and disposal measures shall be implemented, such as:

- deletion (to prevent the dissemination of the prohibited information)
- saving relevant records of the incident
- reporting the incident to the relevant competent departments

Network operators are required, according to the law, to cooperate with the supervision and detection implemented by cyberspace administration authorities and the relevant departments. If the Cyberspace Administration of China discovers the publication or transmission of prohibited information, network operators are also obliged to take the aforementioned measures. Operators refusing or impeding the supervision and detection shall be ordered to rectify. Where the operator refuses to rectify or the circumstances are serious, a fine of between CNY 50,000 to CNY 500,000 shall be imposed, and a fine of between CNY 10,000 and CNY 100,000 shall be imposed on the person(s) directly in charge or other directly responsible persons.

Persons failing to execute the aforementioned disposal measures (stopping transmission and using disposal measures to remove information or save relevant records prohibited by relevant government departments) shall be ordered to rectify, issued a warning and any illegal gains confiscated. Where the network operators refuse to rectify or the circumstances are serious, a fine of between CNY 100,000 and CNY 500,000 shall be imposed and the authorities may enforce the following:

- Suspension of relevant business
- Prohibit business for internal rectification
- Shut down the website
- Revoke relevant business permits or business licences
- Fine of between CNY 10,000 and CNY 100,000 imposed on the person(s) directly in charge and other directly responsible persons

Service providers of electronic information distribution services and application software downloads are obliged to fulfil security administration duties. Upon discovery of individuals or entities providing electronic information and application software with malwares installed or containing prohibited information, service providers shall implement the following measures:

- Deletion (to prevent the dissemination of the prohibited information)
- Save relevant records of the incident
- Report the incident to the relevant competent departments

Persons failing to fulfil security management obligations shall be ordered to rectify and be issued a warning, and any illegal gains shall be confiscated. Where the network operators refuse to rectify or the circumstances are serious, a fine of between CNY 100,000 and CNY 500,000 shall be imposed and the authorities may enforce the following:

- Suspension of relevant business
- Prohibit business for internal rectification
- Shut down the website
- Revoke relevant business permits or business licences
- A fine of between CNY 10,000 and CNY 100,000 imposed on the person(s) directly in charge and other directly responsible persons

15.2.7 Cybersecurity Monitoring, Early Warning and Emergency Disposal

15.2.7.1 Overall Monitoring

The State shall establish a cybersecurity monitoring and an early warning and information notification system. The Cyberspace Administration of China shall coordinate with the relevant departments under an overall plan to execute the following:

- Strengthen the work of collection, analysis and notification of cybersecurity information
- Uniformly release cybersecurity monitoring and early warning information in accordance with regulations
- The establishment and perfection of cybersecurity risk evaluation and emergency work mechanism
- Establish contingency plans for cybersecurity incidents
- Organise drills periodically

15.2.7.2 Key Information Infrastructure

Departments responsible for the protection of key information infrastructure shall undertake the following:

- Establish and perfect cybersecurity monitoring
- Establish and perfect an early warning and information notification system for their respective industry or field
- Submit the cybersecurity monitoring and early warning and information notification in accordance with the relevant provisions
- Formulate contingency plans for cybersecurity incidents
- Organise drills periodically

In cybersecurity contingency plans, incidents are required to be classified on the basis of factors such as degree of harm and scope of influence after the occurrence. Additionally, corresponding emergency disposal measures shall be prescribed for the incident.

15.2.7.3 Cybersecurity Incidents

15.2.7.3.1 Early Warning

Where the probability of a cybersecurity incident increases, relevant departments of the People's Government at provincial level or above shall, in accordance with the authorisation and procedures stipulated, adopt the following measures according to the characteristics and possible harm of the cybersecurity risks:

- Request relevant departments, institutions and personnel to promptly collect and report relevant information
- Strengthen the monitoring over cybersecurity risks
- Organise the relevant departments, institutions and professionals to analyse and assess cybersecurity risks and predict the occurrence likelihood, scope of influence and degree of harm from the incidents
- Release an early warning concerning cybersecurity risks to the public
- Implement measures to prevent and mitigate any harm to the public arising from the incident

Upon discovery of relatively high security risks or security incidents on the network, the relevant departments of the People's Government at provincial level or above may hold an interview with the legal representative or principals of the network operators in accordance with prescribed authorisations and procedures. Network operators shall take measures to effect rectification and eliminate hidden dangers as required.

15.2.7.3.2 Emergency Disposal

Upon the occurrence of cybersecurity incidents, the following disposal measures may be taken:

- Immediate activation of contingency plans for cybersecurity incidents
- Investigation and assessment of incidents
- Request network operators to take technical measures and other necessary measures to eliminate potential security hazards and prevent expansion of harm
- Promptly issue public-warning information affecting public society

In social emergency security incidents and in order to protect the national security and social public order, network communications within specific regions may be restricted or subject to temporary measures of a competent government department upon the decision or approval of the State Council.

Emergency incidents or work-safety accidents caused by cybersecurity incidents are handled in accordance with the Emergency Response Law of the People's Republic of China, the Work Safety Law of the People's Republic of China, and other relevant laws and administrative regulations.

15.3 Data Security Law

15.3.1 Scope

The Data Security Law (DSL) defines the scope of data to encompass both electronic and non-electronic forms. Companies that handle data – including collection, storage, use, processing, transmission, provision, and disclosure of data – shall be subject to the DSL.

15.3.2 Security Obligations for Companies Handling Data

Obligations are dependent on the type of data handled. For all companies conducting data-handling activities, the DSL stipulates the following obligations:

Non-important Data	Important Data
• Establish and perfect a data security management system across the entire workflow • Adopt lawful and proper methods in collecting data and forbid obtaining data by illegal means • Organise and conduct data security education and training • Adopt the corresponding technical measures and other necessary measures to ensure data security • Take immediate disposal measures, notify users as required and report the matter to the relevant competent department	• Specify responsible personnel and management bodies for data security • Designate a data security officer and establish a data security management body

For companies handling data classified as important data, the following obligations are provisioned.

The data security management body is led by the data security officer and shall perform the following responsibilities:

- Studying and making recommendations for major decisions related to data security
- Developing and implementing data security protection plans and data security incident emergency response plans
- Conducting data security risk monitoring and disposing of data security risks and incidents promptly
- Organising activities such as data security awareness, education and training and risk assessment, and conducting emergency drills regularly
- Receiving and disposing of data-security-related complaints and reports
- Reporting data security situations to cyberspace authorities and other competent or regulatory authorities promptly as required

The data security officer is a significant role and shall hold relevant data security expertise and management experience. Additionally, they shall be a member of the data processor's decision-making level and be authorised to directly report data-security situations to cyberspace authorities and other competent or regulatory authorities.

15.3.3 Important Data

The DSL identifies two types of data subject to stricter data management and legal liabilities. Firstly, core data is defined as related to national security, the lifelines of the national economy, important aspects of people's livelihood, and major public interests and shall be subject to stricter management. Secondly, the catalogue of important data shall be formulated by the relevant department under the coordination of the data security mechanism of the state. All regions and departments shall, in accordance with the data classification and classification protection system, determine the specific catalogue of important data in their own regions, departments and related industries and fields, and focus on the protection of the data included in the catalogue.

Currently, there are two regulations for comment that specify the general definitions of data grading:

1 The Draft Administration Regulations on Network Data Security

Data Classification		
Ordinary	Important data	Core data

2. Practice Guidelines for Cybersecurity Standards

Data Level	Details
Level One Data	If data is leaked and misused, there are no damages to the legitimate rights and interests of individuals and organisations.
Level Two Data	If data is leaked and misused, there are minor damages to the legitimate rights and interests of individuals and organisations.
Level Three Data	If data is leaked and misused, there are ordinary damages to the legitimate rights and interests of individuals and organisations.
Level Four Data	If data is leaked and misused, there are severe damages to the legitimate rights and interests of individuals and organisations.

The Measures for the Security Assessment of Outbound Data Transfers (the Measures), effective from 1 September 2022, regulates outbound data transfers. The Measures published by the Cyberspace Administration of China supplements the Data Security Law and Personal Information Protection Law, adopted in 2021, by setting forth the security assessment obligations for companies in China transferring data abroad. Although the Measures mainly applies to companies deemed as critical information infrastructure operations or those handling personal information of more than 1 million individuals, **companies should be aware of the legal obligations, since the Measures includes a catch-all clause in the applicable scope.**

15.3.3.1 Applicable Scope

Mainly, the security assessment applies to two types of data handlers who transfer abroad important data and/or personal information collected and generated in the territory of the People's Republic of China:

1. Critical information infrastructure operators (CIIOs)	2. Personal information handlers that have processed personal information of more than 1 million individuals

For companies that do not fall within the above scope, a security assessment is still applicable to those companies meeting one of the following conditions:

- Transferring important data abroad
- Transferring personal information of more than 100,000 individuals, cumulatively from 1 January of the preceding year
- Transferring sensitive personal information of more than 100,000 individuals, cumulatively from 1 January of the preceding year

15.3.3.2 Other Situations Stipulated by the State Internet Information Department that Require Security Assessment

15.3.3.2.1 Applicable Data

Mandatory security assessments concern four types of data, which may cross over. For companies, conducting a data assessment, clarification is essential to understanding the types of data processed and whether a security assessment is required.

15.3.3.2.1.1 Critical information infrastructure operators (CIIOs)

The Regulations on the Security and Protection of Critical Information Infrastructure defines CIIOs as companies engaged in 'important industries or fields', including the following:

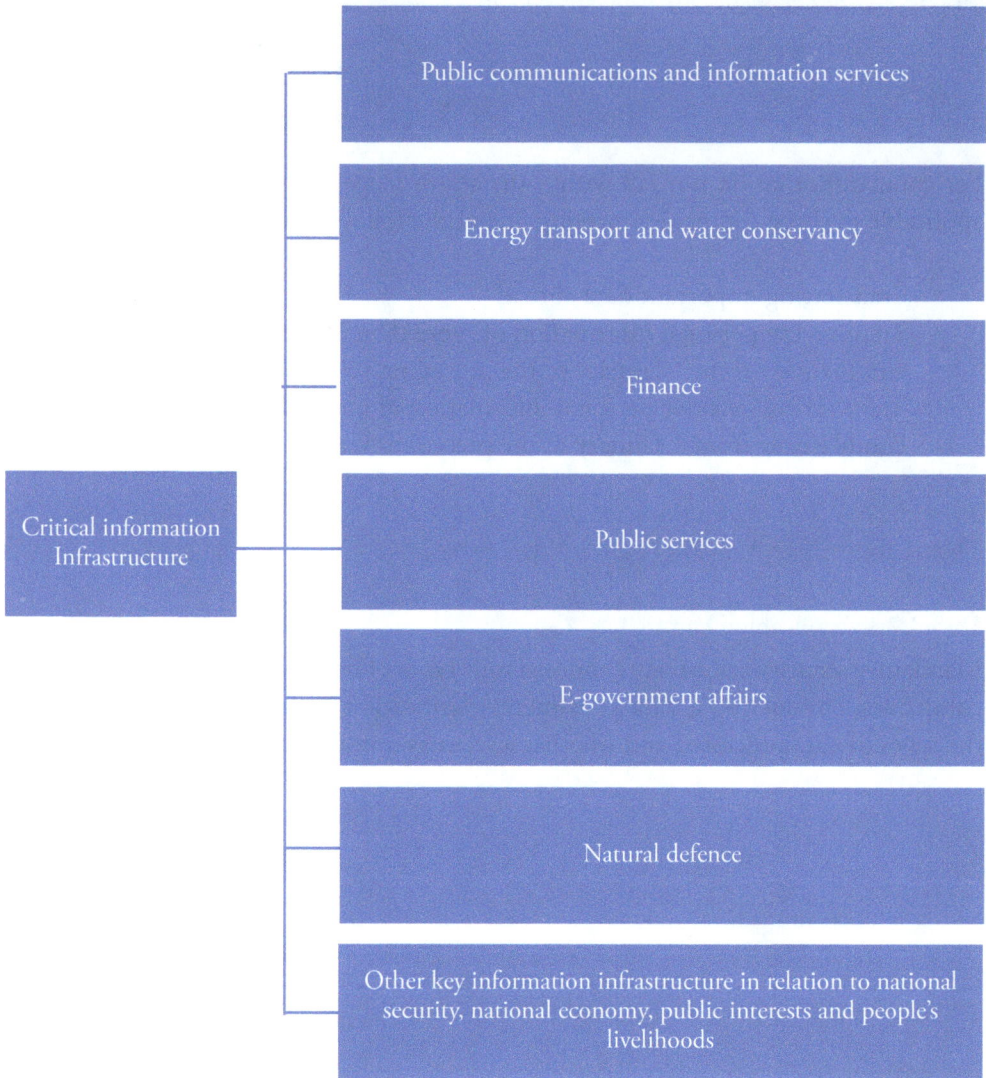

```
                                  ┌────────────────────────────────────────┐
                              ────┤ Public communications and information services │
                             │    └────────────────────────────────────────┘
                             │    ┌────────────────────────────────────────┐
                              ────┤ Energy transport and water conservancy  │
                             │    └────────────────────────────────────────┘
                             │    ┌────────────────────────────────────────┐
                              ────┤ Finance                                 │
 ┌──────────────────┐        │    └────────────────────────────────────────┘
 │ Critical information │     │    ┌────────────────────────────────────────┐
 │ Infrastructure    ├────────────┤ Public services                         │
 └──────────────────┘        │    └────────────────────────────────────────┘
                             │    ┌────────────────────────────────────────┐
                              ────┤ E-government affairs                    │
                             │    └────────────────────────────────────────┘
                             │    ┌────────────────────────────────────────┐
                              ────┤ Natural defence                         │
                             │    └────────────────────────────────────────┘
                             │    ┌────────────────────────────────────────┐
                              ────┤ Other key information infrastructure in relation to national │
                                  │ security, national economy, public interests and people's │
                                  │ livelihoods                             │
                                  └────────────────────────────────────────┘
```

Most foreign companies are unlikely to be deemed a CIIO except those engaged in the energy or finance sectors.

15.3.3.2.1.2 Important data

The Measures echoes the Data Security Law by defining 'important data' as data that may endanger national security, economic operation, social stability, or public health and safety once tampered with, destroyed, leaked, or illegally obtained or used. Companies should also note that specific important data catalogues shall be formulated by each region and department under the Data Security Law. Therefore, companies should be prepared for forthcoming details related to their industry and region.

15.3.3.2.1.3 Personal Information

Personal information refers to any kind of information related to an identified or identifiable natural person as electronically or otherwise recorded, excluding information that has been anonymised.

For companies, personal information is mainly handled by the human resources, finance and marketing departments.

15.3.3.2.1.4 Sensitive Personal Information

The Personal Information Protection Law classifies the following as sensitive personal information:

- Religious beliefs
- Biometrics
- Specific identities, medical and health
- Financial accounts, whereabouts and other information of a natural person
- Personal information of minors under the age of 14

15.3.4 Security Assessment Procedure

Security assessments are required to be submitted to the local cyberspace administration and forwarded to the Cyberspace Administration of China (CAC) for assessment and approval. The assessment and approval are provisioned as 57 days maximum from the submission date, though the authorities may require further supplementary materials or return materials with deficiencies. Assessment results are valid for two years and shall be reapplied 60 working days before the expiration date.

15.3.4.1 Conducting Self-assessment

Applicants are required to conduct a self-assessment of the export of data as part of the security assessment application. The self-assessment focuses on the risks posed by the data export to national security and the personal rights of the individuals and organisations of the collected data. The Measures stipulate that applicants shall consider the following points in the self-assessment:

- The legality, legitimacy and necessity of the purpose, scope and method of the cross-border data transfer, and the processing of the data by the overseas recipient
- The scale, scope, type and sensitivity of the data being transferred, and the possible risks that the cross-border data transfer could pose to China's national security, public interests and the legal rights of individuals and organisations
- The responsibilities and obligations undertaken by the overseas recipient [of the data], and whether the management and technical measures and capabilities for fulfilling the responsibilities and obligations can ensure the security of outbound data
- The risk of the data being tampered with, destroyed, leaked, lost, transferred or illegally obtained or used during the overseas transfer or after it exits the country, and whether the channels for safeguarding the rights and interests of the subjects of personal information are unobstructed
- Whether or not the data-export-related contracts or other legally binding documents (hereinafter collectively referred to as 'legal documents') that are entered into with the overseas recipient fully stipulate the responsibility and obligations of data protection
- Other matters that may affect the security of data export

15.3.4.2 Material Submission

Applicants are required to submit the following material for the security assessment:

- A declaration
- A self-assessment report
- A data processing agreement between the data controller and the foreign recipient
- Other materials required for safety-assessment work

15.3.4.3 Security Assessment and Re-assessment

In the security assessment, the CAC shall also consider the following:

- The impact of data security protection policies and regulations and the network security environment of the country or region where the foreign recipient is located
- Whether the level of data protection of the foreign recipient meets the requirements of the laws and administrative regulations of the PRC and mandatory national standards
- Compliance with the laws of the PRC, administrative regulations and departmental rules
- Other matters that the CAC deems necessary to be assessed

Where the assessment is rejected, a re-assessment can be applied for within 15 working days of the assessment result. However, the re-assessment result is final, and no further appeal is permitted.

15.3.4.4 Amendments

During the assessment validity period, companies are required to notify the authorities if any of the following changes occur:

- Changes to the purposes, methods, scope and types of data exported, as well as the purposes and methods for which foreign recipients process data that affect the security of exported data or extend the period of overseas retention of personal information and/or important data
- Changes in the data security protection policies, regulations and network security environment of the country or region where the foreign recipient is located, as well as other *force majeure* circumstances, such as changes in the actual control of the data controller or the foreign recipient, changes in the legal documents of the data controller and the foreign recipient, and other changes that affect the security of exported data
- Other circumstances that affect the security of exported data

Where the CAC finds that the approved cross-border transfer no longer meets the security requirements for transferring data, the transfer can be terminated. In such a case, the company shall rectify and resubmit the security assessment.

15.4 Personal Information Protection Law

The Personal Information Protection Law (PIPL) was officially adopted by the Standing Committee of the National People's Congress on 20 August 2021 and was effective from 1 November 2021. The PIPL has formulated very strict norms for the protection of personal information and is widely applicable. It can be said that it covers all enterprises (because enterprises will at least collect the information of their employees). At the same time, since it adopts the dual jurisdiction standard of person and territory, it may also be applicable to overseas enterprises. There is also a very high penalty ceiling for violations, so enterprises should pay attention to and take corresponding compliance measures.

15.4.1 Applicable Scope

The PIPL regulates not only enterprises in China, but also overseas enterprises processing personal information of individuals within China for the purpose of offering products or services to, or for analysing and assessing the behaviours of, such individuals, which means that an international enterprise without presence in China but that conducts the above-mentioned business is still subject to the PIPL. For enterprises with physical presence in China, any personal information processing activities shall be subject to the PIPL.

15.4.2 Principles of Personal Information Protection

The Personal Information Protection Law puts forward five principles for personal information protection. It shall be noted that these five principles are mandatory.

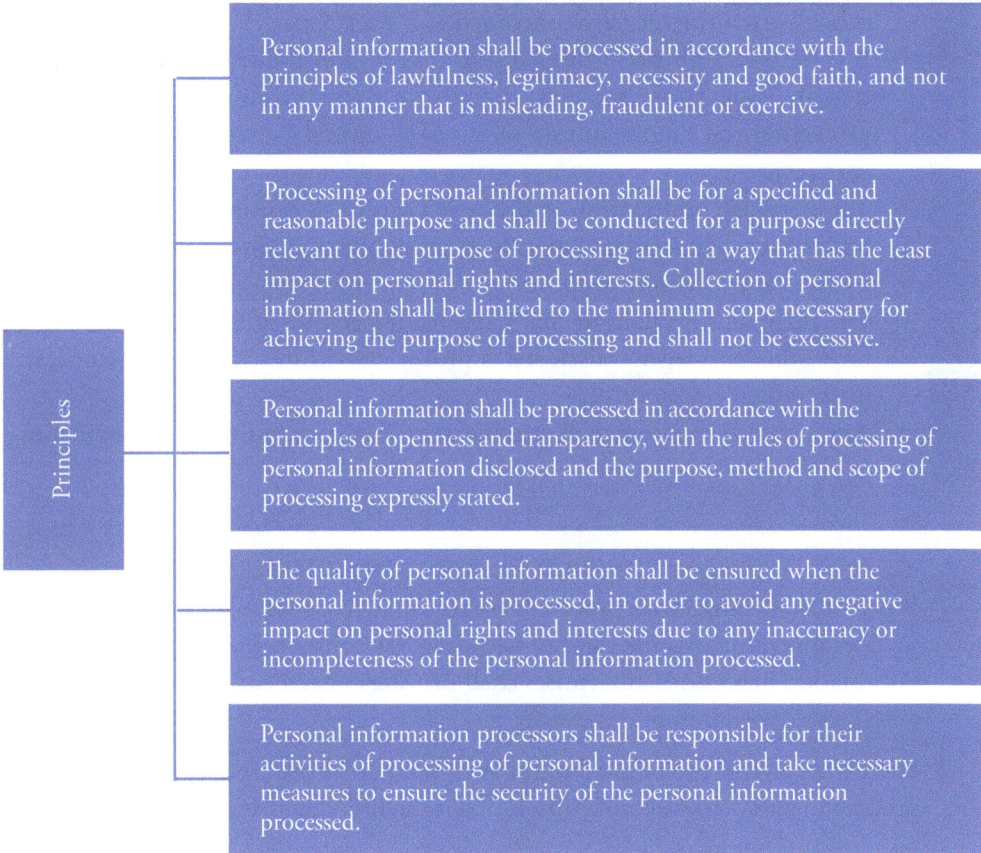

Principles

Personal information shall be processed in accordance with the principles of lawfulness, legitimacy, necessity and good faith, and not in any manner that is misleading, fraudulent or coercive.

Processing of personal information shall be for a specified and reasonable purpose and shall be conducted for a purpose directly relevant to the purpose of processing and in a way that has the least impact on personal rights and interests. Collection of personal information shall be limited to the minimum scope necessary for achieving the purpose of processing and shall not be excessive.

Personal information shall be processed in accordance with the principles of openness and transparency, with the rules of processing of personal information disclosed and the purpose, method and scope of processing expressly stated.

The quality of personal information shall be ensured when the personal information is processed, in order to avoid any negative impact on personal rights and interests due to any inaccuracy or incompleteness of the personal information processed.

Personal information processors shall be responsible for their activities of processing of personal information and take necessary measures to ensure the security of the personal information processed.

15.4.3 General Cases of Processing Personal Information

The basic premise of processing personal information is to obtain personal consent. Of course, in view of the complexity of practice, this law also stipulates several cases where consent is not required. A personal information processor may process personal information of an individual only under any of the following circumstances:

Waived Consent

- Consent is obtained from the individual
- It is necessary for the conclusion or performance of a contract to which the individual is a contracting party, or it is necessary for carrying out human resources management under an employment policy legally established or a collective contract legally concluded
- It is necessary for performing a statutory responsibility or statutory obligation. It is necessary for responding to a public health emergency, or for protecting the life, health or safety of a natural person in the case of an emergency
- The personal information is processed within a reasonable scope to carry out any news reporting, supervision by public opinions, or any other activity for public-interest purposes
- The personal information that has already been disclosed by the individual or is otherwise legally disclosed is processed within a reasonable scope and in accordance with this law
- Any other circumstance as provided by law or administrative regulations apply

---

Important Notes: Consent

1) If personal information is processed based on the consent of an individual, such an individual has the right to withdraw his consent, and, as personal information processors, enterprises shall provide convenient ways for consent withdrawal (withdrawal of consent).

2) For any change of the original purpose or method of processing, the processing party shall obtain consent from the individual anew (reconsent).

3) The processor shall obtain separate consent from relevant individuals in cases of providing personal information it processes to others, disclosing personal information it processes, processing sensitive personal information, cross-border transmission, etc. (separate consent).

15.4.4 Personal Information Management in Business

If in the business development of the enterprise an enterprise needs to obtain, transmit and process any personal information, the enterprise must strictly perform the obligation of disclosure and obtain the consent of the relevant person(s). The enterprise shall inform the individual of the following matters in a conspicuous way, in clear and easy-to-understand language and in a truthful, accurate and complete manner:

- Organisational or personal name and contact information of the personal information processor
- Purpose and method of processing personal information, the type of personal information to be processed and its retention period
- Method and procedure for the individual to exercise his rights provided for by this law
- Any other matter to be informed as required by the law or administrative regulations

Any change to any matter stated in the preceding paragraph shall be informed to the individual. Where any matter stated is informed by personal information processors through established rules of processing of personal information, such rules shall be made available to the public and be easy to access and store.

In addition, enterprises shall not disregard consent matters, shall not force individuals to give consent and must provide a convenient way to withdraw consent. In specific scenarios – such as, processing sensitive personal information, cross-border transmission of personal information, provision of data to third parties, etc. – separate consent is required, and such processing shall only be conducted when it is really necessary. Enterprises also need to manage these situations strictly.

The PIPL has also given requirements to the standardisation of enterprise compliance:

- Developing an internal management system and operating procedures
- Managing personal information based on classification
- Taking appropriate technical security measures, such as encryption and de-identification
- Reasonably determining the authorisations to operate the processing of personal information and conducting security education and training for employees on a regular basis
- Developing and organising the implementation of emergency plans for personal information security incidents
- Taking any other measure as required by law or administrative regulations

In addition, the enterprise shall regularly conduct an information security compliance audit and a prior personal information protection impact assessment for the following situations and record the handling situation:

- Processing of sensitive personal information
- Use of personal information in automated decision-making
- Contracting of the processing of personal information to another party, provision of personal information to another personal information processor, or disclosure of the personal information
- Provision of personal information to an overseas recipient
- Any other activity of processing of personal information of an individual that will have a material impact on personal rights and interests

15.4.4.1 Employee Personal Information Management

At the stage of labour contract execution, it is usually not necessary to obtain the employee's consent for the use of personal information.

> ## Important Notes: Personal Information of Employees
>
> 1) Personal information of employees shall not be collected excessively. The personal information of employees that can be collected is limited to 'basic information directly related to the labour contract', mainly including name, gender, nationality, identity certificate number, address, personal email, health status, education and degree, work experience, emergency contact, etc. In the recruitment process, the enterprise shall determine the scope and content of information according to the actual needs and ensure that the collected employee personal information is reasonable and in line with the principle of minimisation, and avoid excessive collection. For sensitive information that really needs to be collected, the explicit consent of employees shall be obtained.
>
> 2) Employees' personal information shall not be provided to third parties without consent. In the recruitment process, if the enterprise introduces a third party to assist in recruitment or conduct background investigation, the enterprise must obtain the written authorisation of the employee – that is, the third party must work with the employee's knowledge and consent – otherwise, the enterprise may infringe the candidate employee's right to personal information.

During the period of employment, the enterprise shall properly keep the collected personal information of employees, including paper materials, such as employees' certificates, files and documents with personal information, as well as digital information, such as employees' fingerprints and face recognition information (if any). The storage equipment, transmission equipment and use equipment shall be encrypted to ensure the security of employees' personal information. The enterprise shall sign a confidentiality agreement and conduct professional training with the employees who manage personal information.

In addition, employees' personal information is very likely to be left on mobile phones, computers and other devices provided by the company. To avoid compliance risks to the greatest extent, before providing office equipment, the enterprise shall inform employees in writing in advance that it shall not be used for personal affairs, and the enterprise reserves the right to inspect and monitor the information on office equipment. The written signature of employees shall be obtained. Before repairing, inspecting or recycling the equipment, employees can be reminded to clean the personal information on the equipment. Once any employee's personal information is found, it must be kept strictly confidential.

For multinational companies or enterprises with multinational business, if they need to transmit employees' personal information across the border, they shall obtain the written authorisation and consent of employees and employ network security agency services, firewalls and other means to ensure the security of information.

When an employee is leaving an enterprise, the enterprise should only archive the necessary information and delete the sensitive personal information and information that no longer needs to be stored. After an employee leaves the enterprise, the enterprise should be very cautious if the employee's new enterprise wants to do a background check. Unless the employee agrees in writing before leaving the enterprise that the enterprise can disclose his information to other enterprises, the enterprise is very likely to infringe on the employee's personal information rights and interests.

15.4.4.2 International Transfer

The cross-border provision of information has always been the focus of multinational enterprises doing business in China. The PIPL establishes the following provisions for providing personal information to overseas recipients.

First of all, before providing information overseas, the individual shall be informed of the name of the overseas recipient, contact information, purpose of processing, processing method, type of personal information, and the ways and procedures for an individual to exercise his rights under this law. Separate informed consent must be obtained from the individual, then the processor can transfer the personal information overseas through different ways, depending on whether it is the critical information infrastructure operator (CIIO) or whether the amount of personal information processed exceeds the amount specified by the CAC. If so, it shall pass the security assessment organised by the CAC. If not, personal information can be provided overseas through one of the following options: completing voluntary security assessment, carrying out personal information protection certification by professional institutions or signing a standard contract for information provision, etc.

15.4.4.3 Person in Charge

If the amount of personal information processed exceeds the standard set by the CAC, the PIPL requires the enterprise to appoint a person in charge of personal information protection. The enterprise must disclose the contact information of the person in charge of personal information protection and submit the name and contact information of the person in charge of personal information protection to the authorities performing the responsibility of personal information protection.

Personal information processors outside China shall establish a special agency or appoint a representative within the territory of China to be responsible for personal-information-protection-related affairs and submit the name of such an agency or the name and contact information of the representative to the authorities performing personal information protection duties.

Personal information processors shall have the compliance of their activities of processing of personal information with laws and administrative regulations audited on a regular basis.

15.4.5 Connections to Data Security Law and Cybersecurity Law

As the three most important laws in the field of data and information compliance, in terms of scope of application, the Personal Information Protection Law is applicable to the protection of personal information, the Data Security Law is applicable to the processing of data, and the Cybersecurity Law is applicable to the processing of personal information and data by all network operators in China. Therefore, for enterprises other than network operators, especially Internet enterprises, compliance work needs to combine the Data Security Law and the Personal Information Protection Law. Compliance requires that the enterprise shall spontaneously carry out data classification and differentiated management, establish a data security management system for the whole process, arrange technicians to take technical measures and other necessary measures to maintain data security, ensure that data is stored domestically and ensure that domestic data is not provided to foreign judicial or law-enforcement agencies without approval.

15.4.6 Classified and Hierarchical Data Protection

Classified and hierarchical data protection is a requirement of the Data Security Law, which can maximise the value of data while ensuring data security. All regions and departments shall determine the specific catalogue of important data of relevant industries according to the national regulation of classified and hierarchical data protection and provide extra protection of the data listed in the catalogue. If there are temporarily no relevant documents, the enterprise shall also spontaneously carry out the classification – including core data of the state, key data, personal information, sensitive personal information, public data, etc. – and carry out differentiated management.

15.4.7 Data Security Management System

Similar to the personal information protection, enterprises need to determine the data security management system in the form of written documents. Enterprises can improve the overall data security compliance awareness of employees through regular training and organisational learning and retain relevant certificates (for example, training materials, training participants' signatures, etc.). Enterprises involved in important data-processing shall specify the department and person in charge of data security management and regularly carry out risk detection and assessment with the technology, IT and other departments and establish early warning and emergency response mechanisms.

16 Current: Export Control Law

16.1 Introduction

The Export Control Law of the People's Republic of China (ECL) took effect from 1 December 2020. Previously, export controls were scattered across several laws and regulations and lacked a unified regulatory system. The ECL establishes the regulatory framework for export control and defines the controlled items subject to export control. For foreign companies specifically engaged in import and export trade or related business, the ECL may require changes to export licences, administration and/or procedures.

16.1.1 Purpose

The ECL highlights the necessity to establish a unified export control list and export control system coordinated by the State Council, the Central Military Commission, and relevant ministries. The enactment of the ECL safeguards national security and interests, performs non-proliferation and other international obligations, and strengthens and standardises export control.

Additionally, the ECL shall stay in line with the overall national security outlook, maintain international security, balance security and development and improve export control administration and services.

16.2 Controlled Items Subject to Export Control

The ECL defines controlled items subject to export control as including the following:

- Dual-use items that can be for civil purposes and military purposes or for helping to improve military potentials, especially goods, technologies, and services in design, development, production or application utilised for weapons of mass destruction
- Military products comprising of equipment, special production facilities and other related goods, technologies and services utilised for military purposes
- Nuclear materials, including nuclear equipment, non-nuclear materials used for nuclear reactors, and related technologies and services
- Technical materials and data related to the items listed above

Controlled items could affect companies in international supply-chain or cross-border research and development; for example, foreign items containing components assembled or manufactured in China could be deemed as controlled items. For companies engaged in cross-border research or technology transfer, activities such as research, inter-company research (where the research-and-development centre is in China) or technology sales to foreign enterprises could be classified as related technical material and data, thus are subject to export control.

Furthermore, the ECL also stipulates that the State Export Control Authorities (SECAs) may – subject to the approval of the State Council or the approval of both the State Council and the Central Military Commission, together with relevant departments – impose a temporary control on the export of any goods, technologies or services outside the control lists. The term of temporary control shall have a maximum duration of two years.

Also, if an item does not fall in the above scope but the exporter knows or ought to know or is notified by the State Export Control Authorities that any relevant goods, technologies or services outside the control lists that are to be exported by it may pose any of the following risks, it shall apply to the State Export Control Authorities for a licence.

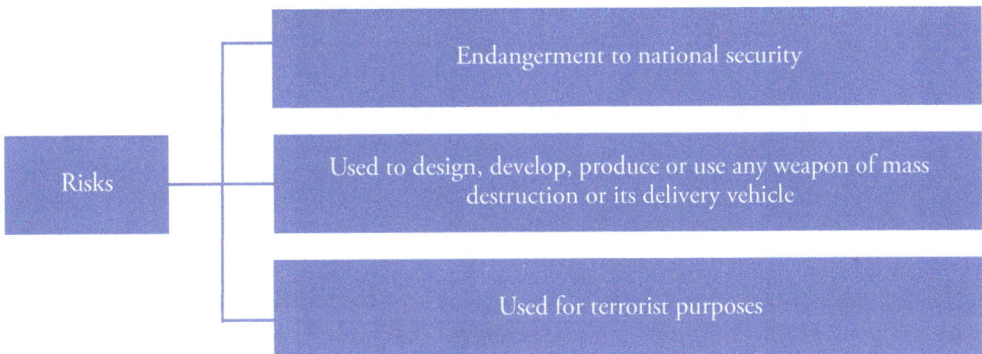

Risks	
	Endangerment to national security
	Used to design, develop, produce or use any weapon of mass destruction or its delivery vehicle
	Used for terrorist purposes

With a wide scope of controlled items, companies should regularly assess their export risk and business operations by establishing an export compliance system. Equally, company policy and implementation should be adjusted to ensure that employees are trained and equipped to implement the system efficiently and violations are avoided.

16.3 Natural Person and Entities Subject to the ECL

Export controls are applicable to any citizen or incorporated or non-incorporated organisation of the People's Republic of China (PRC) and to any foreign organisation or individual. In other words, any export of the controlled items from an individual or organisation in the PRC to an overseas individual or organisation is obliged to obtain the relevant licence first from the State Export Control Authorities.

The scope of the ECL also extends to indirect exports. Specifically, third parties including transportation, importers and end users, and export from bonded areas, export processing zones, and other areas subject to special customs supervision are subject to the ECL. As a result, companies should note the following two aspects:

- Service providers such as import-export agencies, freight, delivery, customs declaration, third-party e-commerce transaction platforms and finance services, and so forth, are forbidden to provide services to exporters who violate the ECL. In practice, in order to migrate logistical problems, companies should ensure that licences are applied for on time
- The ECL extends to both importers and end users. The SECA shall forbid exports to importers or end users within control lists. Exporters are required to certify end users and the end use of the controlled items. Specifically, end users shall not alter the end use of the controlled items, nor assign them to any third parties, without the approval of State Export Control Authorities

16.4 Export Control System

Exporters engaged in the export of controlled or temporarily controlled items are required to apply for a licence to export items. The State Export Control Authorities shall review the application and determine the approval of the licence based on the following factors:

International obligations and commitments to foreign parties
Type of export
Export destination country or region
The end user and end use
Relevant credit records of the exporter
National security and interest
Other factors as prescribed in law or administrative regulations

Factors

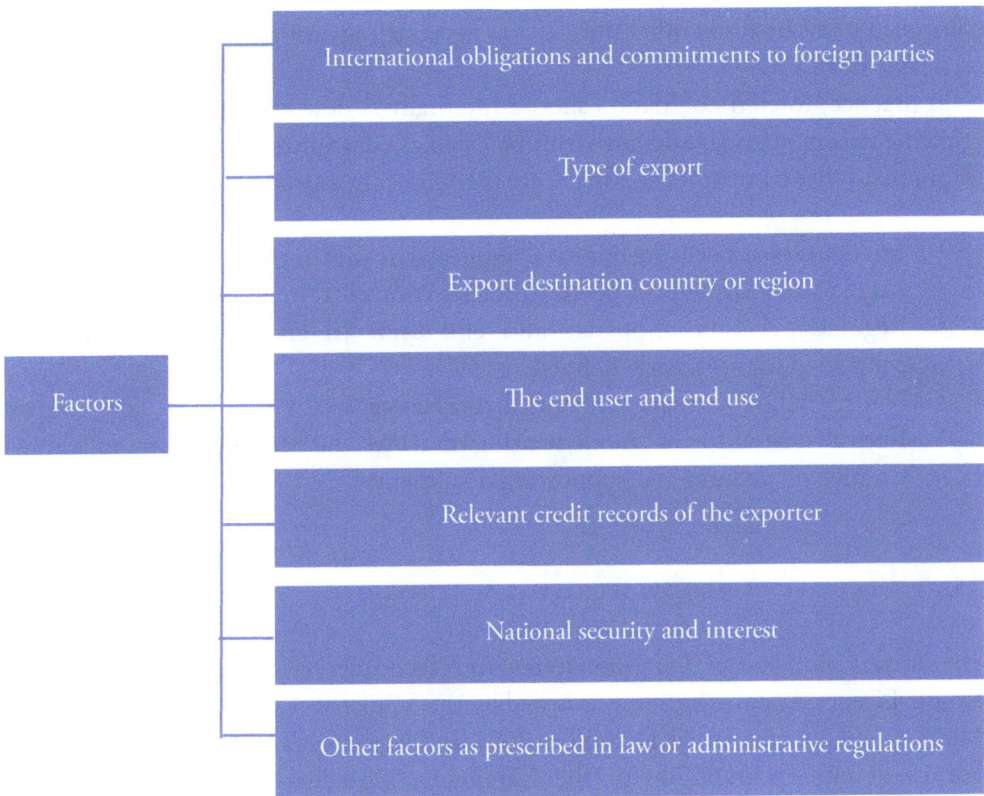

The ECL states that exporters engaged in the export of controlled items shall establish an internal export control compliance review system. Where the system operates well, the exporter may be granted facilitation measures, such as a general licence for the export of relevant controlled items.

16.4.1 Controlled List of Importers

A controlled list of importers and end users shall be established. Importers and end users who are identified under the following circumstances shall be placed on the controlled list:

- Breach of the regulatory requirements regarding end users or end uses
- Potential endangerment to national security and interests
- Use of any controlled item for any terrorist purpose

The State Export Control Authorities may suspend the export of the relevant controlled items or adopt other measures as necessary against any exporter or end user on a controlled list.

In practice, foreign companies should internally review exported items and draft implementation plans should any items be listed as controlled items. For example, we recommend that companies at risk ensure the following aspects are evaluated:

- Import/export licensing approval applications within time, where applicable
- Regularly classify export goods to ensure controlled items are clearly defined
- Regularly classify importers and end users to ensure those within the controlled list are clearly defined
- Notify trading partners and amend contract clauses
- Keep abreast of further implementing measures and lists and adhere to administrative procedures and supporting documents

16.5 Licence Administration Catalogue

The latest Catalogue of Dual-use Items and Technologies Subject to Import and Export Licence Administration was issued by the Ministry of Commerce and General Ministry of Customs on 31 December 2021 and was effective from 1 January 2022. For items and technologies in the Catalogue, regardless whether the customs commodity number is listed in the catalogue or not, the import and export licence for dual-use items and technologies shall be applied according to law, which mainly includes: regarding import, chemicals subject to control, precursor chemicals, radio-isotope and commercial encryption; and regarding export, nuclear items and technologies, biological items and technologies, chemicals subject to control, precursor chemicals, commercial encryption, etc.

16.6 Supervision and Regulation

16.6.1 Investigation

The State Export Control Authorities may adopt the following measures to investigate any activity suspected of being in violation of the law:

- They may enter the business premises of the subject of the investigation or any other relevant places to carry out an inspection
- They may interview the subject of the investigation, any stakeholders and any other relevant organisations or individuals and require them to provide statements on matters related to the subject matter of the investigation
- They may access and copy relevant vouchers, agreements, accounting records, business correspondence and other documents and materials of the subject of the investigation, any stakeholders or any other relevant organisations or individuals
- They may inspect any vehicles used for export transportation, stop the loading of any suspicious items to be exported and order the return of any illegally exported items
- They may seize or detain any relevant items involved in the case
- They may inquire into the bank account of the subject of the investigation

16.6.2 Penalties

Violation of the ECL can result in criminal and/or administrative penalties. For foreign companies established outside of China in violation, extraterritorial enforcement jurisdiction of the law can be applied.

Administrative penalties range from general penalties to prohibited activities:

- General penalties include warning, ordering to cease the illegal act, confiscating illegal gains, imposing a fine, ordering to suspend the business for rectification, and even revoking the qualification of engaging in the export of relevant controlled items
- Prohibited activities include refused application for an export permit for five years, prohibiting the person(s) directly in charge or in liability from engaging in the relevant export business activities for five years or for life.

Additionally, some violations of the ECL, such as exporting controlled items or exporting without permission, can result in criminal penalties.

Companies with business involving controlled items should assess the risks and draw a contingency plan. Where there is intercompany research with the parent company or affiliate from abroad, a wider risk assessment should be conducted and internal policies updated.

www.ingramcontent.com/pod-product-compliance
Lightning Source LLC
Chambersburg PA
CBHW080935220326
41598CB00034B/5785